LEGENDARY LOCALS

OF

NORWICH

CONNECTICUT

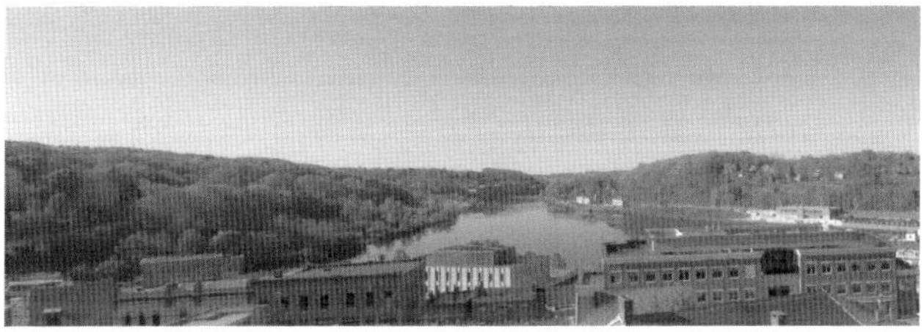

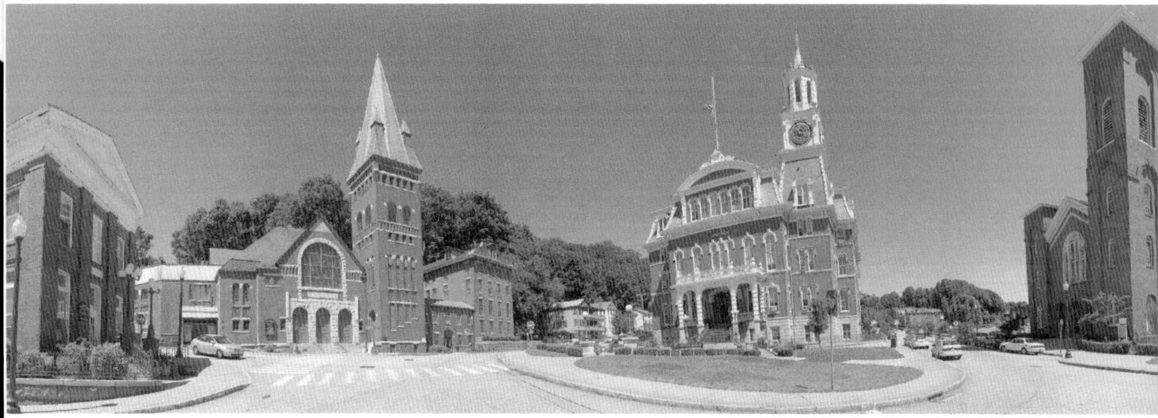

Norwich City Hall Panorama

At the encouragement of his pastor, Joseph Otis purchased land and built the Otis Library building in 1850. The library moved to a new Main Street location in 1962 (far left), and the building is now an annex of Norwich City Hall, located across the street. The cornerstone of the Central Baptist Church (left of center) was laid in 1891.

From the settling of Norwich in 1659, until 1829, the town hall was located on the Norwichtown Green. From 1829 until a fire in 1865, the town hall was located atop Jail Hill, overlooking the harbor. The Second Empire structure on Union Square (right of center) was inspired by the Louvre, with a facade of Philadelphia pressed brick and window trims of granite. It has served without interruption as Norwich City Hall since 1873. (Courtesy of Chris Hetzer.)

Page 1: Norwich Harbor Panorama

The Thames River was the major transportation route from Norwich to New London and the Long Island Sound, from before Norwich's settling in 1659 to the early 20th century. Norwich is a city of three rivers, the Thames, the Shetucket, and the Yantic. While the city continues to move forward, it never tires of remembering the sights, beauty, and glory of its past. (Courtesy of Chris Hetzer.)

LEGENDARY LOCALS OF NORWICH CONNECTICUT

BERYL FISHBONE

LEGENDARY LOCALS

ISBN 978-1-4671-0078-6

Legendary Locals is an imprint of Arcadia Publishing
Charleston, South Carolina

Printed in the United States of America

Library of Congress Control Number: 2012955778

For all general information, please contact Arcadia Publishing:
Telephone 843-853-2070
Fax 843-853-0044
E-mail sales@arcadiapublishing.com
For customer service and orders:
Toll-Free 1-888-313-2665

Visit us on the Internet at www.arcadiapublishing.com

On the Front Cover: Clockwise from top left:
Hortencia Torres, purveyor of authentic Mexican food (Courtesy of Akil Peck; see page 57), "Joe" Geer, printer and community asset (Courtesy of Terri Geer; see page 113), Cam Fogg, consignment shop owner (Courtesy of Cam Fogg; see page 46), Mike Quarto, Navy hero (Courtesy of the Quarto family; see page 26), Zoey the dog, All Friends Animal Hospital outreach program (Courtesy of All Friends Animal Hospital; see page 119), Harry Swatzburg and Jeff Hodkinson of Uncas Pharmacy (Courtesy of Jeff Hodkinson; see page 43), Tim Wawrzynowicz, shop owner known as Johnny Kielbasa (Courtesy of Tim Wawrzynowicz; see page 46).

On the Back Cover: From left to right:
Donald Pavlak, Tony Turano, and Anthony Vocatura, of Vocatura's Bakery, one of the most popular bakeries in the history of Norwich (Courtesy of Vocatura's Bakery; see page 59), Members of Scout Pack 17, Troop 4, who came through in a time of need (Courtesy of Boy Scouts of America Pack 17; see page 120).

CONTENTS

ACKNOWLEDGMENTS

Since its founding in 1659, Norwich, Connecticut, has always been a city. Even when it belonged to England, and ever since the American Revolution 100 years later, Norwich has called itself a city. In 1659, Norwich was roughly nine square miles. Parts of the old Norwich broke away and formed new towns, and other communities formed with their own identifying names appropriate for their times. Today, Norwich occupies about 29.5 square miles.

I anticipated the work that would go into this project, including locating photographs of residents past and present and relating a short story about them. However, I never counted on how reticent and shy the residents would be to share their stories and personal photographs.

To those who gave me permission to place their words and photographs in this scrapbook collection, I give my thanks. I hope I have told your story in a way that makes you proud. To those who declined to give me permission but told me their stories anyway, I thank you for sharing your time and trusting your treasures with me.

I did my best to be kind. I did my best to be accurate. I documented where I could, and hope for the leniency of the reader and understanding where I could not.

My unending gratitude goes to Erin Vosgien, senior acquisitions editor of Legendary Locals, for her encouragement and for putting up with my frequent moments of terror and frustration as I worked on this project.

My deepest thanks to my friends Barbara, Carmen, Cindy, Dianne, George, Jerry, Lisa, Nancy, Sandee, and Vivian, who let me prattle on about this project with endless patience. Thanks also go to Richard, for lending me a camera and for his endless picture digitizing, and to the contributors of the "You're probably from Norwich if . . ." Facebook page. And, thanks go to Frank O., Chris H., and Brian K., and everyone who reassured me with the words "Yes you can. Now get busy!"

Unless otherwise noted, all images are from the author's collection.

INTRODUCTION

Norwich historians refer not to its founding as a city, but to its settling as a community. Norwich sits at the juncture of three rivers: the Thames, the Shetucket, and the Yantic. The history of the area begins not with its settling by the British, but with its habitation and use by Native Americans. The rivers were rich with fish, and their navigability made travel into the more fertile lands of the interior easier. The forests were thick with old growth, and the animals that enjoyed its food and protection were plentiful. Settlers from Old Saybrook purchased nine square miles of land from the Mohegan tribe, with great thought for its future. One story says the farmers wanted to leave Old Saybrook to escape crows. Supposedly, the smart birds had learned to follow the farmers as they planted their crops and would dig up the seeds that had just been planted.

There is no established record of the first settlers of Norwich. The list of the "founding fathers" came about through the later registration of land and property, after the settlement had been established. Some of the first settlers may have seen what awaited them and returned to Old Saybrook or moved on to another part of the colonies. For some, a notation in an account book is the only evidence that they existed at all. Others are known only as "wife of," "son of," or "daughter of," and they rest without a name of their own.

Norwich is lucky to have been the home of Frances Manwaring Caulkins (1795–1869), who wrote a very complete *History of Norwich, Connecticut; from its possession by the Indians to 1866*. It was her second attempt at writing a history book, and she tried to make it as complete as possible, with stories of locations, land types, and genealogies and the occasional addition of a personality. Her first edition created such a stir among its readers that she was immediately asked to revise it with corrections. The second edition was better received, and later editions have continued the tradition of correcting information where necessary.

Caulkins was the first woman elected to membership in the Historical Society of the United States, and was its only female member for over a century. Born and educated in New London, Connecticut, she was fascinated early on by historical and genealogical research. For seven years after finishing school, she lived with an uncle, Christopher Manwaring, and began contributing articles to local newspapers on historical figures and events in the area. When her stepfather's death left the family destitute, Caulkins became a schoolteacher for girls in Norwichtown from 1820 to 1829, served as a principal in New London (1830–1832), and returned to teaching in Norwichtown (1832–1834). Then she lived with various relatives, performing evangelical work until her death in 1869.

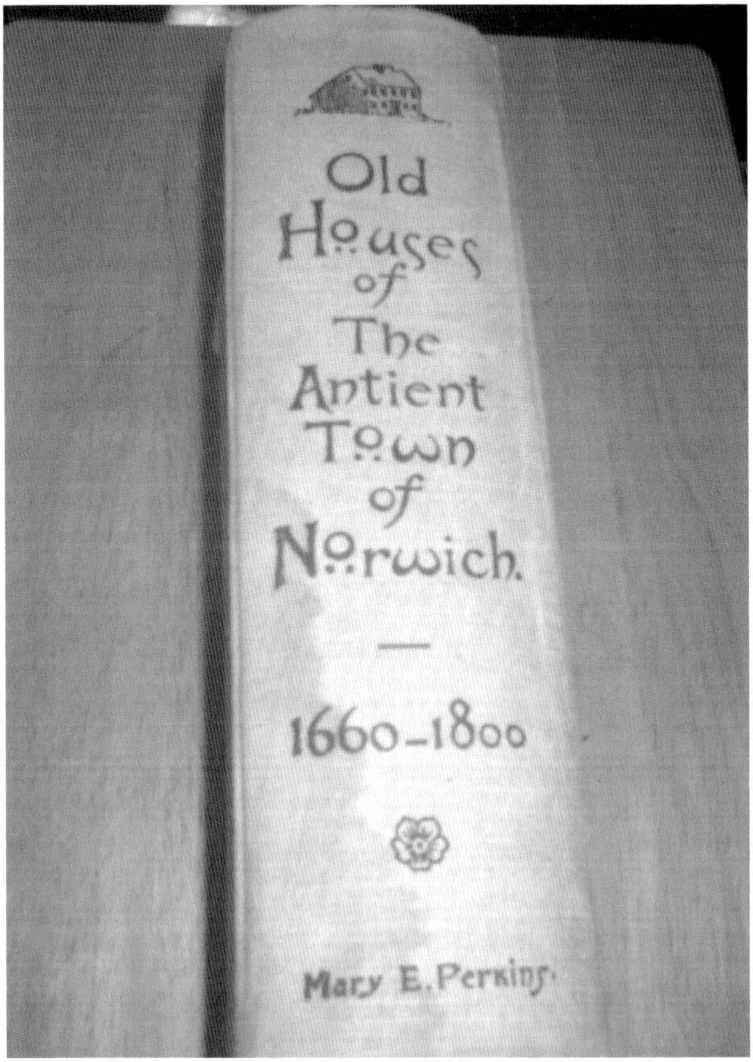

Mary E. Perkins

Mary Perkins published the first volume of *Old Houses of the Antient Town of Norwich, 1660–1800* in 1895, with the knowledge that errors would need to be corrected and with the full intention that this volume would be the first of many to follow the changing architecture of Norwich as well as the genealogy of its residents. She was so enthused that readers might be able to provide documentation she had been unable to locate, she kept post office box No. 63 in her name and checked it on a regular basis, until her death. Perkins left instructions for checking the box for a period of time afterward.

Perkins documented her work using the early paper trails as closely as possible and employing the technology of her publisher, the Bulletin Company, to include 105 illustrations and half-tone prints and 27 portraits and miniatures. Unafraid of anyone finding fault with her presentation, she clearly stated her sources and, as the frontispiece of the book, included a colored map by Heliotype Printing Company of Boston, titled "Norwich Circ. 1830 A Boyish Remembrance by Donald G. Mitchell." Mitchell made it clear that the map was based on his boyhood memories and was not a historical document. Anecdotes and stories are used to enliven Perkins' 600-page book, making it an easy and enjoyable reading experience.

CHAPTER ONE

Settling In

In the 1600s, winters were harsh, springs were wet, and summers were hot and dry. If all had gone right, the fall would bring a harvest. Produce to be sold was taken to markets via roads that were not much more than potholed paths that threatened to break a wagon axle. What is more, the roads were surrounded by woods that might hide thieves. The easiest way to travel to the more fertile interior lands was by boat, then by land until reaching the next river. Norwich has three active rivers, the Shetucket, the Thames, and the Yantic. The Shetucket River is really a 20-mile-long tributary of the Thames River, beginning north in Willimantic, where the Willimantic and Natchaug Rivers join. They flow south-southeast before joining the Quinebaug River, which then widens into an estuary that stretches southeast for almost five miles, joining the Thames estuary on the south side of Norwich.

The Thames River begins where the Yantic and Shetucket Rivers join, then flows south to Long Island Sound. Throughout history and in legend, it has been known by many names, including the Pequot River, the Great River of Pequot, Little Fresh, the Mohegan, and the New London. This is among the most confusing aspects of history. The same person, place, thing, or event may be called by many different names at different times.

The Yantic River begins west of Norwich, where Exeter Brook, Sherman Brook, and Deep River meet. It eventually flows into the Shetucket River and then the Thames River.

The three rivers are the reason that much of Norwich's early business was in trade and manufacturing. In addition to providing easier transportation, the rapid speed of the water became a source of power for machinery and, later, for electricity. Today, Norwich Public Utilities provides four services to the City of Norwich: natural gas, electricity, water, and wastewater collection.

Miantonomo

Miantonomo was chief of the Narraganset Indians. He was friendly to the white settlers but was constantly at war with Uncas, sachem of the Mohegan tribe. Uncas killed Sequassen, a relative or friend of Miantonomo. The chief complained to the governor of Hartford, who denied any action by the settlers. Miantonomo decided to take revenge, but Uncas found out about the plot. In the chase that followed, one story has Miantonomo leaping over Yantic Falls and breaking his leg. Uncas, following, makes the leap unharmed. Another story involves Miantonomo running in a suit of armor borrowed from a friend, and this slows him down.

In any case, Uncas captured Miantonomo and took him to Hartford to be tried. He was found guilty of attempted murder. The commissioners of the United Colonies of New England recommended the death penalty and gave Miantonomo back to Uncas, with instruction to carry out the execution on Mohegan land.

Only through another story is it known that Wawequa, brother of Uncas, buried a tomahawk in the head of Miantonomo at a signal from his brother on September 28, 1643, killing him in one blow. The story always ends with the climax of Uncas slicing off a piece of flesh from the dead Miantonomo and eating it, saying, "It is very sweet and it makes my heart strong."

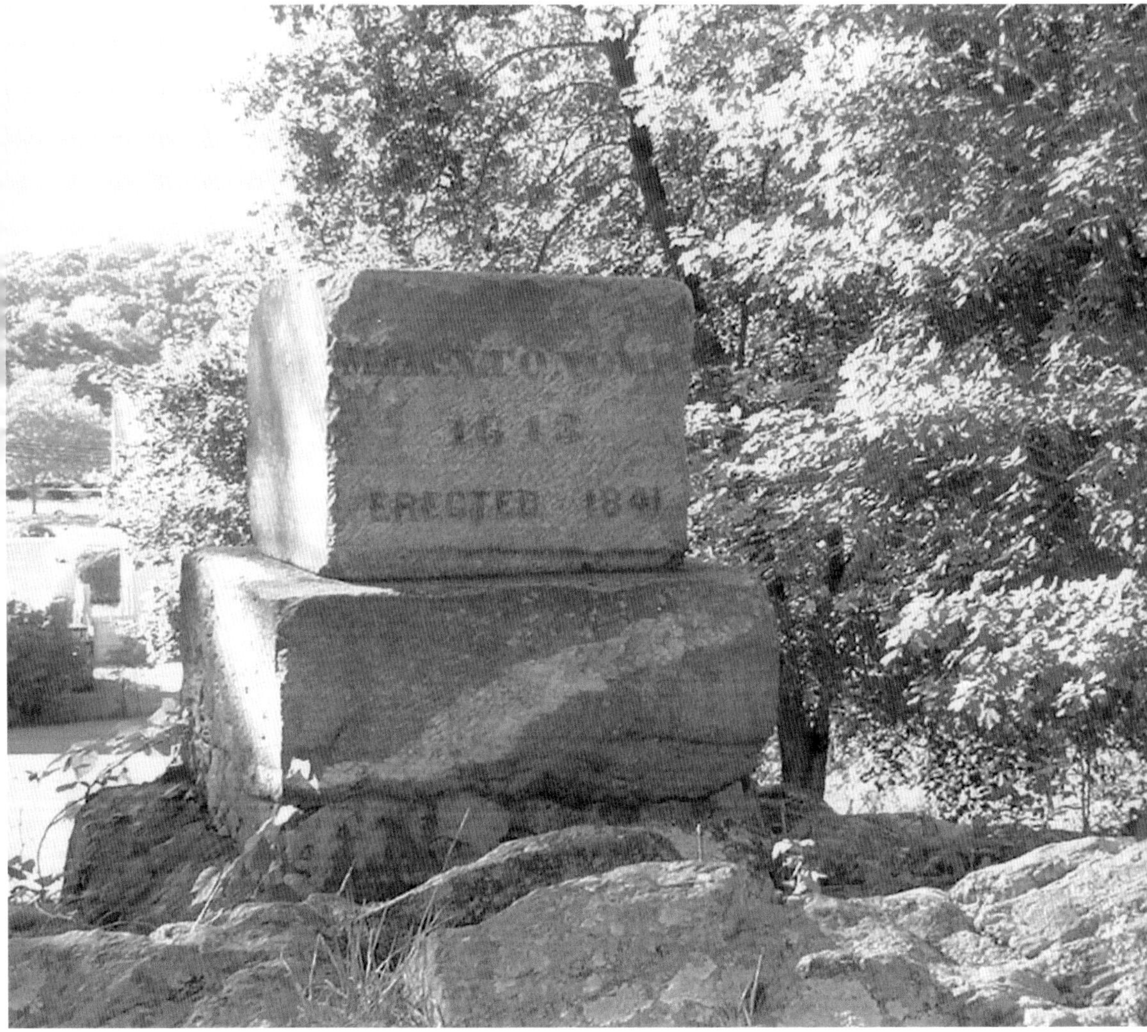

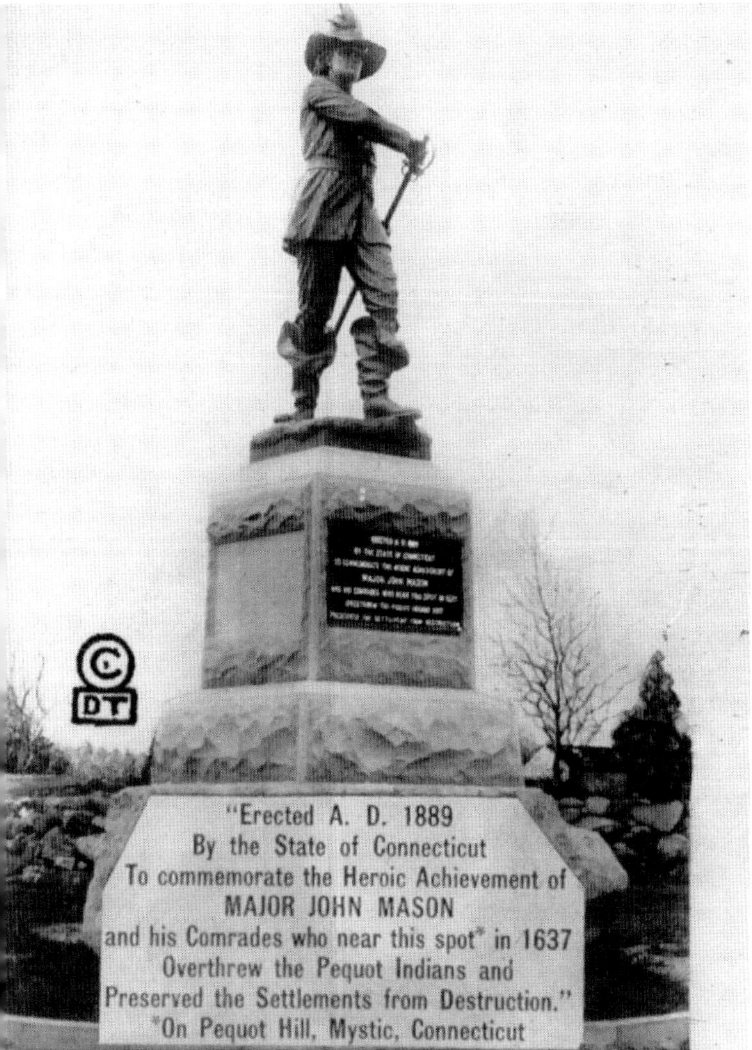

This Major John Mason was the only trained soldier among the first settlers of Norwich, Connecticut, 1659-1660, which made him the leader in the defence of the settlement—hence his name appears conspicuously on the "Founders' Monument."

Copr. Dwight Tracy

(The three vacant panels on the monument were undoubtedly for the Heroic Comrades. Who can supply their names?)

Dwight Tracy, 46 West 51st St., New York

John Mason

John Mason, or "The Major," was already known for getting a job done by whatever means necessary when he helped settle Norwich in 1659. In the spring of 1640, grain was scarce and cattle were starving. Mason was commissioned to travel to Springfield with "money in one hand and a sword in the other." He threatened the local natives with war if they did not sell their corn at a "reasonable price." The natives finally capitulated and sold the colonists the corn. Today, only the Administrative Office Building for the Norwich Department of Education carries the John Mason name in Norwich.

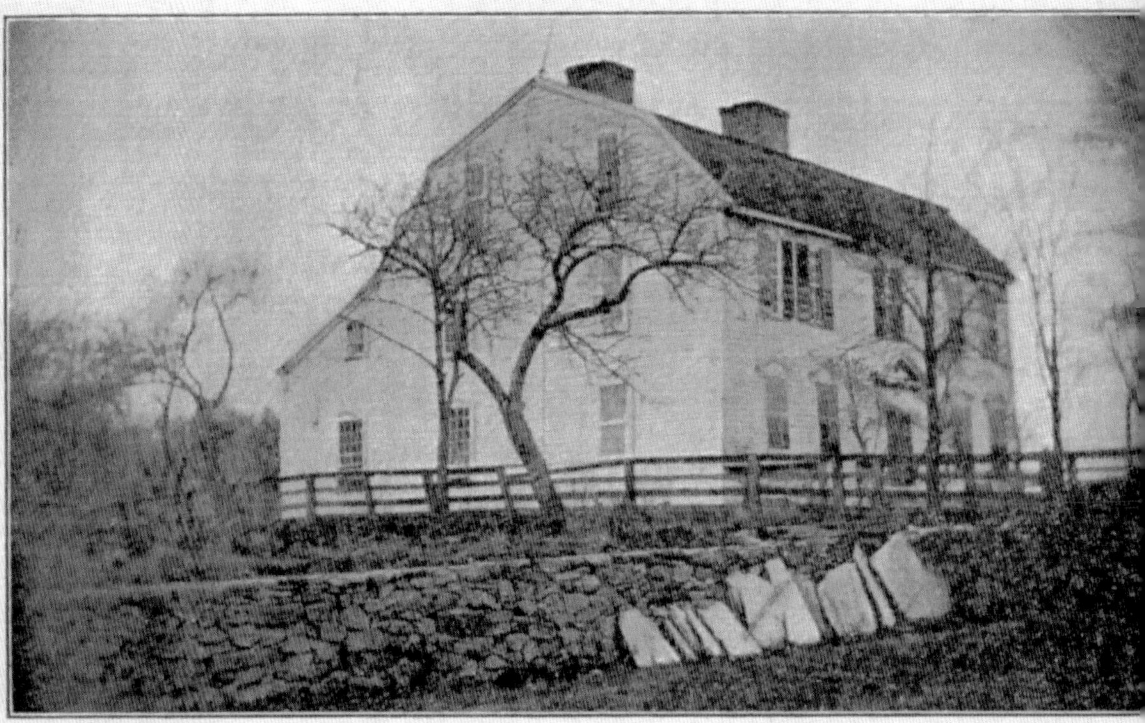

Norwich, Conn. BENEDICT ARNOLD'S BIRTHPLAC

Benedict Arnold

As a boy, Benedict Arnold, in petticoat and bib, played in a Norwich garden halfway between the harbor and Norwichtown. He worshipped his mother, and he admired the father he knew in his early years but pitied the later man. Benedict was an admired student, known for his pride, strength, beauty, and bravery. He provided the full support for his family until his mother's death in 1759 and his father's death in 1761.

An ambitious and aggressive businessman, he repurchased the family homestead in Norwich that his father had sold when deeply in debt, and resold it a year later for a substantial profit. In 1764, he and a partner bought three trading ships, and Arnold often commanded one of his own ships throughout New England, Quebec, and the West Indies.

The classroom and life lessons he learned while in Norwich served him well all his life. The decisions that led him to betray the fledgling country and made him a notorious and untrustworthy figure in America and England, he learned in other places.

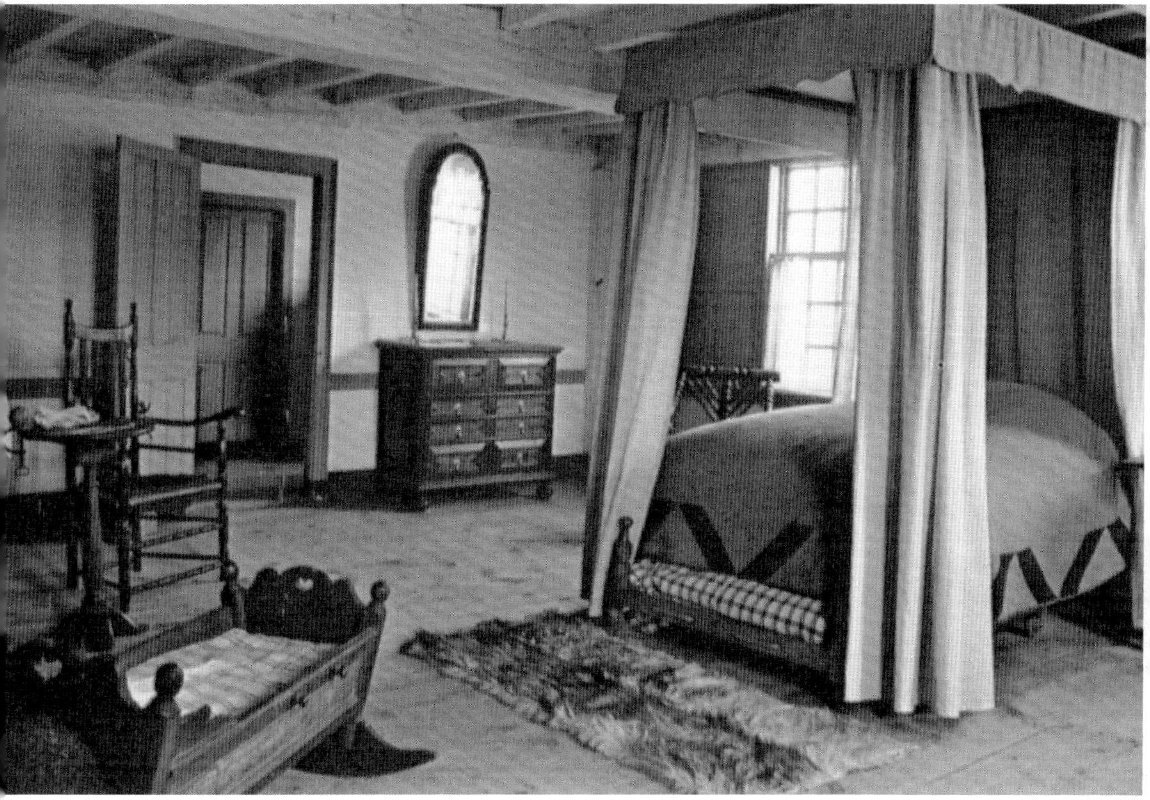

Christopher Leffingwell

A patriot and businessman, Christopher Leffingwell came from an old and firmly established Norwich family by the time of the American Revolution. In 1765, he petitioned against the Stamp Tax. Within a year, he had established a paper mill to make paper for the *Connecticut Gazette* and paper for British musket bullet cartridges.

By 1770, he had also built Connecticut's first chocolate mill; mills for fulling and dyeing, which made wool cloth cleaner and produced thicker stockings; and a pottery.

In 1775, he became a member of the Committee of Correspondence, passing along full private letters from England that made a difference in preparations for the Battles of Lexington and Concord, fought on April 19, 1775, in the Province of Massachusetts Bay, that began the American Revolution and helped finance Benedict Arnold's expedition to Fort Ticonderoga. Today, his home is the completely furnished Leffingwell House Colonial Museum.

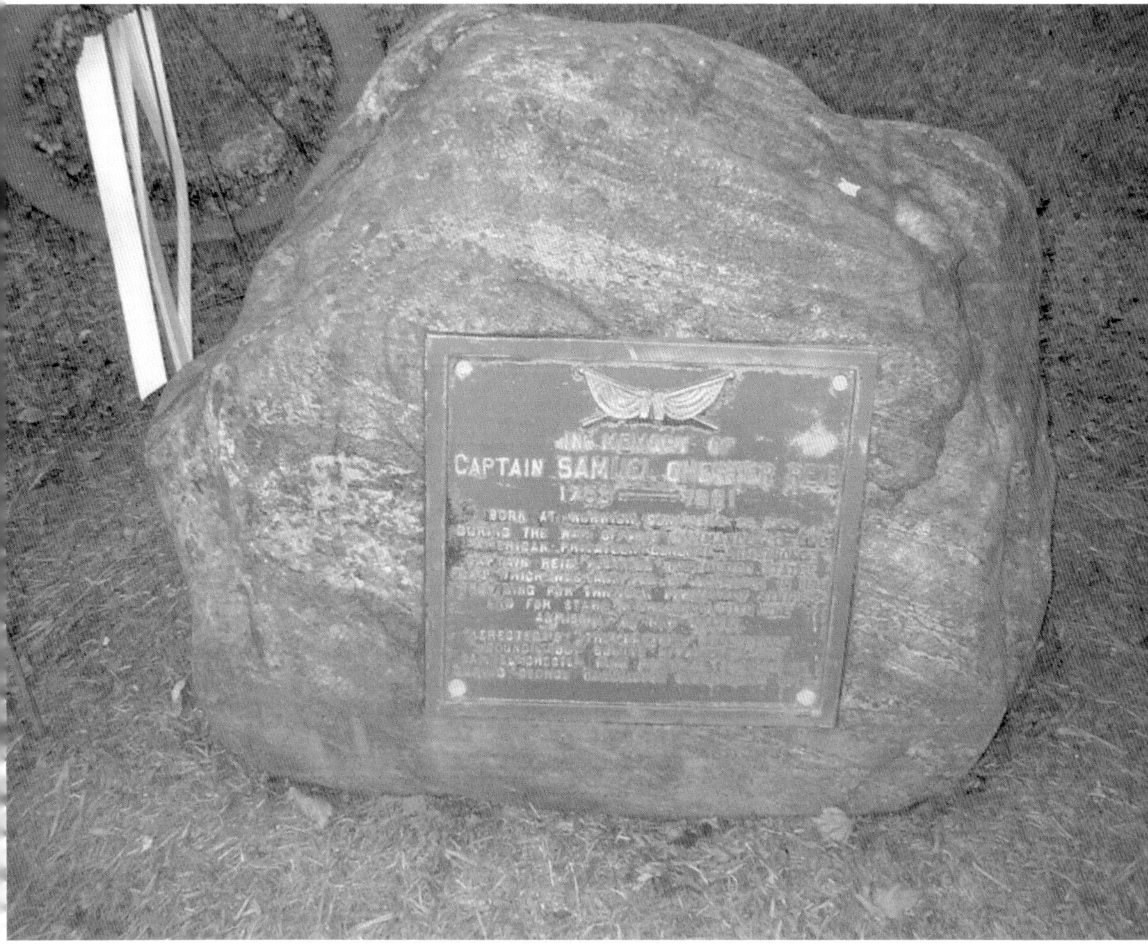

Samuel Chester Reid

During the War of 1812, Reid was in command of the privateer *General Armstrong.* The small brigantine weighed 246 tons, carried seven guns, and mounted six long nines with a 42 pounder, also known as a "Long Tom," on a pivot amidships. The ship had a crew of 90 men, including officers.

In September 1814, the ship escaped pursuit by a British squadron as it left New York during light winds by pumping water on the sails and towing the ship with rowboats. On September 26, in the harbor at Fayal in the Azores, three British ships arrived with 136 guns and 2,000 men. Captain Reid was called upon to surrender. His answer was a simple "No," and the battle began.

The *General Armstrong* was responsible for inflicting severe damage on the British ships. Knowing he could not escape, Reid deliberately sank his ship, but the damage done to the enemy made it necessary for the British fleet to remain in the Bay of Fayal for repairs. This delay made it possible for Gen. Andrew Jackson to reach New Orleans and score the victory that won the war for the United States. Captain Reid was responsible for the turning point in the War of 1812.

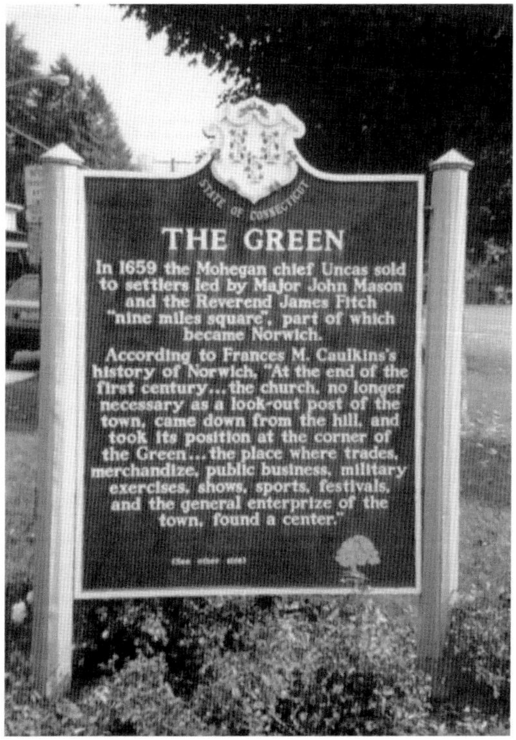

Samuel Bailey

Bailey served with John Paul Jones during the American Revolution. In the 1790s, Bailey returned home and became a tavern-keeper on the Norwichtown Green. He called his establishment the Crossed Keys, because the jail was on the second floor. He was quickly elected jailor and was informed that he would need to get a bondsman, and a wife. He said, "I'll get them both before night." The bondsman was easy, but when he asked one of two sisters to marry him, she said, "This is so sudden. I will have to think it over." A wiser man, Bailey turned to her sister and said, "The Lord says that you should marry me." "The Lord's will be done," she said, and put on her bonnet. The minister married them that night. (Courtesy of Ginny Dubois Edmundson.)

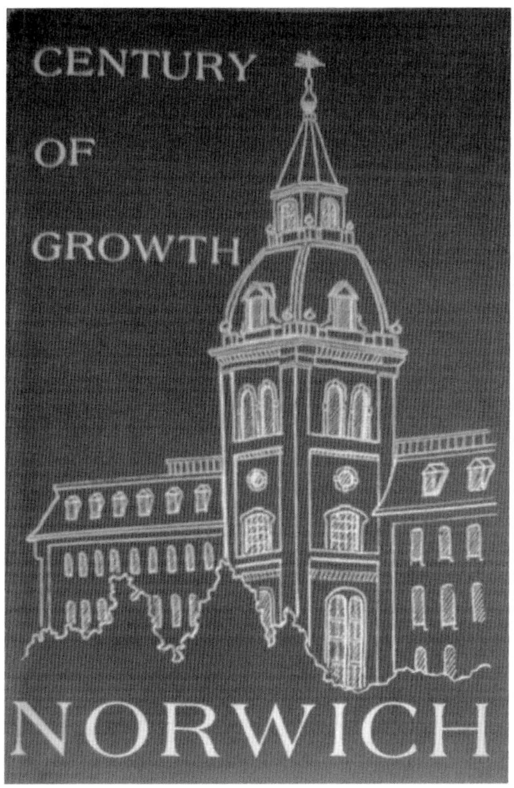

Eleanor B. Read

With enthusiasm and insight, Eleanor Read taught social studies and American history to the students of Norwich Free Academy. So great was her insight that, as early as 1972, the Bicentennial Committee of Norwich asked her to write the economic history of the city for publication, documenting the growth of Norwich to 1975.

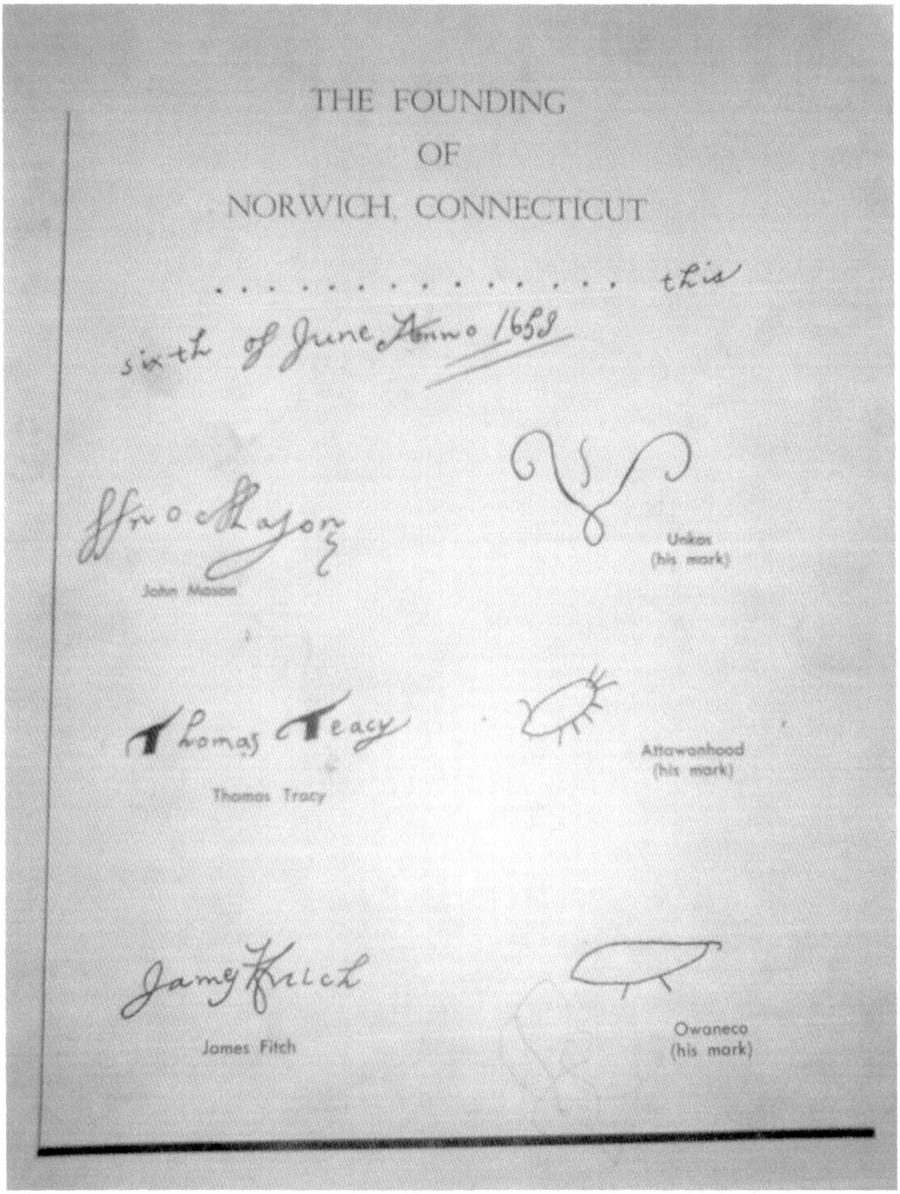

Mary Turner Shugrue

While Shugrue was teaching her students to be proud of their city's history, she became aware that a new resource was needed. She sought to condense 300 years of history into smaller bites that students would be interested in. With the photographic assistance of Beatrice Willey, Shugrue set about creating a 25-page pamphlet, "The Founding of Norwich, Connecticut 1659," published by the Franklin Press of Norwich in 1971.

In addition to presenting the students with Colonial history, Shugrue introduced local Indian names, early enterprises and their history, and two pages of locations of historic points of interest in the Norwich area, for use as the basis for field trips and walkabouts for classes, schools, and families. For over 25 years, the pamphlet and its extensive bibliography were used to teach local history in the Norwich schools.

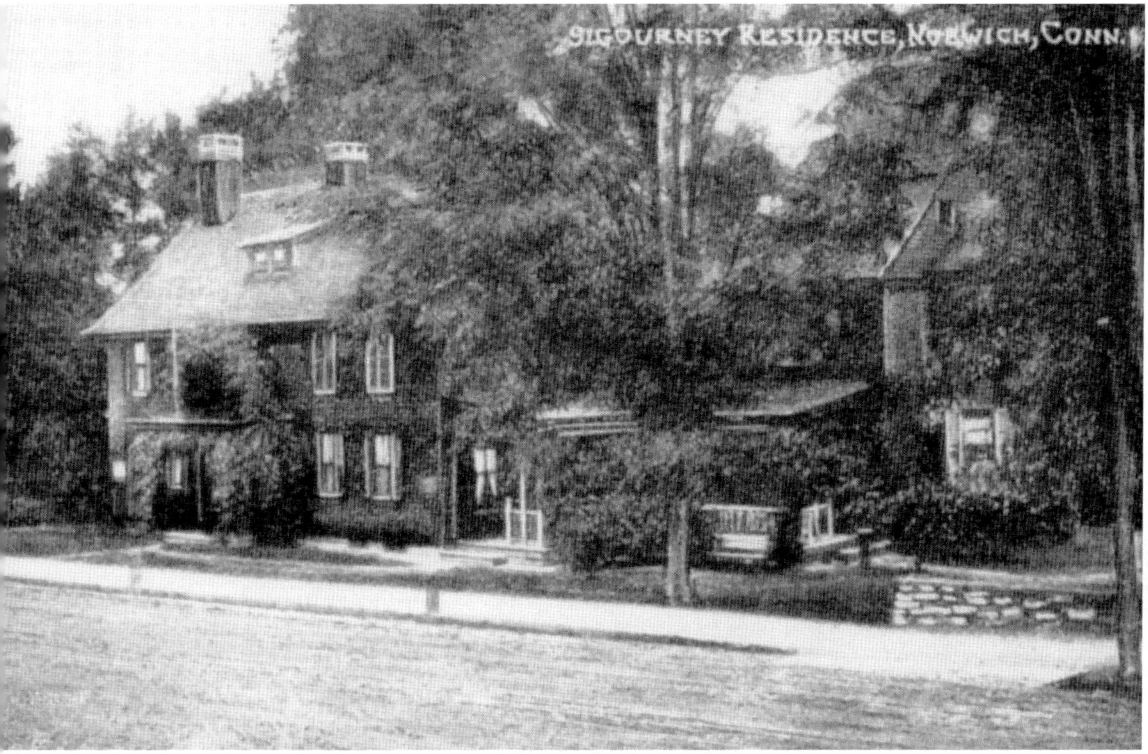

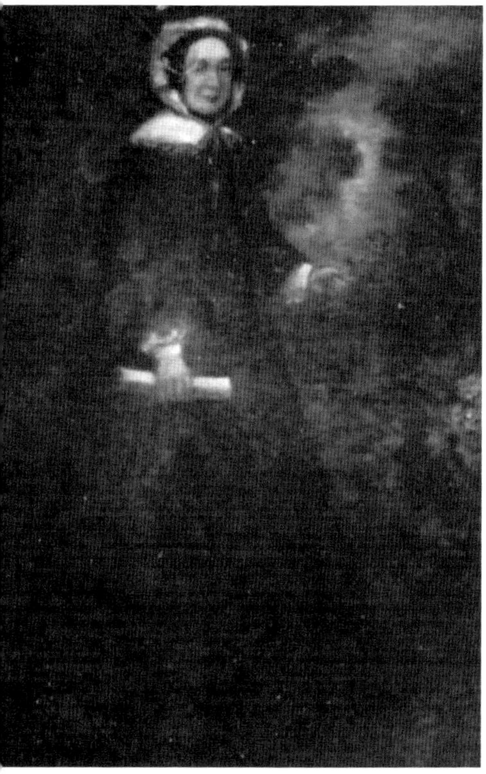

Lydia Howard Huntley Sigourney
One of the first women to achieve a successful career as a writer was Lydia Howard Huntley Sigourney (1791–1865). From 1809 to 1811, Sigourney and a friend operated a school for black and white students, stressing reading comprehension, the practice of reading aloud, and the skills of letter writing and memorization. In 1815, she published *Moral Pieces in Prose and Verse.*

In *Sketch of Connecticut* (1824), she used her experiences in Norwich to discuss cross-class obligations and the diversity of people. Her works were among the first to give voices to blacks, Native Americans, members of diverse religions, farmers, and the poor. Sigourney gave away many copies of her 67 published books and contributed more than 2,000 articles to nearly 300 periodicals, edited *The Religious Souvenir* from 1839 to 1840. From 1839 to 1842, she was listed as an editor of *Godey's Lady's Book*. Many women's literary societies were organized in her name, and in 1844, Sigourney, Iowa, was named in her honor. The image above is from a postcard of the Sigourney residence. The portrait at left is from the mural on the courthouse wall in Sigourney, Iowa. (Image at left courtesy of Clerk's Office of Sigourney, Iowa.)

Joseph Williams

Williams married Abigail Coit on May 30, 1778, and began his investments in West Indies trading, privateering, and other maritime interests. The American Revolution was good to Williams. He became a correspondent and friend of George Washington and Gov. Jonathan Trumbull, and his interests soon grew to include two warehouses, a shipyard, a fleet of more than 20 sailing ships, and an interest in the portion of the Western Reserve of Connecticut, which became Cleveland, Ohio.

In 1783, he was appointed a lieutenant of the Home Guards. By 1793, the men of the Home Guards regularly paraded together on "the Great Plain," the unimproved land near his home. In 1796, he was appointed brigadier general of the 3rd Brigade, Connecticut Militia. In April 1797, "the Great Plain" was dedicated as a public parade thanks to the military reviews General Williams conducted there. For almost all of the 19th century, the park was known as Williams Park in his honor. In the 20th century, the name was changed to Chelsea Parade.

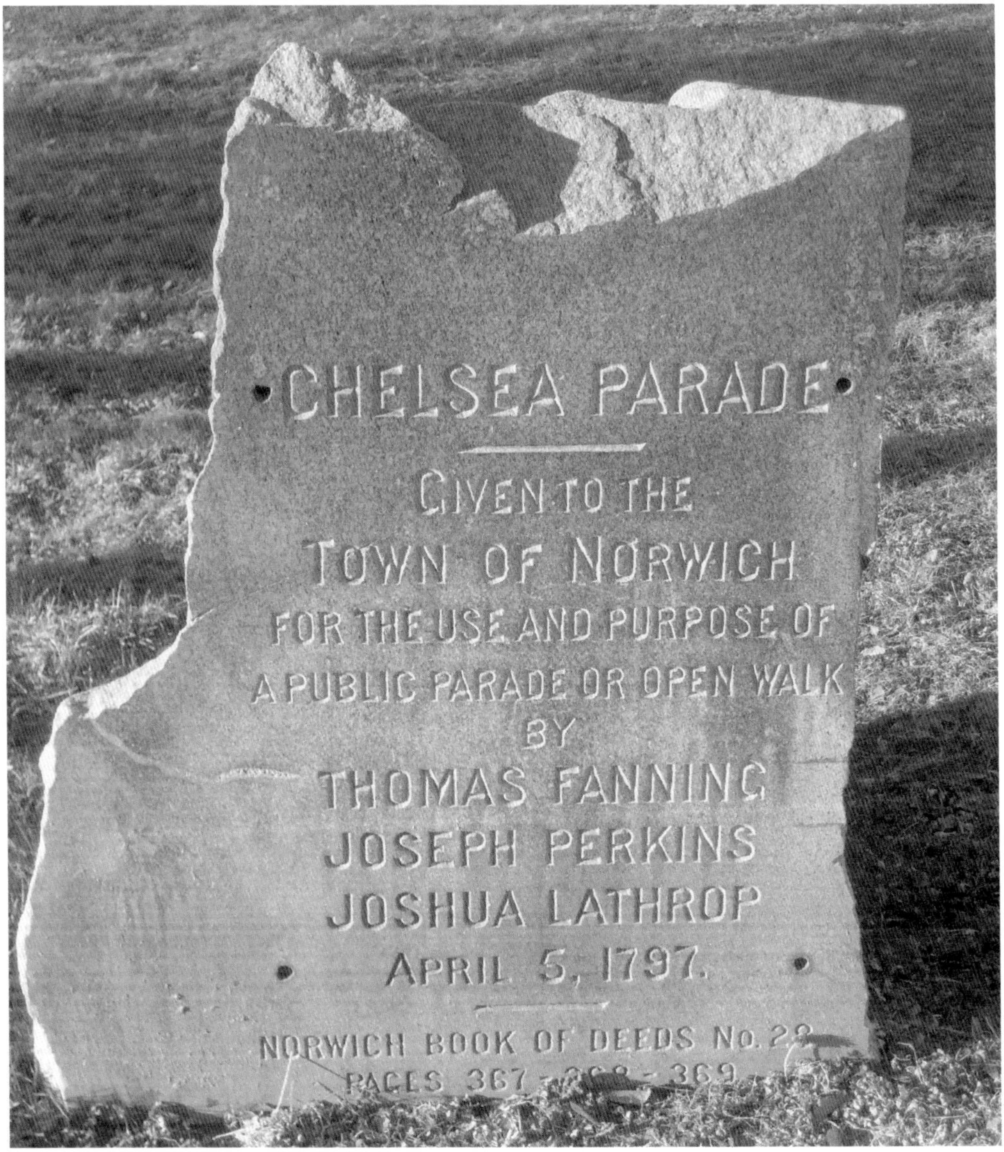

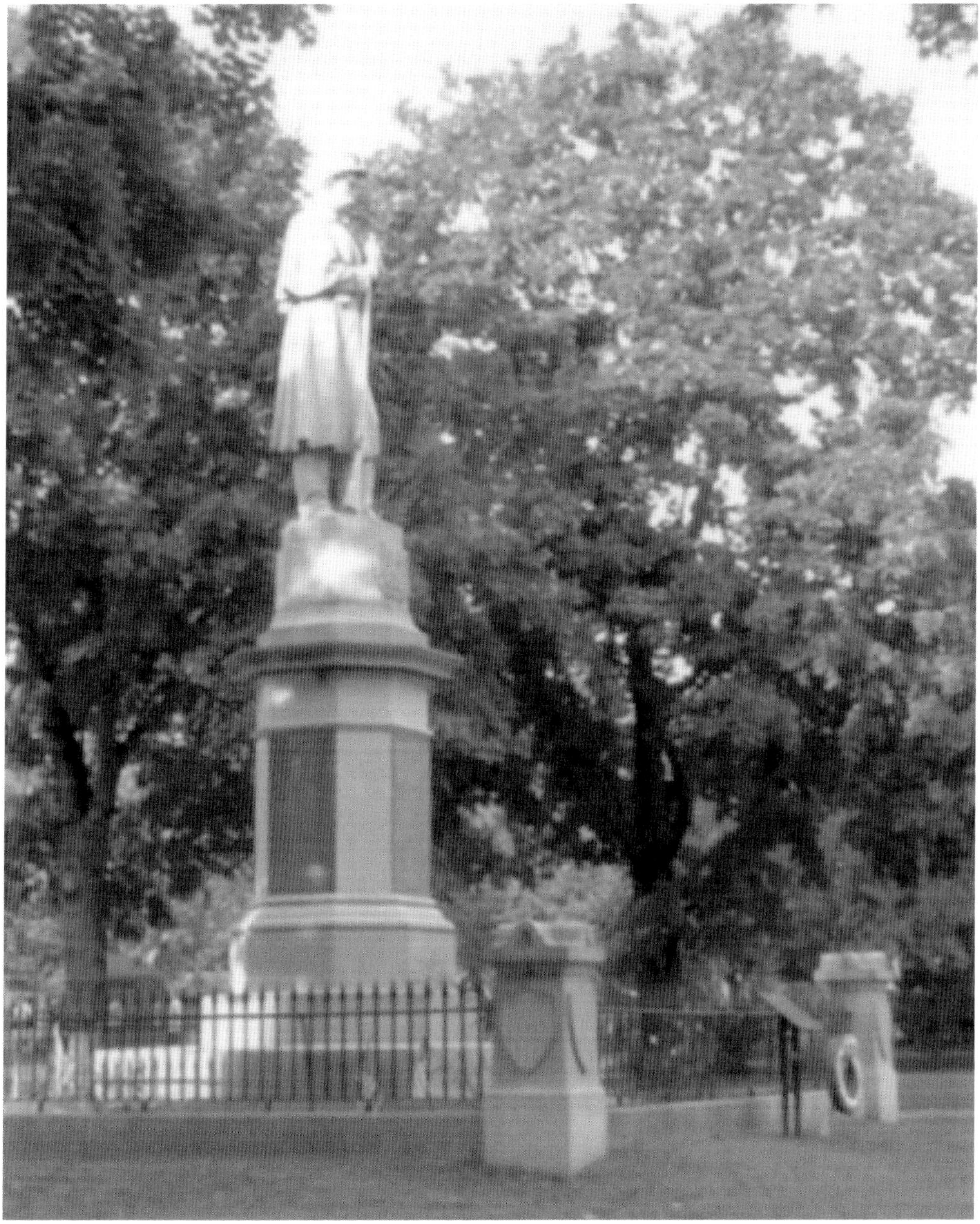

The Soldier
Standing 12 feet high on a taller-than-usual, octagonal base, *The Soldier* was the first of the monuments placed at the northern point of Chelsea Parade since April 14, 1873. Nearby and below the statue stand the memorials for those who have served in times of war and peace, up to the present day. The soldier's last duty is to guard the time capsule, buried in 1959 at the 300th anniversary of the settling of Norwich. The capsule will be opened in 2059.

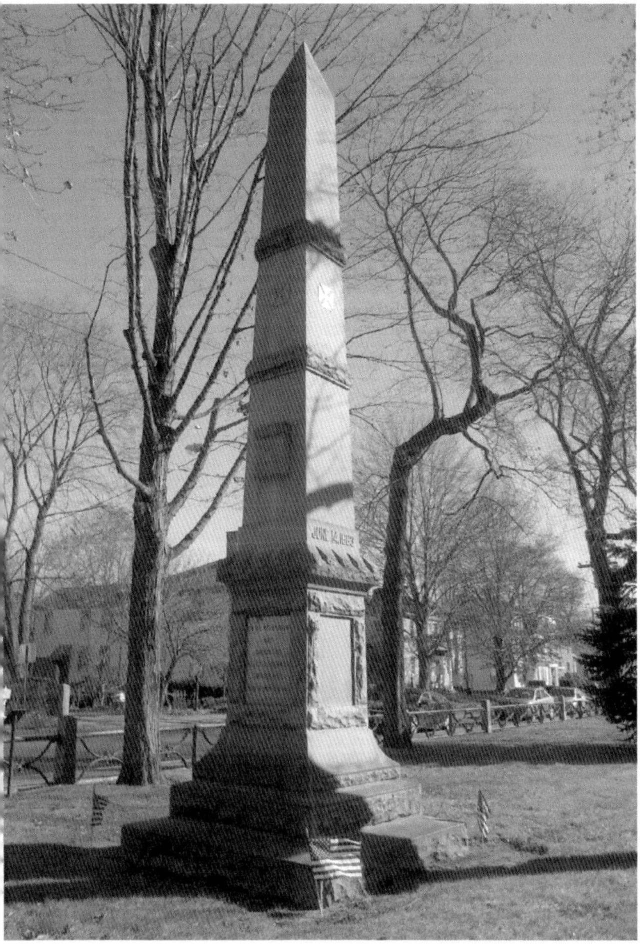

Edward P. Manning

On November 10, 1862, Edward Manning joined the service as a commissary sergeant, creating the 26th Regiment of the Connecticut Volunteer Infantry. The regiment arrived on December 16 at Camp Parapet, a Confederate fort north of New Orleans that had been captured by Union forces. The regiment participated in two assaults of Port Hudson on May 27 and June 14, 1863. Manning was promoted to second lieutenant. The Confederate leaders at Port Hudson surrendered on July 9, and the regiment returned home to Norwich. On August 14, Manning received his commission as a lieutenant. He died on August 17, 1863, the same day the 26th Regiment was mustered out of service to its country.

James Lindsay Smith

In 1881, James Smith, successful shoemaker and Methodist minister, wrote a first-person account of his life in the South and his journey to Norwich, where he got married and raised and educated his children.

Few other cities have such a document, which relates the details of a black businessman's experience in the North just after the Civil War and the importance he placed on education. His son James H. Smith attended Normal Grammar School and followed his father into the shoemaking trade. His eldest daughter, Sarah Ann Smith, was also a graduate from the Normal Grammar School, and his two younger daughters went on from the Normal Grammar School to Norwich Free Academy. They graduated, having taken courses in classical education and English, and became teachers in Washington, DC.

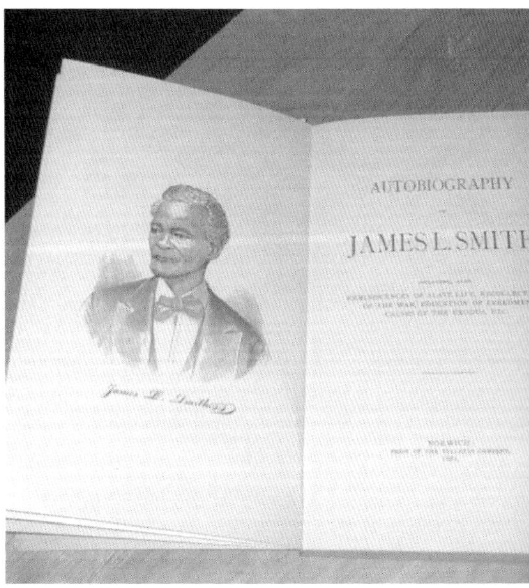

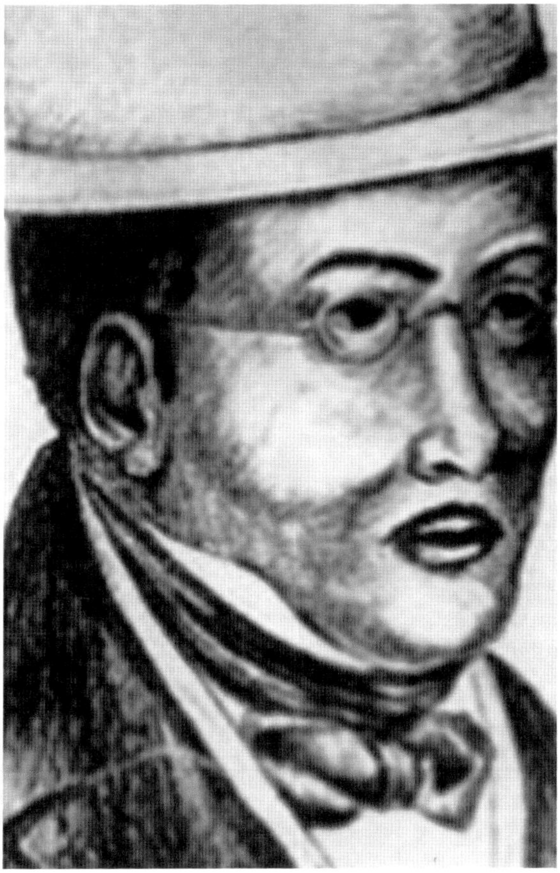

David Ruggles

David Ruggles (March 15, 1810–December 16, 1849) and his family moved to Norwich as free blacks when David was very young. His father was a blacksmith and woodcutter, and his mother was a noted caterer for the area. The family lived simply, and David attended Sabbath schools. He impressed other residents so much, they hired a tutor from Yale to teach him Latin.

Ruggles was once observed in a store placing a ball of chewing gum, clandestinely set aside for a lady friend, into his hat. No accusations were made, and Ruggles headed for the exit. He just happened to be met at the bottom of the stairs by residents who needed help turning the grinding stone. Although suspicious, he could not refuse, and he helped turn the wheel. In the full August sun, the melting wax of the gum began to streak down his face. Ruggles was kindly thanked and discharged with the suggestion "to take off his hat and cool his head," but he declined and left. When he was next seen a few days later, it was with a new cap settled on a newly sheared head.

At 17, Ruggles moved to New York City and worked as a mariner. He then owned a grocery store and sold liquor, until he realized the impact alcohol was having on the black community, at which time he embraced temperance. He advocated an end to slavery in his advertisements and opened the nation's first black-owned bookstore while writing columns for the *Emancipator*, an abolitionist weekly. He later self-published a booklet, the first imprint by a black man in the United States. He was the most visible member of the Underground Railroad in the Northeast. Abolitionist orator Frederick Douglass was one of the 400 slaves that Ruggles guided to freedom and safety. Physical issues led Ruggles to join a health commune in Northampton, Massachusetts. The cure worked, and by 1845, David Ruggles, now a doctor of hydropathy, opened the first water-cure hospital in the United States. His body was retrieved by his family after his death on December 18, 1849, and he was buried in the family plot in Norwich.

Robert Ogden Fletcher

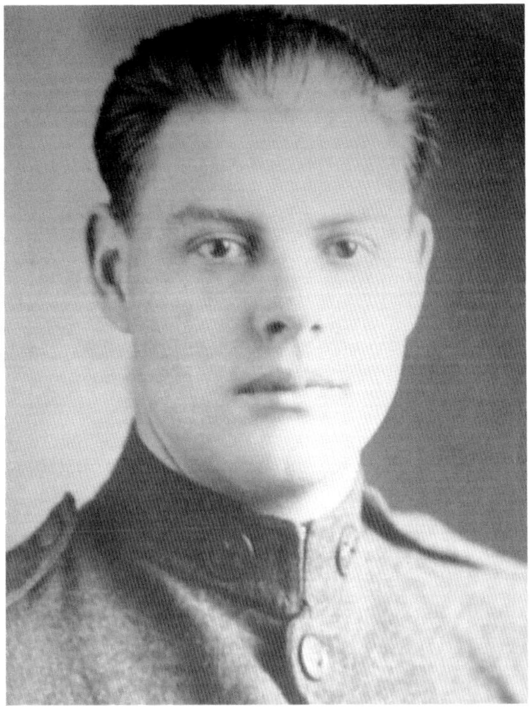

Fletcher was captain of the baseball team in his Norwich Free Academy graduating class of 1912. Immediately after graduation, he worked for Hopkins & Allen Arms Company, assembling a variety of guns. He then worked for the *Bulletin* newspaper as a sports editor. In the early spring of 1917, he enlisted in the 3rd Company, Coast Artillery. Fletcher became company clerk and went to Fort Wright at Fisher's Island in July 1917. When the 56th Artillery Regiment was formed from the Connecticut Coast Artillery, he became regimental supply sergeant, and left for overseas duty on March 20, 1918, where he was promoted to sergeant major. Fletcher died while convoying supplies on August 15, 1918. As a tribute to the friendship he demonstrated to all he associated with, the American Legion Post No. 4 was named in his honor in 1922.

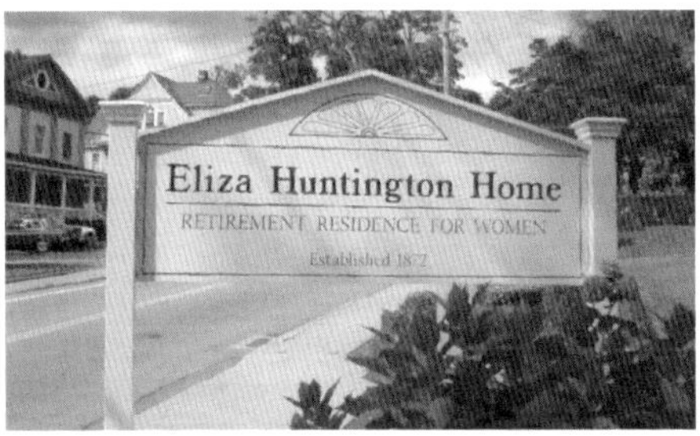

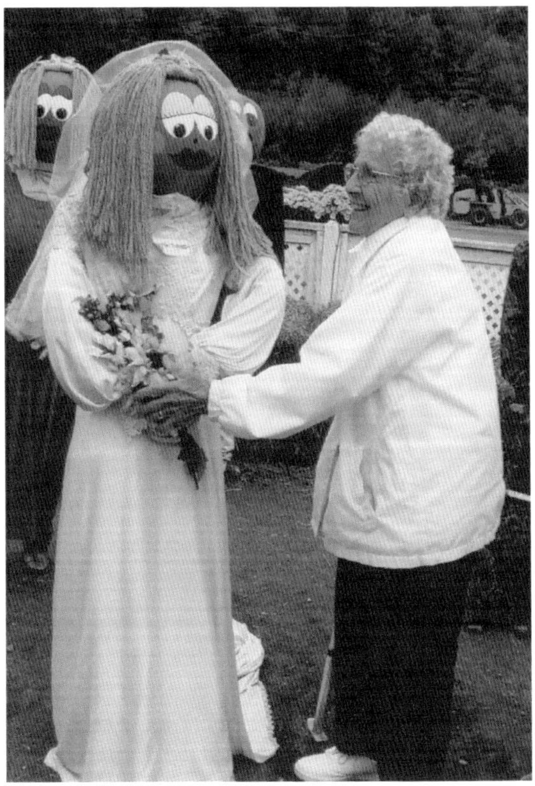

Eliza and Jedediah Huntington

Eliza and Jedediah were married in June 1819 and spent much of their nearly 40 years of marriage in the main house. He was a buyer and seller of various dry goods, bolts of cloth, pottery, salted beef, and other domestic supplies. All visitors were greeted as friends. Jedediah was well known for making large donations to religious and benevolent associations. It was no surprise that, in his last will and testament, he honored the memory of his wife by establishing "a place to call home" for retired women. At right, Ellen Balchunas is pictured during a Halloween pumpkin maze activity. (Both images courtesy of Eliza Huntington Memorial Home.)

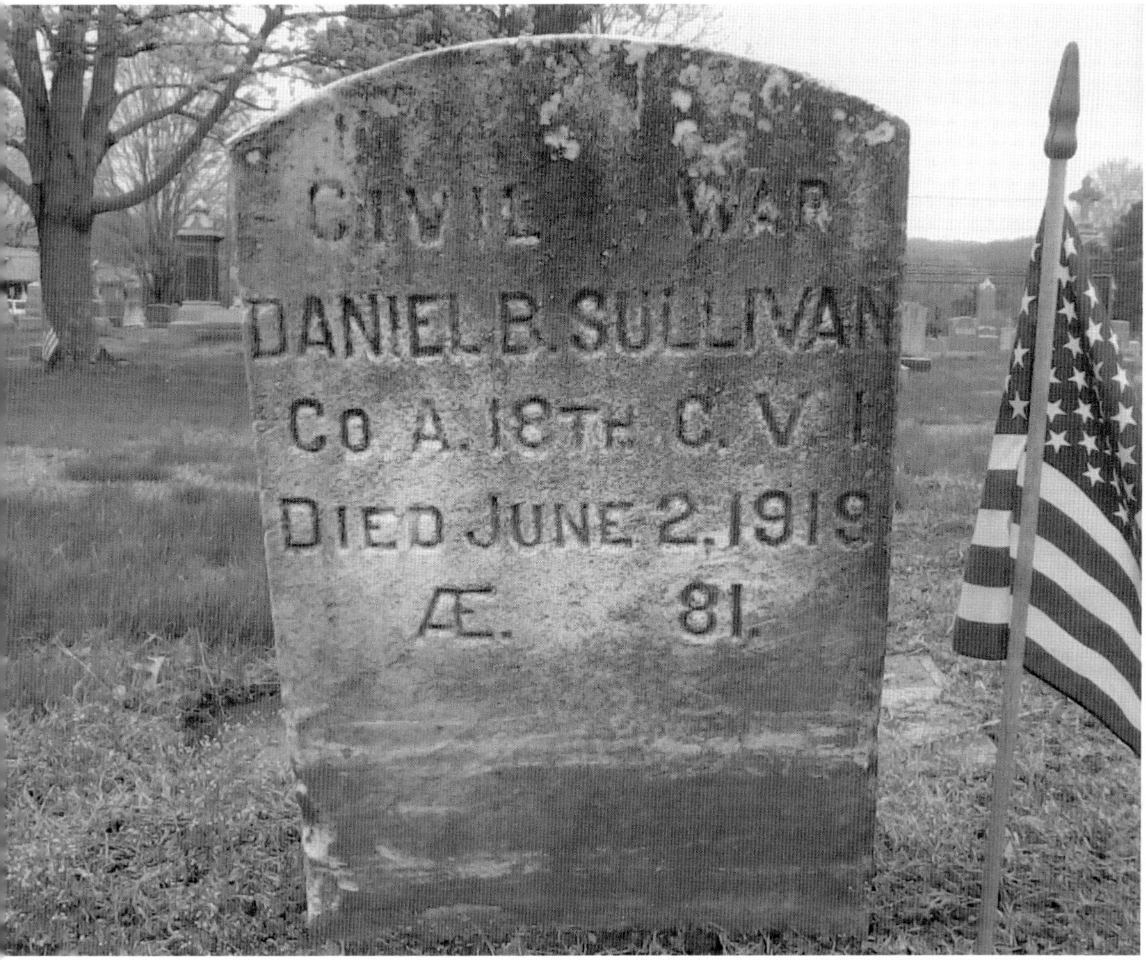

Daniel B. Sullivan

As a member of Company A, 18th Connecticut Volunteers, Daniel Sullivan was shot in the left side during the Battle of Winchester on June 15, 1863. He recovered from his wound and returned home to Norwich. The bullet remained embedded in place for nearly 37 years. Then, suddenly for two or three weeks prior to the event related below, the healed scar became a running sore.

On Monday, March 12, 1900, Sullivan complained of not feeling well, but not so unwell that he missed a shift at his job as a tinsmith in the store of J.P. Barstow & Co. on Water Street. Around 3:30 p.m., when he stooped over to pick up a tool, he felt something run down the line of his clothing. Curious, he picked the object out of his shoe. To his amazement, he saw that it was the troublesome bullet, evidently a Winchester bullet half an inch in diameter, flattened and discolored. The edges were rough and irritating. Feeling greatly relieved, Sullivan continued working. It was presumed that his wound once more healed over, as he lived several more years, until June 2, 1919. (Courtesy of John Sullivan.)

Lafayette Sabine Foster

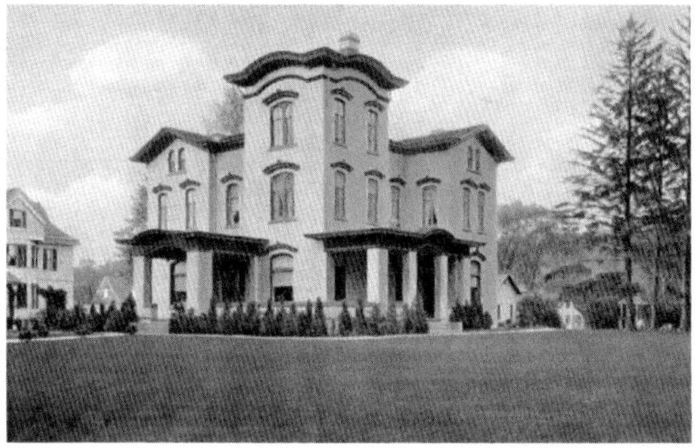

The Foster home served as the Norton-Peck Library on the Norwich Free Academy campus from 1952 to 1992 and is currently home to the academy's board room and community rooms. Lafayette Sabine Foster was an outstanding lawyer, civic official, and educator known for his tact and impartiality. From 1835 to 1838, he was the editor of the *Norwich Republican* newspaper. In 1851, he entered politics, twice serving one-year terms as mayor of Norwich. He was elected for the second term without a single vote being cast against him. He was elected state representative, serving three terms as Connecticut House Speaker, followed by several terms as a US senator. Foster was chosen president of the Senate at the first session of the 39th Congress on March 6, 1865. A month later, on April 15, after Abraham Lincoln's assassination, he became acting vice president of the United States until the end of his Senate term, in 1867. Later, he became a judge on the Connecticut Supreme Court.

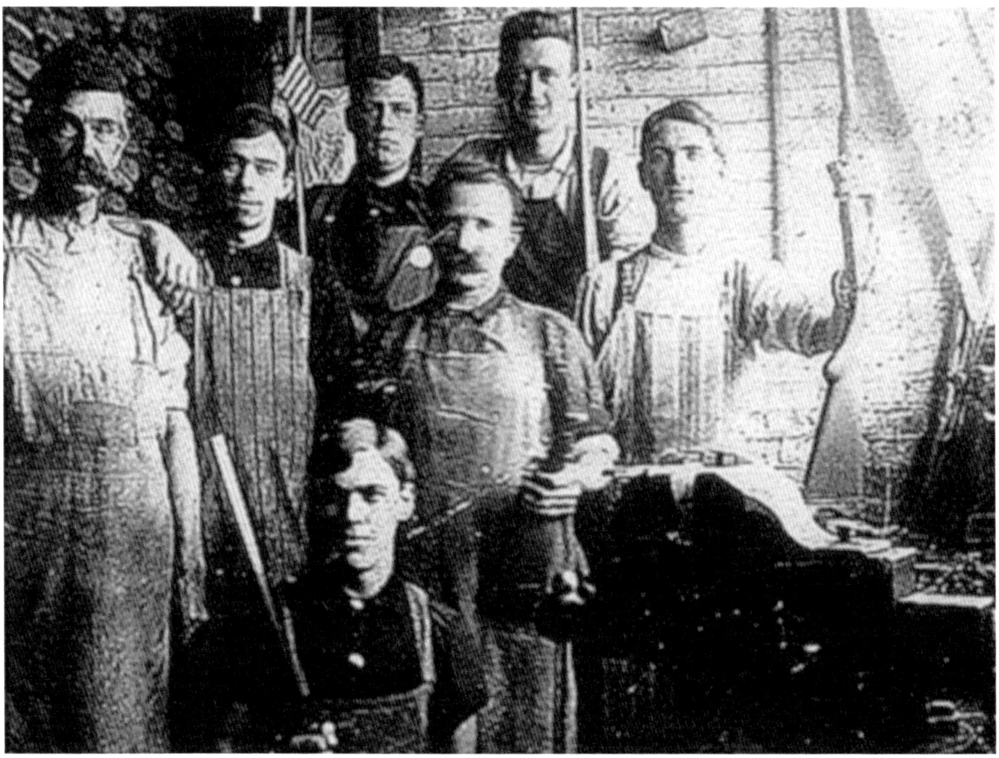

James T. Carey

Before becoming a mail carrier, James T. Carey assembled guns at the Hopkins and Allen Firearms Company in Norwich. He was a mail carrier for 33 years on the West Side, and in the Jail Hill, Laurel Hill, and Washington and Asylum Street areas of Norwich. In retirement, he portrayed Santa for the Norwich Chamber of Commerce for many years. His secret of success, besides liking children, was his great memory. As a mail carrier, he had learned the names of many of the children, their parents, and even their grandparents. (Courtesy of Mary Kelleher.)

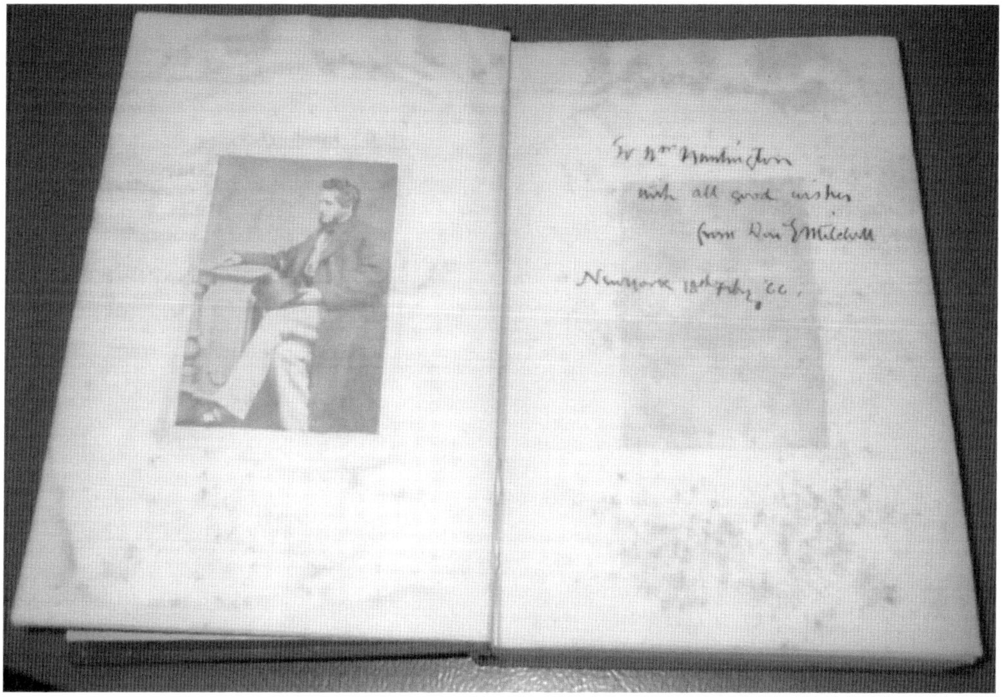

Donald Grant Mitchell

Donald Mitchell was born in the family home on Broadway on April 22, 1822. He graduated from Yale in 1841 at the head of his class and spent the next three years farming. During the next three years, he set out on a walking tour of Europe before publishing *Fresh Gleanings* in 1847. Mitchell wrote in his letter of dedication in *Battle Summer*, published in 1848, that law school lost its appeal. "I conjured up images of the New Order, and the images dogged me in the streets, and at my desk, and made my sleep a nightmare."

Following his return to Connecticut, he wrote under the pen name Ik Marvel. Among his works were *The Reveries of a Bachelor* and *Dream Life*. In 1853, he wrote of his marriage, *Consulship in Venice*, and he wrote of other European experiences in *Seven Stories with Basement and Attic*. He became a settled Connecticut farmer in 1855 and died in 1908.

William Tyler Olcott

Astronomer William Olcott wrote six books and many articles telling the story of stars. Olcott mentored over 100 observers and gave countless lectures to popularize the field of amateur astronomy. In 1911, he and others founded the American Association of Variable Star Observers (AAVSO). NASA honored Olcott by naming a crater on the moon after him. Olcott lived in the c. 1768 home of Rev. John Tyler, his great-great-grandfather.

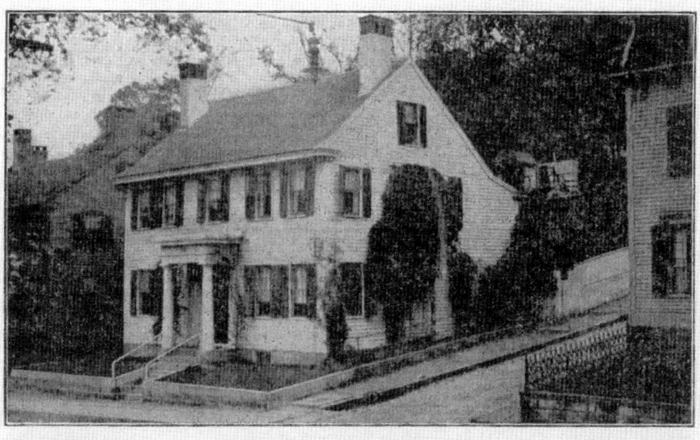

Norwich, Conn. The Globe House, Home of the Rev. John Tyler 1768

Moses "Mace" Goldblatt

The 1930 Norwich Free Academy yearbook states that the highest ambition of "Mace" Goldblatt was to find a new kind of necktie. It also says that he danced beautifully, sometimes wore a derby, and liked a "cosmopolitan" crowd. He enlisted one night in the Abraham Lincoln Brigade, an international band of volunteers who went to Spain to defend the democratic Republican government against the illegally elected Spanish government. Goldblatt was killed at the Battle of Gandesa, Catalonia, on April 3, 1938. His body was not recovered. He was the only person from Norwich to fight in the Spanish Civil War. (Courtesy of the Goldblatt family.)

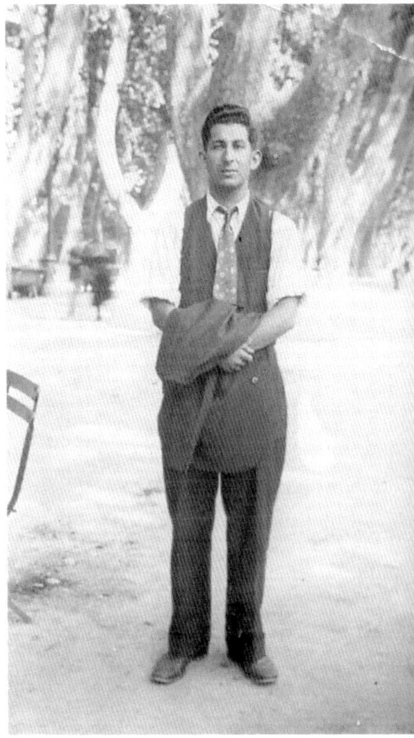

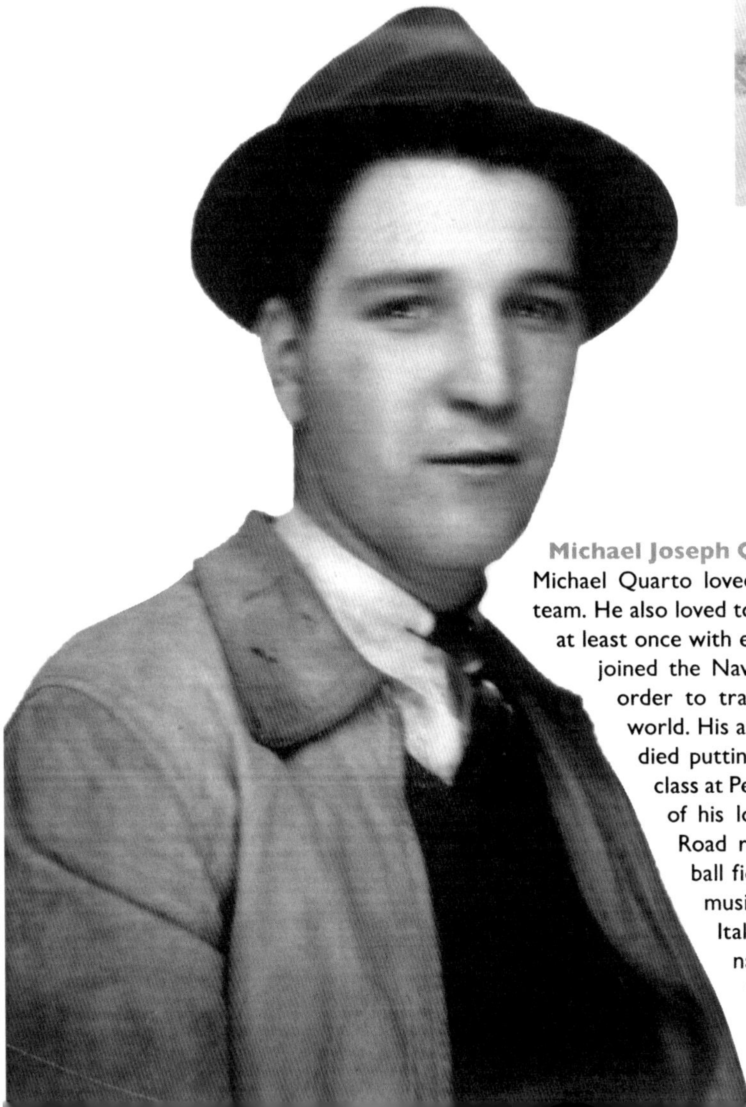

Michael Joseph Quarto

Michael Quarto loved sports and being a member of a team. He also loved to dance, bragging that he had danced at least once with every girl in Norwich. When Quarto joined the Navy, he told his family that it was in order to travel and dance his way around the world. His adventures had barely begun when he died putting out a fire as a Navy seaman first class at Pearl Harbor, Hawaii, in 1941. In honor of his love of baseball and sports, Quarto Road runs by the side of a neighborhood ball field. As it was sure to be the site of music and dancing, the Michael J. Quarto, Italian American Veterans Post 20 was named in his honor. (Courtesy of the Quarto family.)

CHAPTER TWO

Education

Education has been a special feature of Norwich from the time of its settlement. Boys and girls, black, white, and Native American, were taught to read, write, and do sums. The Leffingwell House Museum has Colonial-era copybooks from boys and girls in its library. Many early residents completed their education at Yale University in New Haven.

By 1853, the Reverend Dr. John P. Gulliver was appealing to the wealthiest of Norwich to establish a school to provide equal education for boys and girls, from the very poorest to the wealthiest of the community, at no cost. Through 40 benefactors, $76,000 was raised and the doors of the Norwich Free Academy were opened in 1856 with a student body of 80, a faculty of five, and one classroom building. Today, Norwich Free Academy remains a private institution, serving as the designated high school for Norwich. It has a student body in excess of 2,400, a faculty of 200, and comprises nine classroom buildings.

The passion for education did not stop at the city limits. In 1882, John Fox Slater donated $1 million toward the education of emancipated black slaves in the Southern states. Today, Norwich is proud to be the home of 16 public, private, and charter schools serving students from preschool through grade 12, as well as Three Rivers Community College.

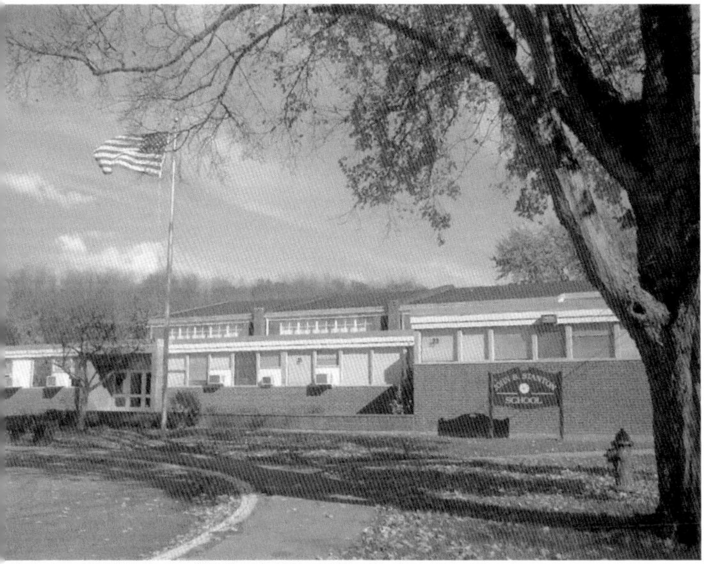

John Byron Stanton
Stanton died in February 1933, but the impact of his 37 years as a teacher, principal, and community leader was so deeply felt that a school was named for him in 1956. Stanton, a leader by example, spoke often of looking to the future. The John B. Stanton Elementary School serves the community with academic and athletic programs and the first health outreach program for students, faculty, and members of the Norwich community.

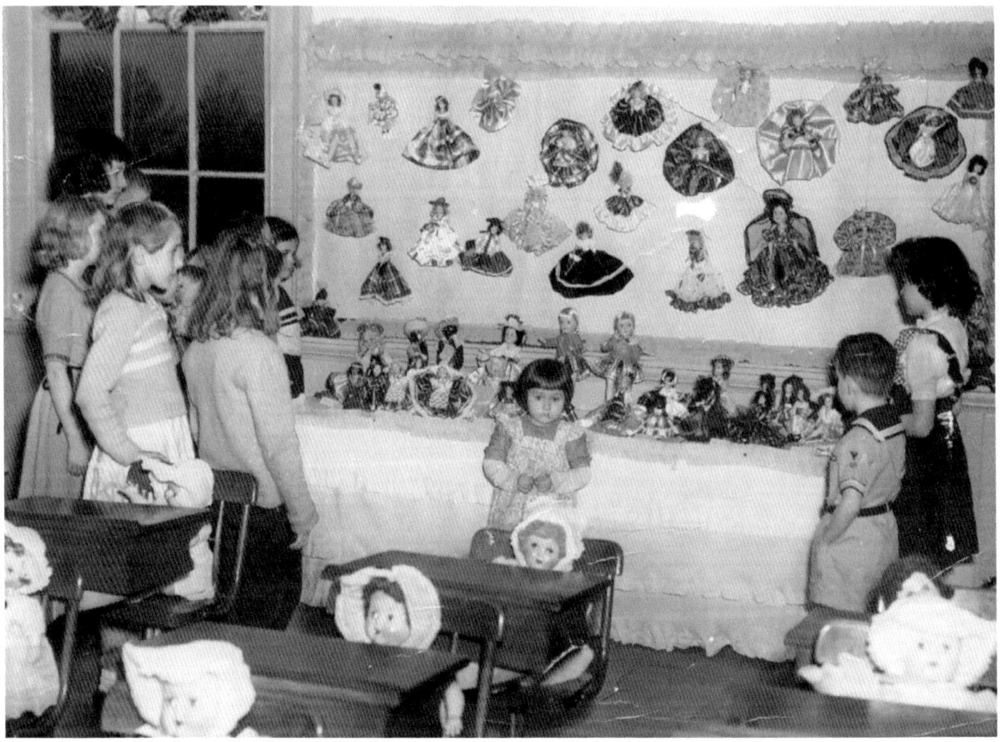

Marjorie McCune
In 1950, Marjorie McCune was teaching third grade at the Falls School in Norwich, at a time when the world was changing. The population of Norwich was rapidly expanding, with immigrants speaking different languages and practicing different customs in their homes. To celebrate the diversity, students from all grades brought dolls to school, dressed to represent different nationalities. The exhibit was so unusual for its time, even residents who did not have children in the school attended and commented in letters to the local papers. (Courtesy of Mary Kelleher.)

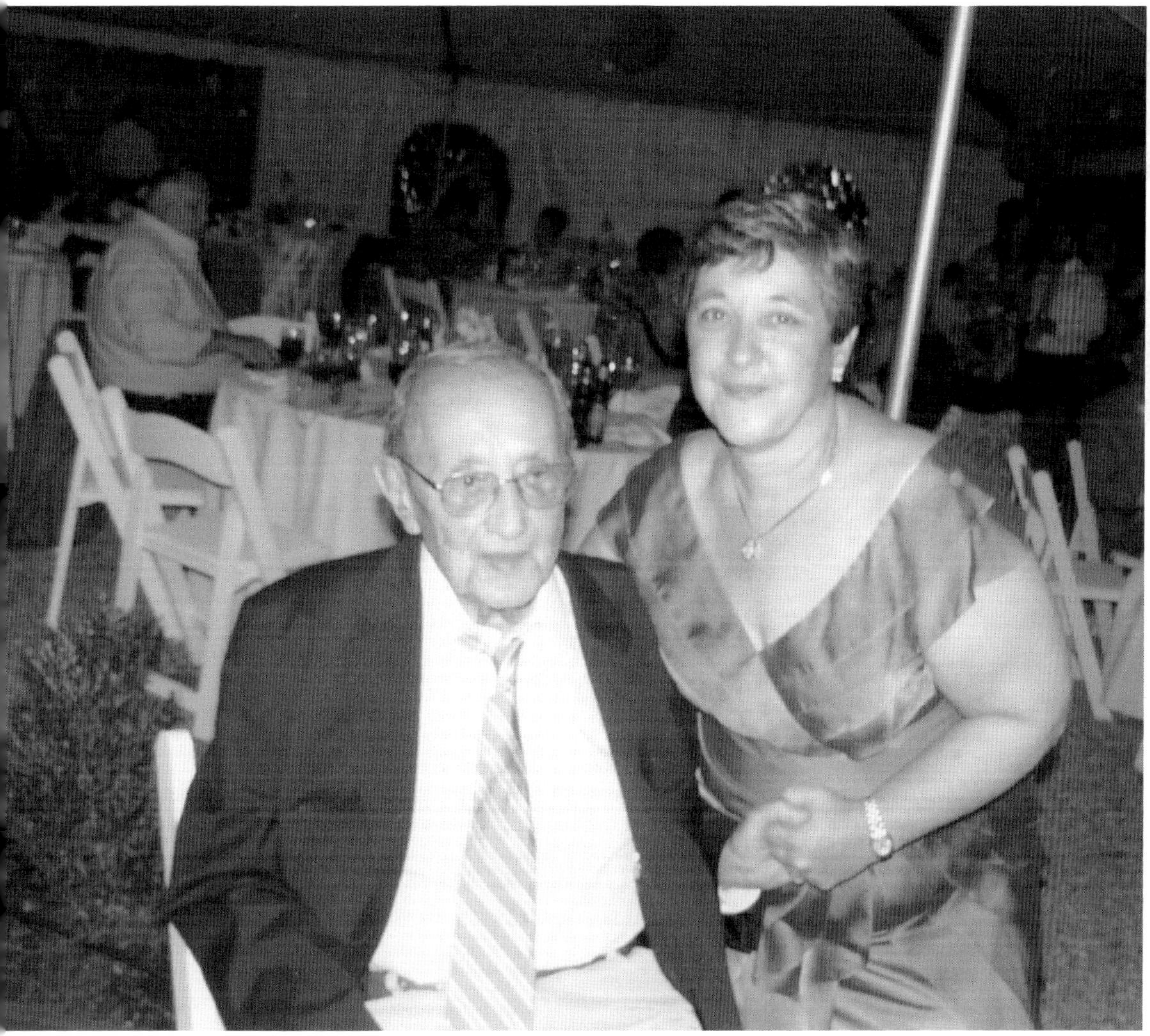

Stanley Israelite and Abby Dolliver

The caption for Stanley Israelite's 1943 Norwich Free Academy yearbook photograph reads, "If you ever need help or assistance call Stanley at #316, he will help you." An assistant for 25 years to Second District congressman Christopher Dodd, Israelite had a plaque on his desk that read, "Either I will find a way or I will make one." Israelite proved that he could make paths where there were none as president of the chamber of commerce, creating one of the first industrial parks in the state of Connecticut in the 1960s. The name Norwich Industrial Park was later changed to Stanley Israelite Business Park to honor his impact and dedicated years of service to the people of Norwich.

Abby I. Dolliver teaches leadership by example. Her career began as a school social worker, and she rose to the position of special education coordinator in Norwich, becoming instrumental in the launch of the 24-town LEARN ABA School Support Network. She was also a member of the board of trustees and a corporator of the Norwich Free Academy. Dolliver was selected to the Educational Leadership Program at the University of Connecticut for certification as a school superintendent. When a superintendent of schools was needed, the Norwich Board of Education did not hesitate, asking Dolliver to serve in that capacity, fully confident that her priority would always be the students, families, staff, and community. (Courtesy of Abby Israelite Dolliver.)

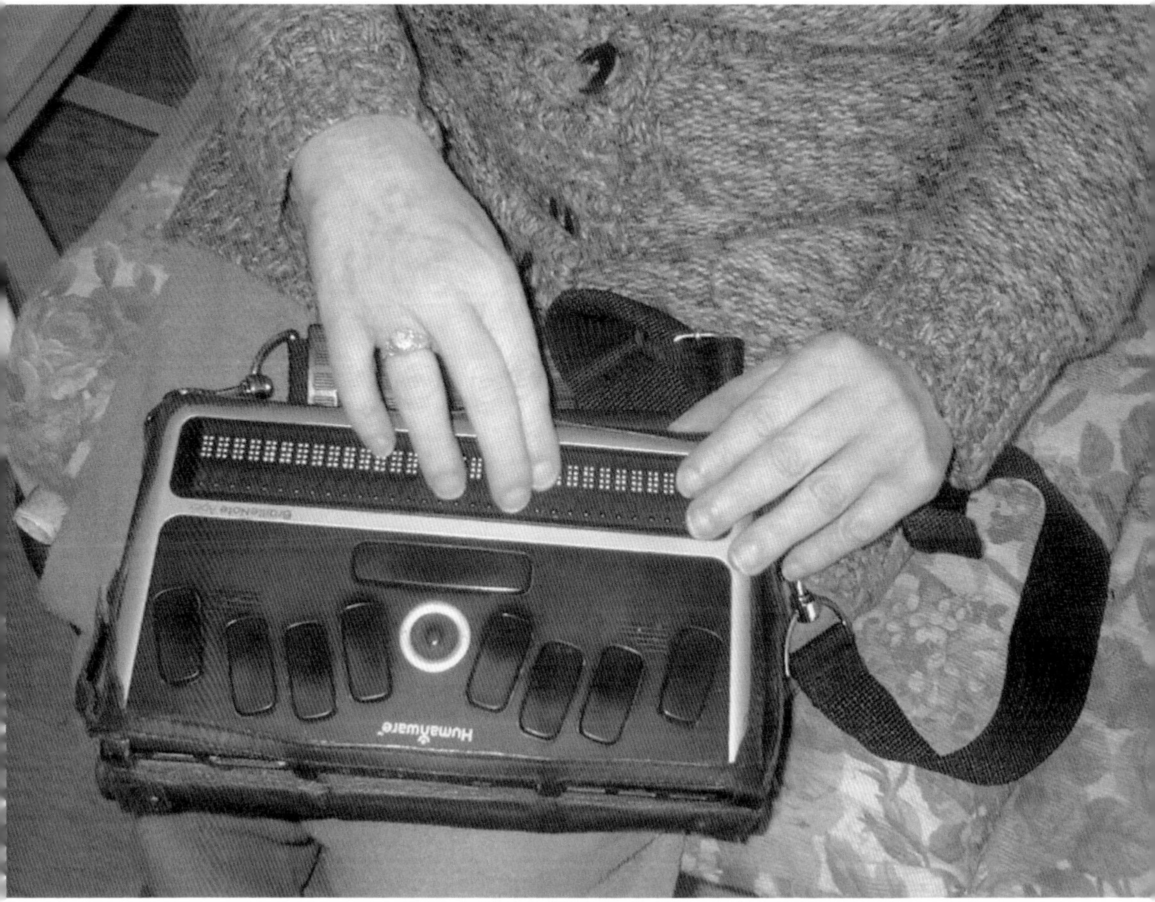

Eileen Akers

"If it is not right, you fix it." Being blind has not stopped Eileen Akers from seeing what is needed and working hard to provide it. She earned her bachelor of arts in English from Connecticut College, a master of arts in English from Trinity, and did doctoral work at Columbia University in special education, receiving a special education certification from Columbia.

Never one to be pigeonholed, in 1966, Akers was one of the first Braille-ready teachers to be hired by a public school system in Connecticut. In 1978, she broke another barrier by bringing her guide dog to work at Teachers Memorial Middle School.

"You have to go beyond the conventional to make progress," Akers said. Much of her teaching has been accomplished with progressive technology, which she demonstrates and uses for the benefit of others. Digital players, synthetic speech, closed-circuit television, and computers have made a tremendous change in what can be accomplished. Akers knows that everybody is different, and so are their needs.

As president of the Connecticut Braille Association, she makes sure that school textbooks are available in large print and Braille. Being on the State of Connecticut Bureau of Educational Services of the Blind, Akers keeps a wary eye on the policies, programs, and services available to the blind and ensures that they are effectively used. An active member of the board of directors of the Otis Library, she encourages her students, families, and friends to make good use of the library and to use interlibrary book loan. Akers also volunteers with the Lion's Low Vision Center of Eastern Connecticut, having served as their president. The organization works with senior citizens who have lost their sight.

"A dynamic community is constantly able to re-shape itself, and for a community to serve itself, it must serve everyone," Akers has said.

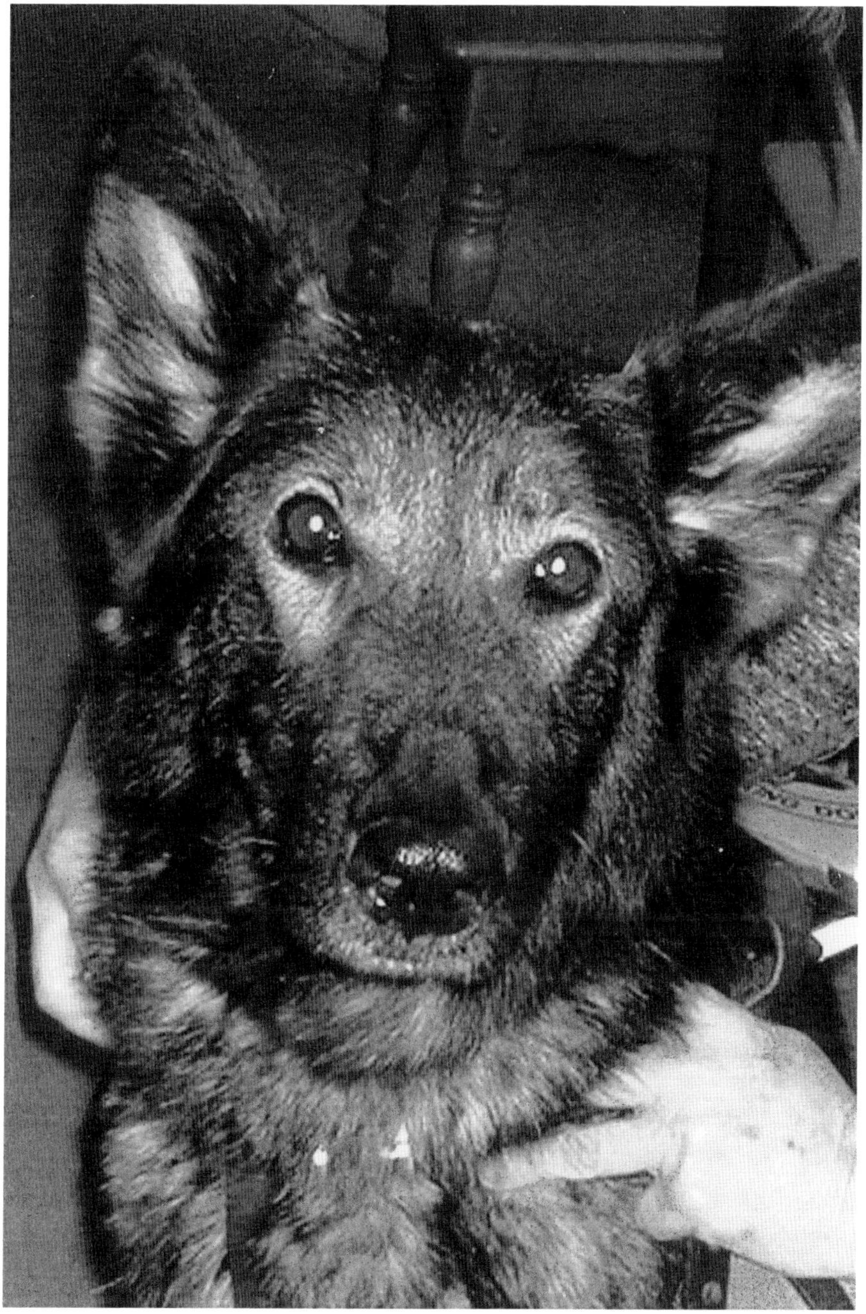

Fiona

Fiona, a Fidelco German shepherd, has been bred and trained to do one thing: correctly guide Eileen Akers, her human partner, and to keep her safe. Fiona goes for walks on the streets and to the supermarket, restaurants, stores, and Akers' workplace in the schools of Norwich, where she is a teacher, low-vision consultant, and advocate. Fidelco pioneered in-community placement in the United States, a process that allows guide-dog users to be trained in the communities where they live and work.

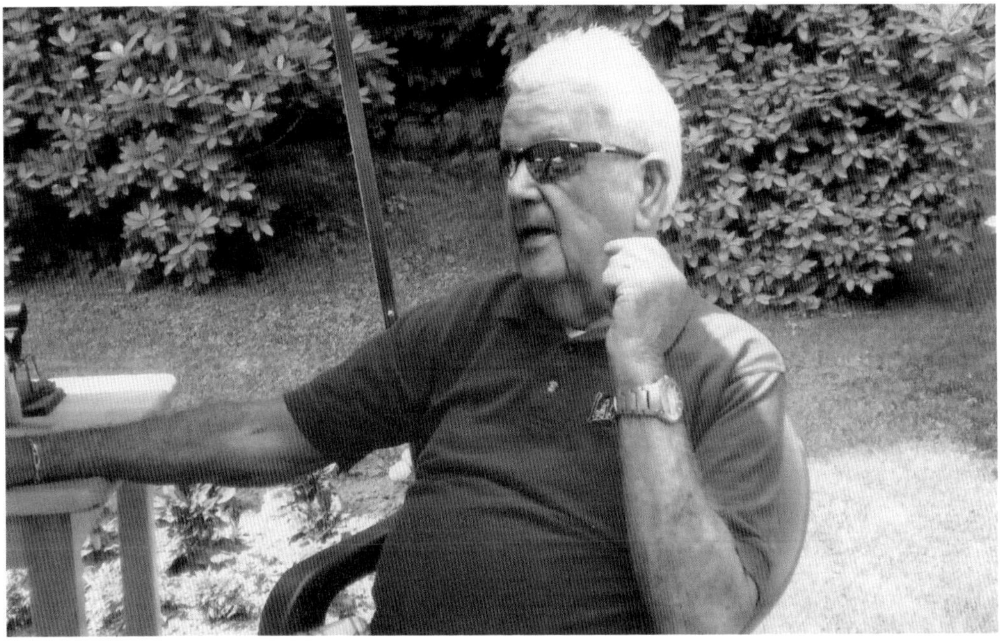

John Anderson
"Norwich is a brighter place to live in because of all the lamps made in my woodworking class," grinned John Anderson. For 30 years, Anderson introduced students to woodworking in the shop class at Kelly Middle School. With authority and skill, he directed the students through the process of choosing or designing a project and seeing it through to completion. Sometimes, it was the first time a student saw a project all the way through to its end.

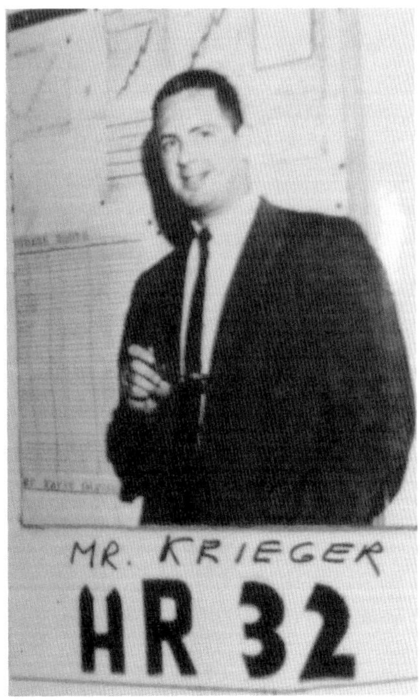

Mort Krieger
Krieger stands out in the memory of many Kelly Middle School students as their favorite teacher. This, despite the fact that he taught math! Realizing that students need to have self-respect and pride in themselves, he created a marching drill team, Kelly Pride. Through this project, with no grades or tests, Krieger successfully taught the skills of following directions, cooperation, and leadership that would last a lifetime. Krieger taught for over 30 years. (Courtesy of Lori Krieger Taylor.)

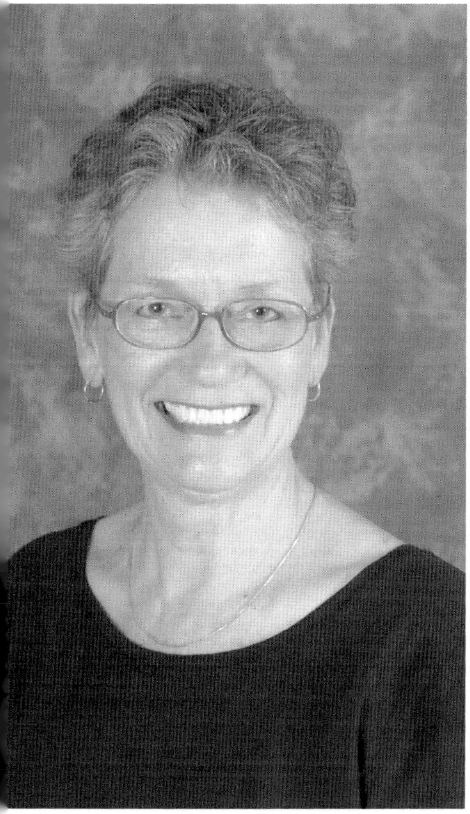

Joyce Werden
In 1970, Joyce Werden relocated from Iowa to Norwich with her husband, who had joined the Coast Guard band. With her education degree in hand, she began substitute teaching in Norwich elementary schools, only to be told by the superintendent that, in order to obtain a teaching contract, she had to have a Norwich address. Werden persevered and, after 30 years, retired from Norwich Public Schools. She was one of three teachers who opened the Integrated Day Charter School in the city. In 2005, Werden was elected to the Norwich Board of Education, and she continues there after eight years. Thanks to the classroom and administrative leadership of Werden, Norwich is a place where fresh faces and ideas in education are welcomed and encouraged! (Courtesy of Joyce Werden.)

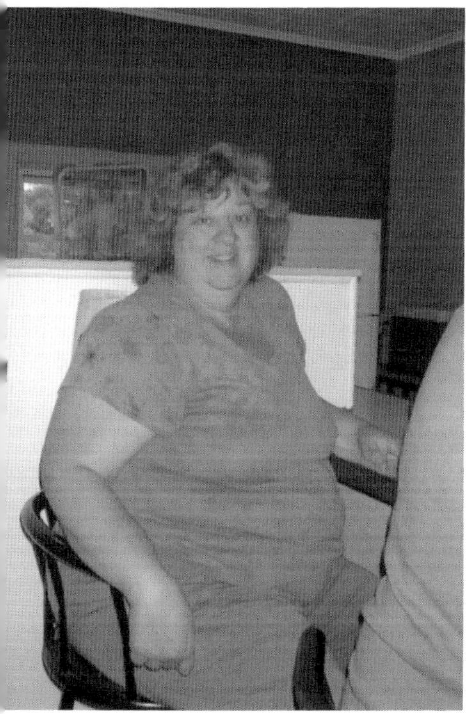

Jodi Martin
Jodi Martin safely drives school buses in the Norwich area. High school students can remember her driving them to kindergarten. Parents greet her in stores with stories of their child's new adventure or milestone. Sometimes, the parents bring greetings, telling their children, "If you see Ms. Jodi, be sure to tell her 'Hi' from me." "That's my favorite thing," says Martin. "When the students remember me. It makes me feel good."

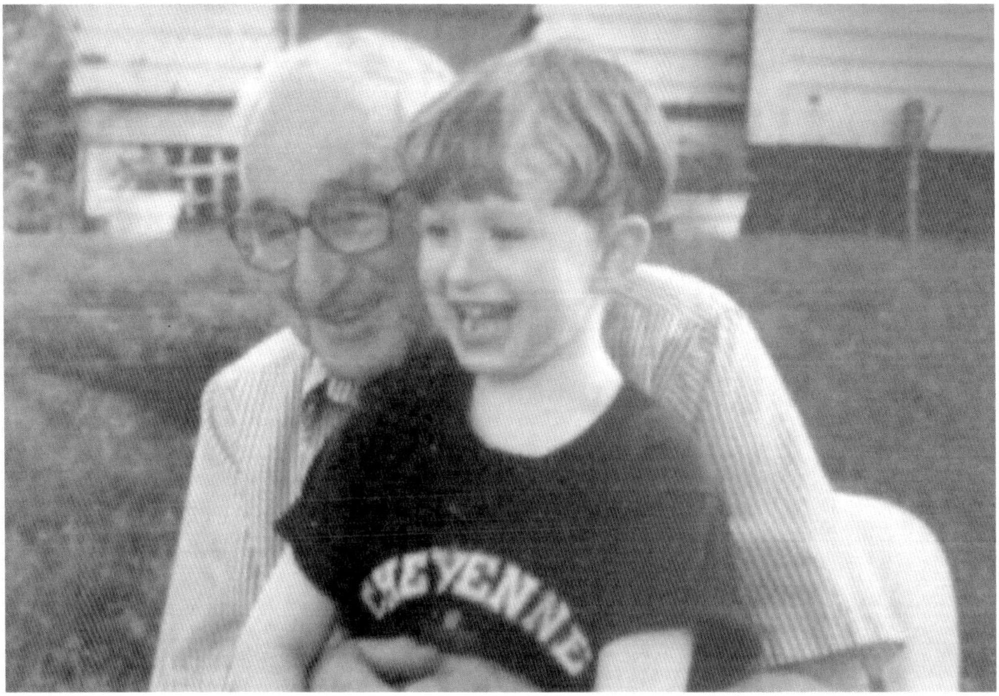

Harold King
More than just the man in the orange vest carrying a stop sign, Harold King was, for 55 years, the crossing guard for Stanton Elementary School. From the first day the school opened, and every day school was in session, he was always happy to see students, and they knew he really wanted them to have a good day. Kids would tell him how they had passed their test, and he would reply, "I told you that you could do it!" King was also the custodian at Stanton School for many years, until the city made him retire when he turned 72. He took great pride in doing a good job. King often said, "If you're not early, you're not on time!" (Courtesy of the King family.)

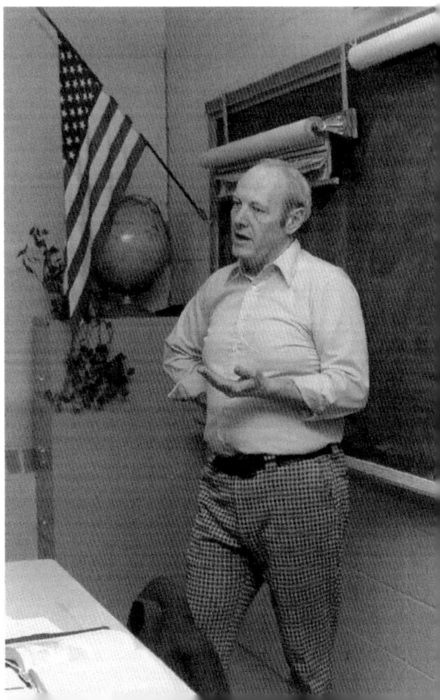

Jack MacAdie
MacAdie was the "time on the console clock" for thousands of students who sat in the homerooms of Norwich Free Academy over the years. Then, he would turn the morning announcements over to students hoping for a career in radio or television or just hoping to build self-confidence through public speaking. MacAdie was also the sports announcer for years at the Norwich Free Academy basketball and football games. He also worked for WICH-AM radio as an on-air personality and salesman. (Courtesy of Bruce MacAdie.)

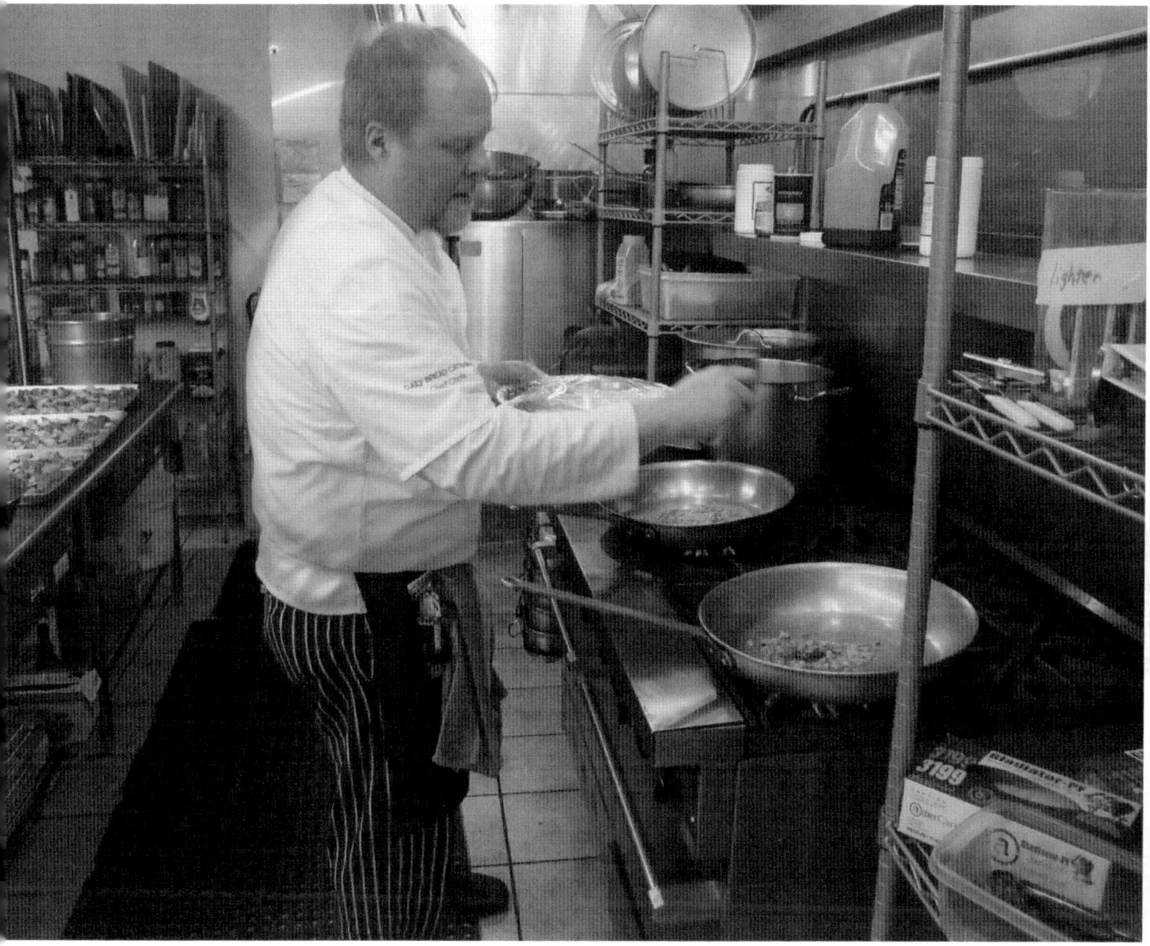

Chris Hetzer
Since late 2008, Chris Hetzer has shared what he has learned about food while traveling and training around the globe. He gives his time and knowledge to the staff and clients of the St. Vincent de Paul Place Kitchen (SVdPP). Hetzer began a catering program as a fundraiser for the soup kitchen while teaching the skills of cleaning, food preparation, and serving for everyday, holiday, and special-occasion meals and events. "The greatest personal gift is the amount of learning I receive when put in the position of teaching," said Hetzer.

"Chef Chris" is well known for his unique combinations of flavors and textures, which elicit smiles and shared glances between staff and guests. The SVdPP's holiday meals of fresh, locally grown turkey or roast beef with all the trimmings is discussed with anticipation throughout the year. Over time, the team's skills have been showcased in the most unexpected arenas, including a five-course meal with service at the old railroad station, a nine-course, nine-wine event at a local winery, and even the food services for an area winery's two-day festival. (Courtesy of Chris Hetzer.)

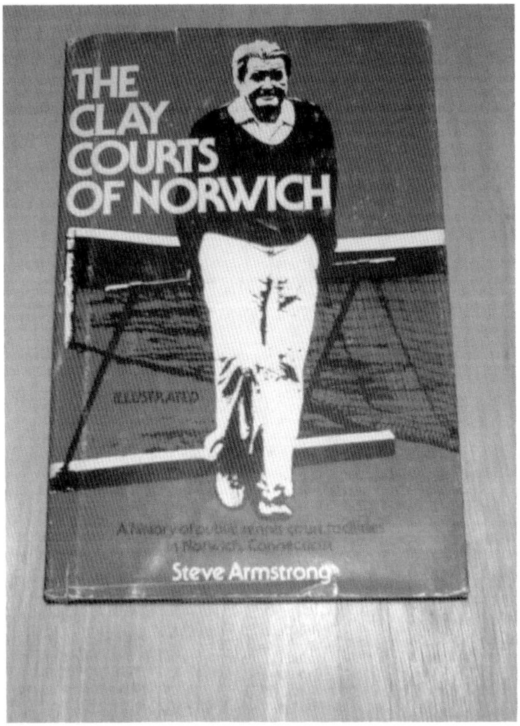

Steve Armstrong

In 1930, Steve Armstrong was introduced to tennis. With much persuasion and perseverance on his part, the recreation department in the 1940s agreed to build municipal tennis courts. The material for the court was not ordered from a supplier. Instead, Armstrong led a convoy of trucks to the site in Connecticut where the clay could be found, so that there could be no error or substitution in the materials that would be used for the final mix. In 1985, he told the story of the convoy in a book, *The Clay Courts of Norwich*, a history of the city's public tennis facilities. Armstrong's dedication did not stop when the courts were built. For many years, he was seen pulling a six-foot drag brush over the courts and supervising the precise painting of the lines and repairs to the court surface, the surrounding fence, and poles.

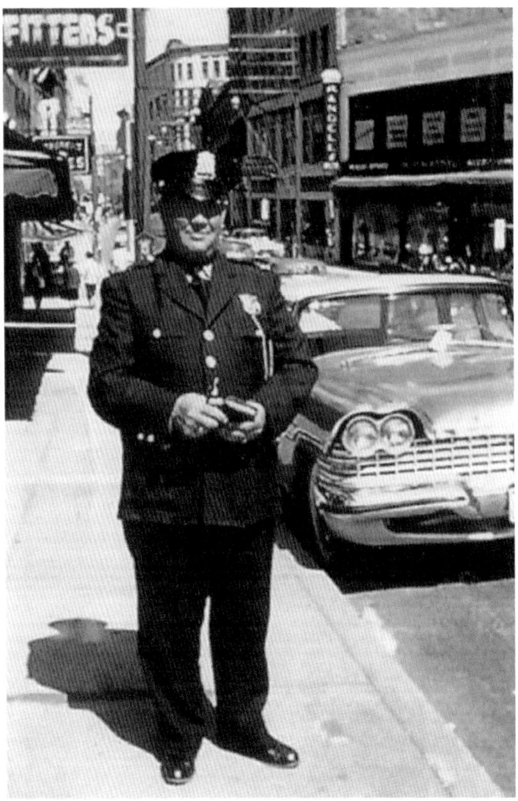

Jim "Brud" Quinn

Norwich Police sergeant Jim "Brud" Quinn was a New England boxing champion and a USA Olympic Boxing alternate when he walked the downtown beat in the 1950s and 1960s. This was a posed photograph, as "Brud" thought issuing tickets was bad for downtown business. He had a reputation for not handing out parking tickets under any circumstances. (Courtesy of John Belli.)

CHAPTER THREE

Together, We Build Our Community

Throughout its history and up to the present day, residents of Norwich have worked to create the community of their choosing. They take to heart the words of Cesar Chavez: "We cannot seek achievement for ourselves and forget about progress and prosperity for our community. . . . Our ambitions must be broad enough to include the aspirations and needs of others, for their sakes and for our own."

Norwich, Connecticut, unlike most cities, did not begin as a small agricultural community. From its beginning in 1659, it was a place destined for manufacturing and industry. Connecticut was forbidden by the British Parliament to manufacture or produce many goods, but in 1659, the town gave John Elderkin a contract to build a gristmill. In 1728, Hezekiah Huntington built the first mill to extract linseed oil from the native flaxseed, on Bean Hill. And by 1717, Capt. Joseph Kelley had established the first shipyard in Norwich, where the Yantic and Shetucket Rivers meet.

Christopher Leffingwell built the first paper mill in Connecticut in 1766, collecting a stipend from the British government. He then built a stocking mill, a fulling mill, a pottery, and a chocolate mill. The American Revolution ended Colonial dependence on Britain, and manufacturing of all sizes found a home in Norwich.

Manufacturing was built by the unlimited power provided by the fast-running rivers. Wholesale and retail establishments developed spaces along transportation routes and hubs. Homes were built close to where the jobs were, and neighborhoods were built and established. By the 1900s, a historic pattern of ebb and flow regarding the locations and types of Norwich businesses was observable. Small businesses grouped together to attract larger businesses, and larger businesses spawned small businesses to support their needs.

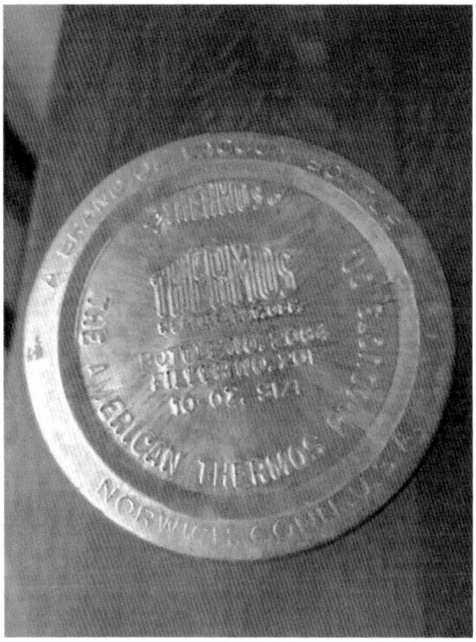

William Walker
Walker came to town in response to advertising by the Norwich Chamber of Commerce. If the city believed in him and helped him bring his company to Norwich, he promised to pay five times the cost before he took title to the property and to include the name "Norwich" in his national advertising. Walker was probably the first industrial leader to offer paid training to employees before they began work in the factory. When Walker died in 1922, the products of his firm, the American Thermos Bottle Company, were stamped "Made in Norwich, CT" as far away as Japan. The company remained in Norwich until 1988, when a merger with a company in Freeport, Illinois, led to the facility's closing. (Courtesy of Ginny Dubois Edmundson.)

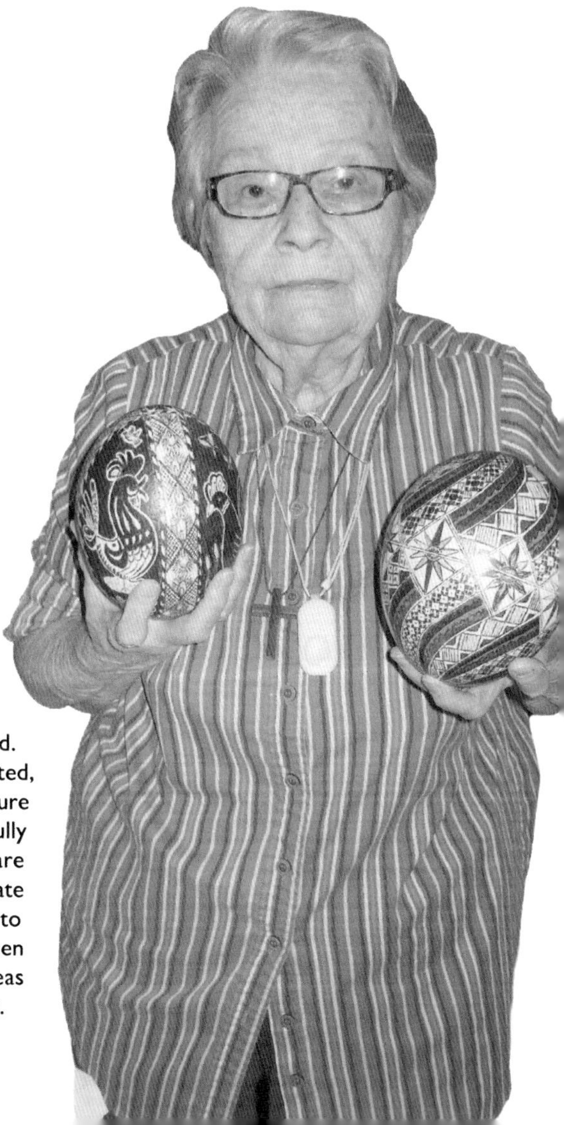

Pat Bromley
Pat Bromley's creative outlet is the art of Pysanky, Ukrainian Easter egg decorating incorporating creative and traditional folk designs using a wax and paint, batik, method. Her baskets of wooden eggs have intricate painted, burned, and carved designs. Hen eggs feature beautiful, brightly painted patterns and are carefully cradled in tissue paper. Large ostrich eggs are colored with markers in designs so intricate that a single egg can take a week or more to complete. Since emu eggs are naturally dark green on the outside, Bromley carves away the areas representing seas to show the earth's continents.

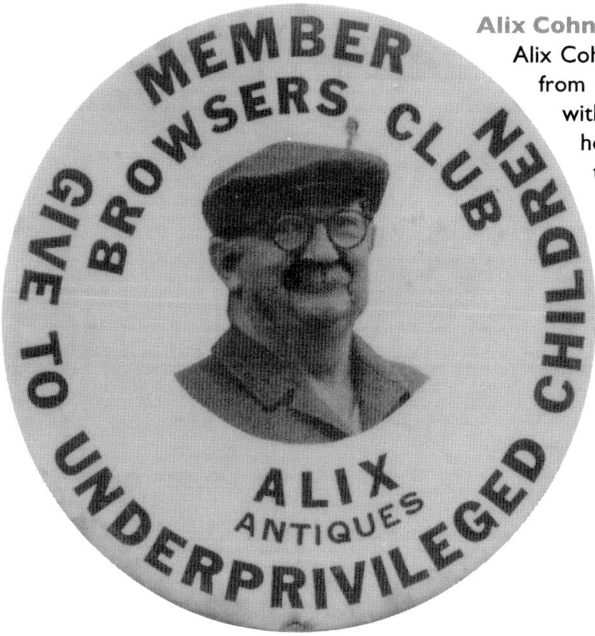

Alix Cohn

Alix Cohn filled the cavernous old trolley garage from floor to ceiling (at least 20 feet high) with everything from jewelry, appliances, horse-drawn sleighs, and a pile halfway to the ceiling of motorcycles with gas still in their tanks. In only one part of the building could a floor be seen. On Friday nights, teenagers crowded onto the floor to dance to the music of local bands. Cohn was forced to close his business and empty the trolley garage of its contents in the 1980s. (Courtesy of Frank Obuchowski.)

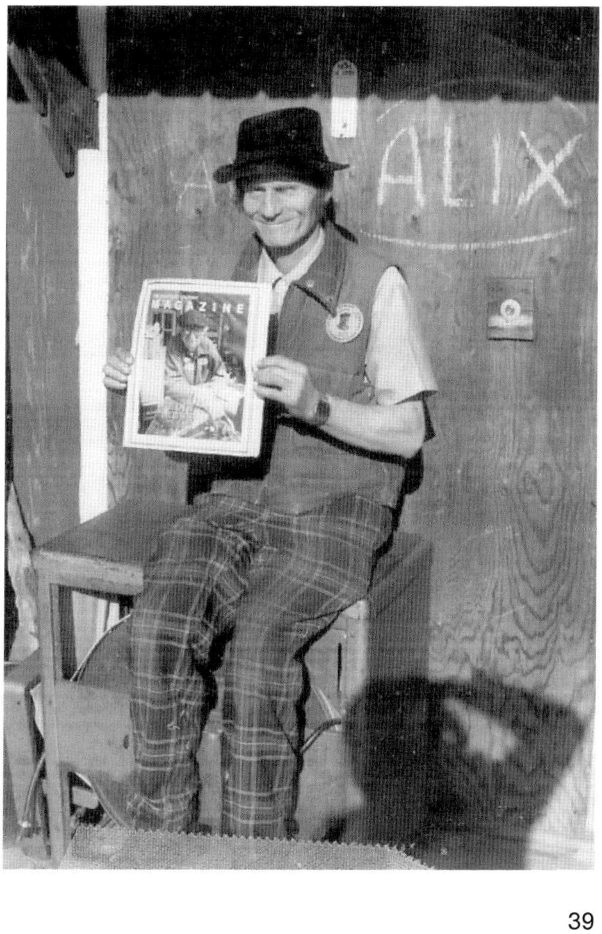

George Eno

Eno was a fixture in Greenville and at the side of Alix Cohn. Eno knew where to find things in the Cohn collection of overflowing stuff that filled the old trolley barn from top to bottom. More important, he knew how to get an item out when it was called for. He proudly wore his yellow "Browsers Club" pin from Alix's place to support the dances. (Members of the community were given a bright yellow pin to wear in support of the teen dances held in the Alix Antiques Trolley Barn.) Wearing the pin every day, it was more of a uniform for Eno than his trademark vest or coveralls. He continued to wear the pin even after Alix's had closed in the 1980s and the dances were no more. (Courtesy of Frank Obuchowski.)

James Cronin
Cronin once said, "Community banking is essential to helping small businesses regain their footing and the key to economic growth." Cronin has been a heavily involved driving force in civic and community organizations that have brought more affordable housing into the area. In 1998, he was instrumental in forming The Dime Bank Foundation, which commits funds to a host of community causes, from affordable-housing initiatives to food and shelter for the homeless. (Courtesy of The Dime Bank.)

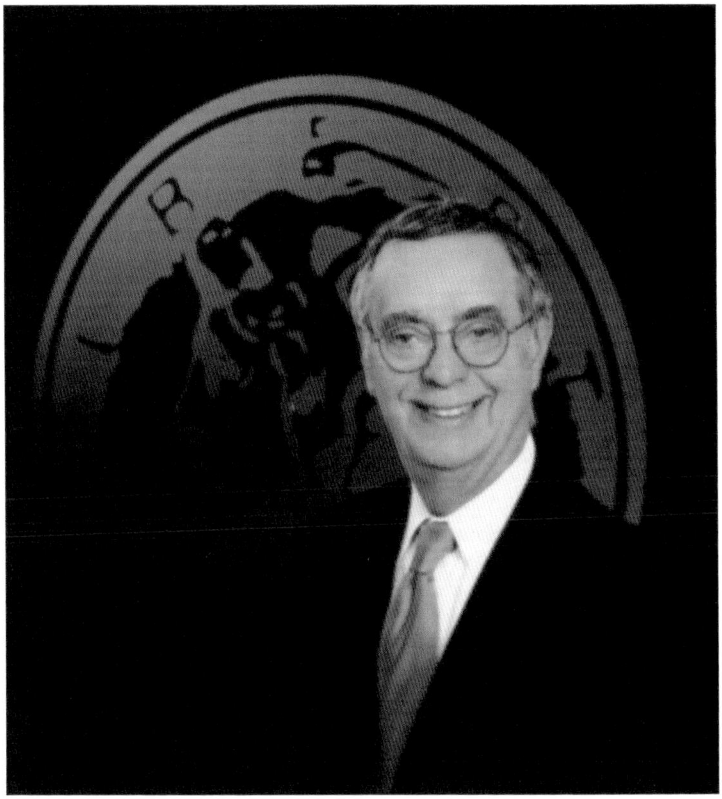

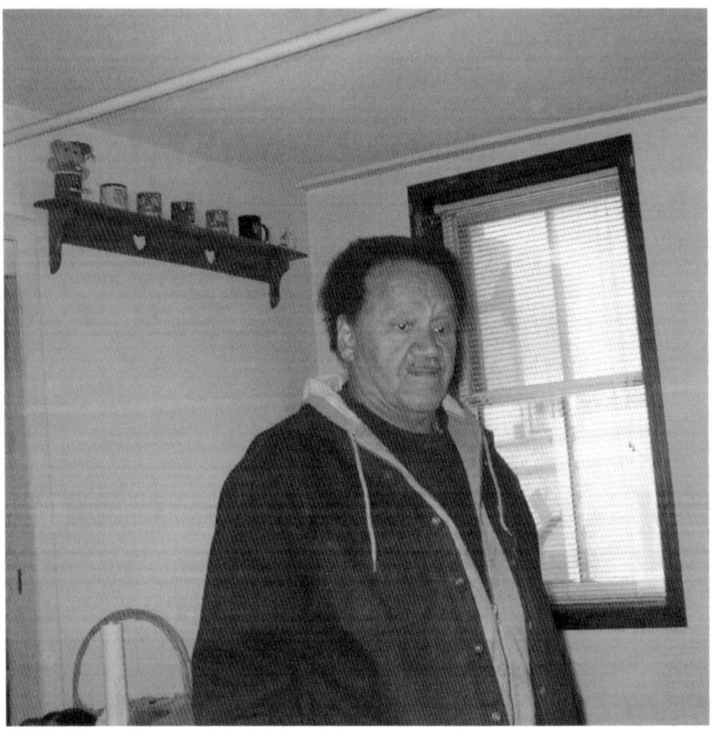

Harry Lawson
Harry Lawson likes people and enjoys being in the thick of things. He also enjoyed the art of selling, whether it was in his discount center, garden store, or grocery and sandwich shop, all of which carried his name. Lawson, an active participant in every revitalization effort in the downtown area, would relate many of his adventures and misadventures in exquisite and remarkable detail. He reminded people of promises and plans, and he offered advice, solutions, poignant questions, and observations.

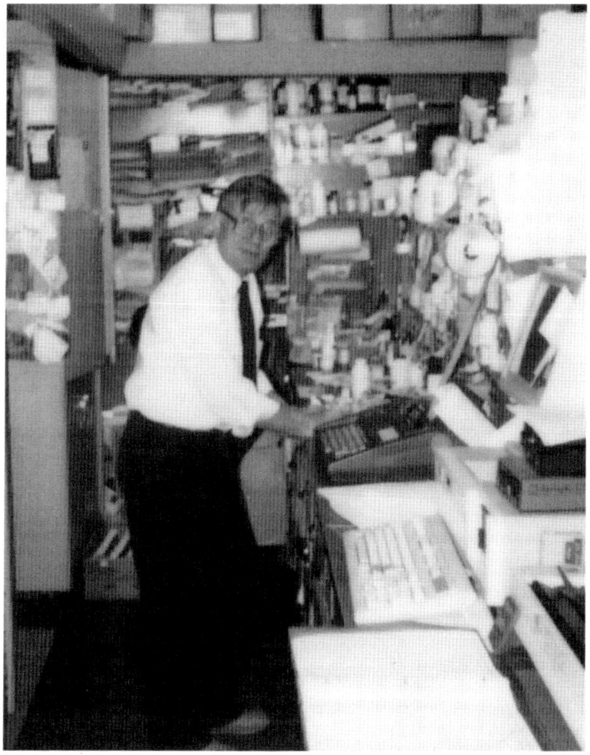

Alvin Sohn

For 41 years, from 1955 until 1996, Alvin Sohn, of West End Pharmacy, was the neighborhood pharmacist. He knew everyone in the community and provided medicines from 9:00 in the morning until 10:00 at night. Children frequented his business, as there was a soda fountain at the front of the store until 1977, serving ice cream, milk shakes and 5¢ sodas. (Courtesy of the Sohn family.)

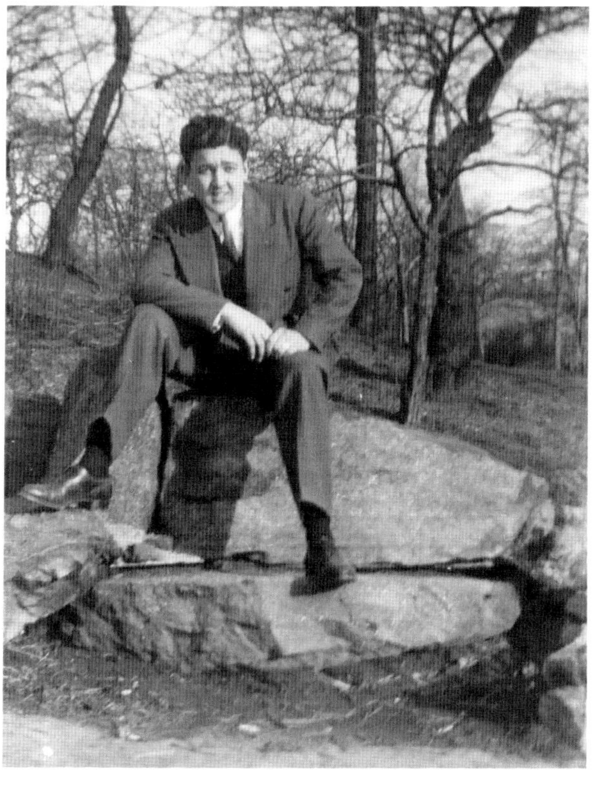

Henry Miranda

Henry Miranda tells jokes and stories that endear him to people and make casual, one-time acquaintances and loyal customers friends for life. His stories from sales, marketing, and delivering Lay's potato chips in the Norwich area tell of fun and exciting adventures. One story involved the local sandwich shop that had no room for a potato-chip rack. Every day for a month or so, Miranda stopped there for lunch. And every day, he leaned on a soda cooler while he waited for his sandwich. Every day, the cooler moved just a little bit, less than an inch. But eventually, Miranda was able to show the owner that there was room for a small rack of Lay's Potato Chips. (Courtesy of Maria Miranda.)

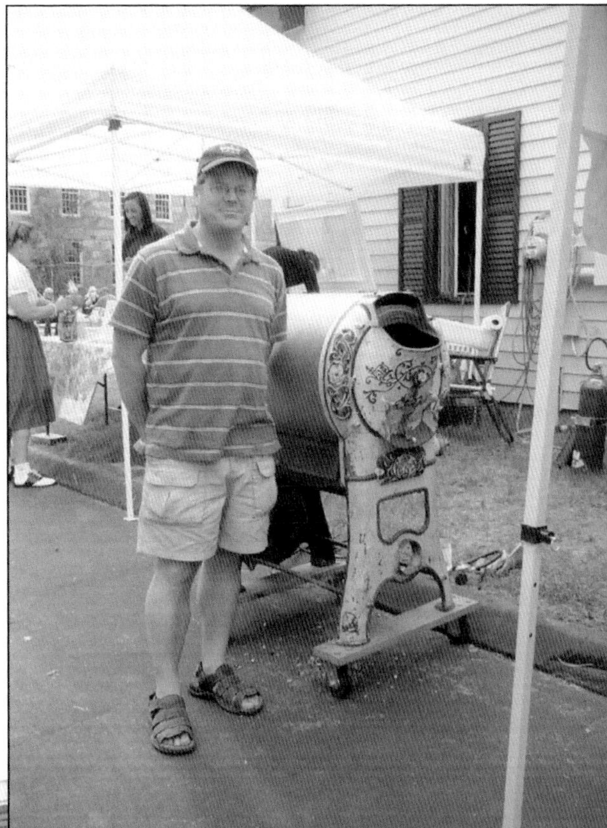

Tony Longo

Tony Longo ran Longo's Fruits and Vegetable Market on the corner of Bath and Franklin Streets. But he also sold roasted peanuts to commuters, providing a snack that warmed the hand or pocket. Longo's granddaughter Mary-Kay Kelleher and her husband, Tim (above), bring the peanut roaster out of retirement for fundraisers for the Yantic Fire Department, to the delight of children and adults.

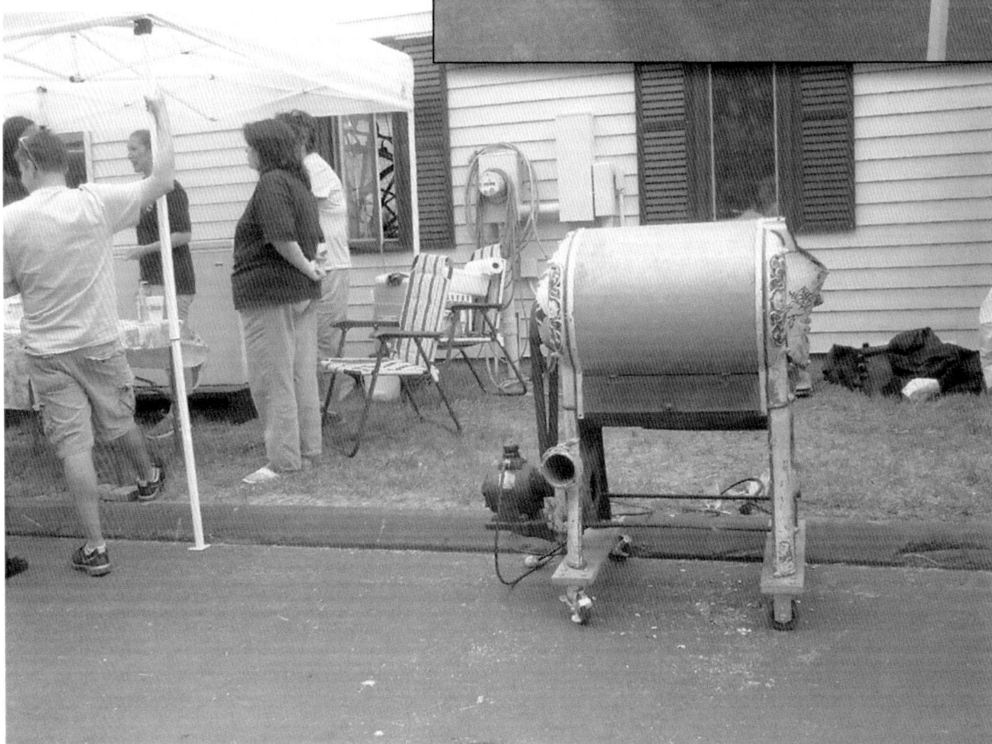

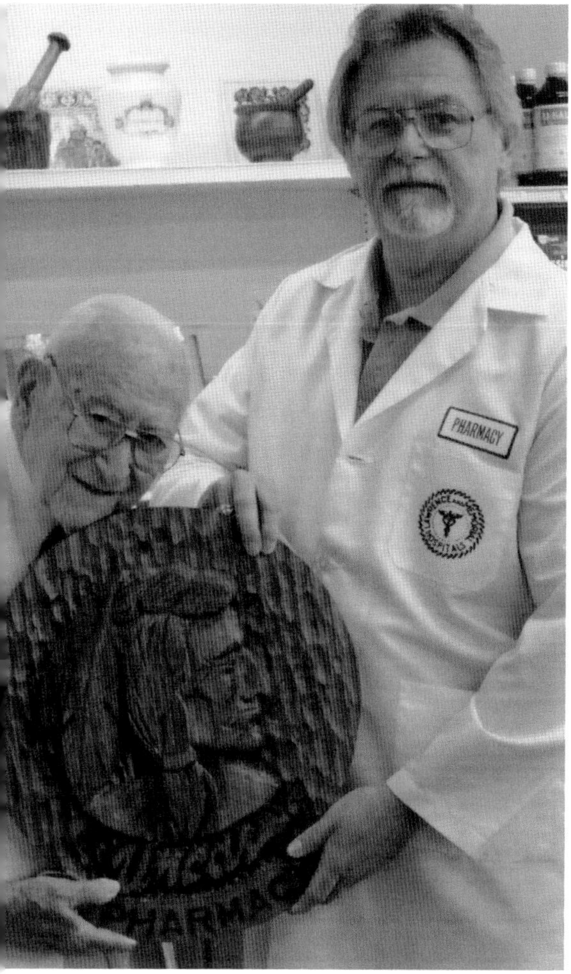

Harry Swatzburg
In 1951, Harry Swatzburg (left), with his wife, Selma, opened the Uncas Pharmacy. As the area grew with customers and neighbors, Harry and Selma made friends of them all. The business expanded, and the Swatzburgs hired delivery and counter help. With practiced ease, they encouraged the staff to do what was right and to do what made them feel proud. They communicated a faith in their employees and their customers and were repaid with lasting loyalty and friendship. In 1991, Jeff Hodkinson (right), once a delivery boy for Harry and Selma, returned to Norwich with his wife, Shirley, and purchased Uncas Pharmacy. They practice pride and goodwill toward all in the tradition of Harry and Selma. (Courtesy of Jeff Hodkinson.)

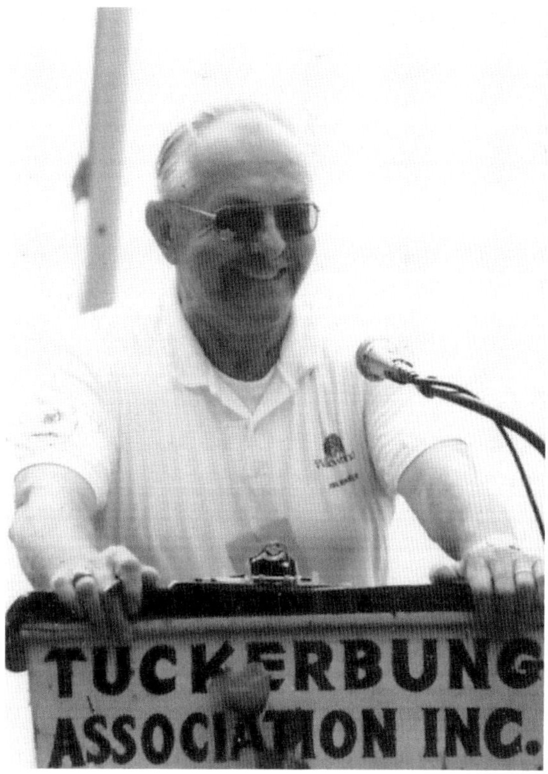

Sam Mereen
Sam Mereen enjoyed making people happy and bringing them a smile. His oft-repeated refrain was, "Attitude is everything." With never a misstep, and in all sorts of weather, Mereen was the early-morning deliverer of the *Norwich Bulletin* newspaper to patients in the William W. Backus Hospital. He performed this deed for over 20 years, thanks to the financial support of the local Kiwanis and the Masonic lodge. (Courtesy of J.P. Mereen.)

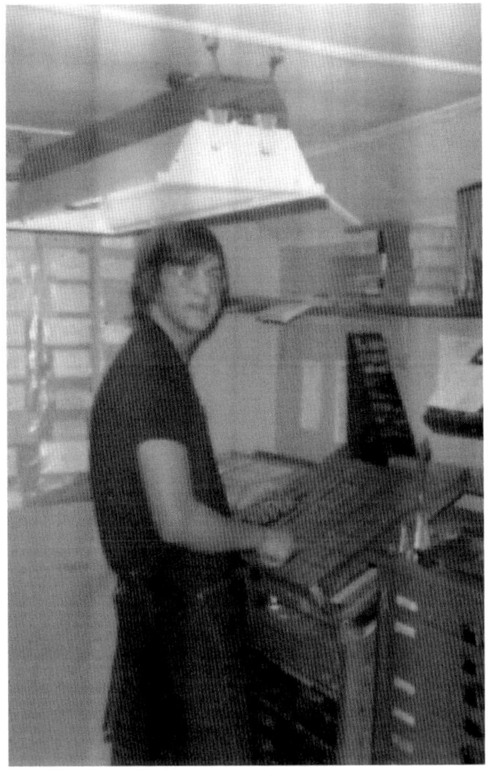

Frank Obuchowski
With glee, pride, and a twinkle in his eyes, Frank Obuchowski relates stories of poker games, impromptu jam sessions, antics, and backstage drama of acts from Frank Sinatra to Kenny Rogers and the First Edition. From the 1960s to the 1980s, entertainers who came to Norwich to perform would mingle in his White Eagle print shop. The business printed programs, tickets, and advertising posters for all of the big events in Norwich. (Courtesy of Frank Obuchowski.)

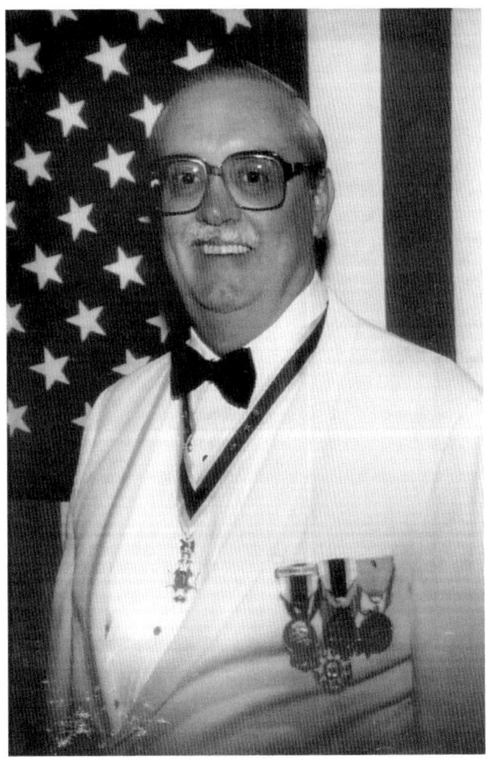

"Jack" Ricketts
A dedication to historic education led Ricketts to The Society of the Founders of Norwich, which maintains a Colonial history museum in Norwich. The facility contains artifacts and documents dating to before the settling of the city in 1659. His efforts brought authentic paint colors to the historic building and the sounds of children's laughter to the Colonial house during well-attended holiday story times. (Courtesy of Barbara Ricketts.)

CHAPTER FOUR

It Is Just Business

Business is the art of making money. It can be done in a variety of ways and to different extents. The most successful businesspeople are the owners and managers who maintain a sense of self, allowing them to share their vision of what they are and what they want to be to the world.

Norwich has always been a city that welcomes the big and the little with enthusiasm. In manufacturing, it is not just being able to repeatedly offer the highest quality or the greatest quantity, but the ability to improve the product.

Norwich enjoyed a variety of small retail shops in its downtown, while the largest manufacturing mills settled on the banks of the rivers. Trolleys, taxis, buses, and motor cars connected them all in an expanding web of streets and avenues. As transportation changed, so Norwich adapted, with broadened avenues and the construction in Taftville of one of the earliest alphanumeric street grids in the country. Norwich was also the site of the first industrial park in the state of Connecticut. Now, Norwich has pockets of commerce convenient to each of its neighborhoods and to each other.

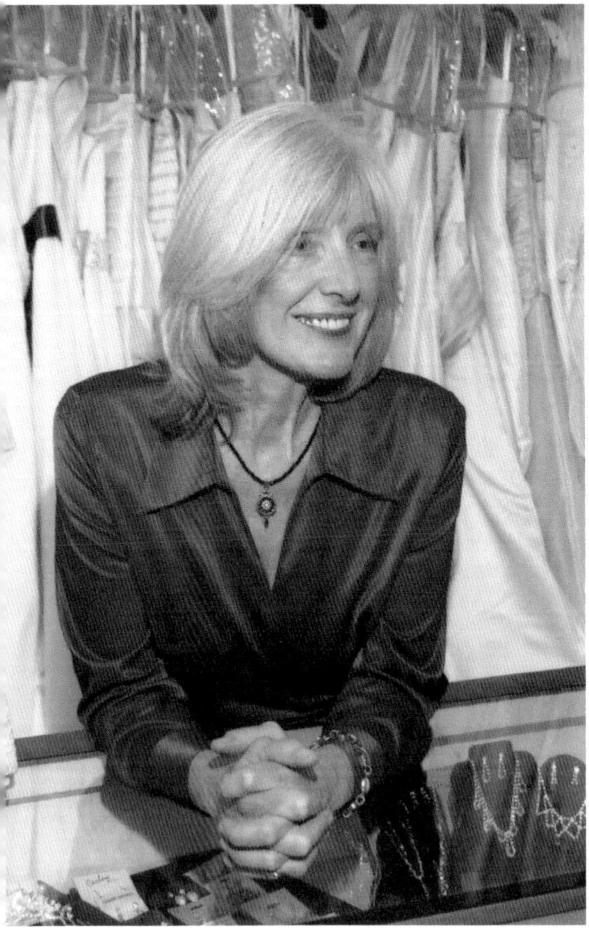

Cam Fogg

Norwich women have been going to Cam Fogg and her consignment shop, Love Me Two Times, for everyday clothes and formal wear. Fogg always enjoyed clothing and the excitement of finding the greatest bargain for herself and for others. Consignment shopping was a new concept in 1981, but it rapidly found a home on the main street of Taftville.

Once, a mother of the groom needed to have seven clothing changes for an upcoming wedding day, and she was on a limited budget. Fogg listened, asked a few questions, then helped the woman choose and assemble everything she needed for one of the happiest days of her life, all well within her budget. (Courtesy of Cam Fogg.)

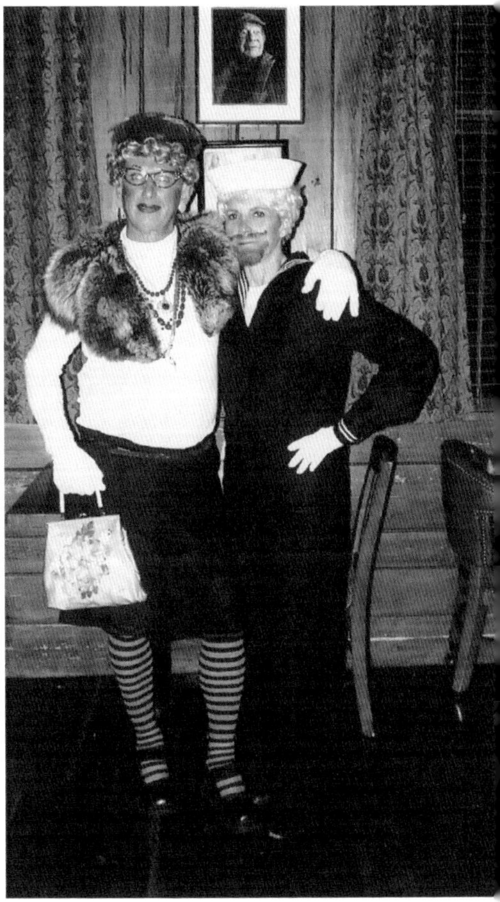

Timothy Wawrzynowicz

On three nights a week and on weekends, Timothy Wawrzynowicz goes dancing, bringing with him a smile, a laugh, and a never-ending supply of Henny Youngman one-liners. During the day, he answers to the name Johnny Kielbasa of Johnny Kielbasa's Stuff Shop.

Wawrzynowicz's shop was ready to open in 1974. Its shelves and spaces were crammed with new and used items for all ages and sizes. All that was left to do was order the sign. In a serious voice, he asked his 10-year-old niece Cindy what he should call the shop. With wide eyes and with great wisdom in her voice, she declared, "Johnny Kielbasa's Stuff Shop." So the business was named and a new identity for Wawrzynowicz created. In the 40 years since, he has sold everything from breast pumps to coffins, and a few things that have defied identification. Wawrzynowicz (left) is pictured here with Joyce Marcinek. (Courtesy of Timothy Wawrzynowicz.)

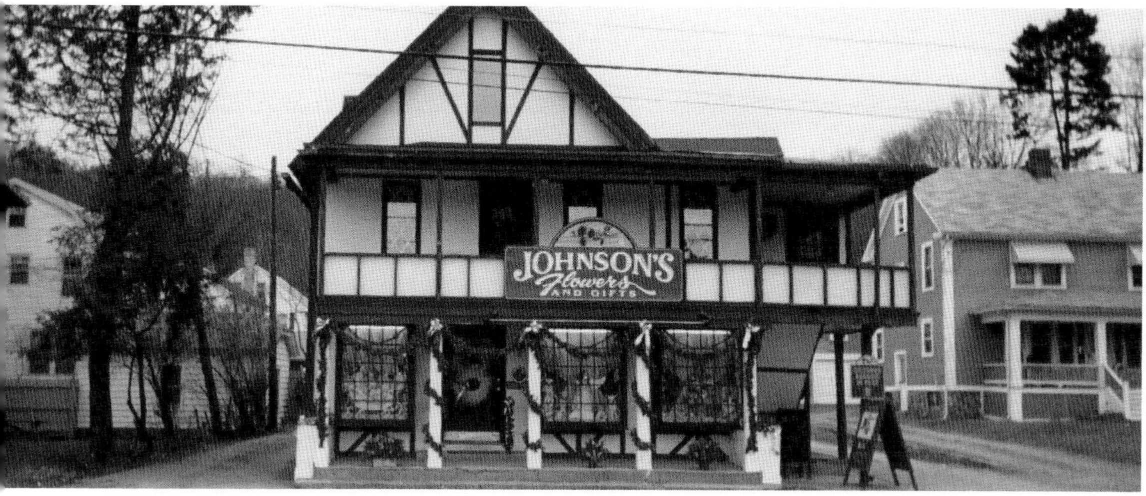

Claire Wallen

Claire Wallen began working at Johnson's Flowers and Gifts in 1976 and purchased the business in 1984. Wallen and her staff make each arrangement unique, telling a story through the container, flower, and leaves. The recipient easily recognizes the sentiment, whether the arrangement says "Congratulations," "Get well soon," "Thank you," "I'm sorry," or, a favorite, "Will you marry me again?"

Wallen, cognizant that some plants are more delicate than others and are susceptible to the changeable New England weather, makes it a point to deliver arrangements and plants into the recipients' hands and not just leave them at the door if no one is available. (Courtesy of Claire Wallen.)

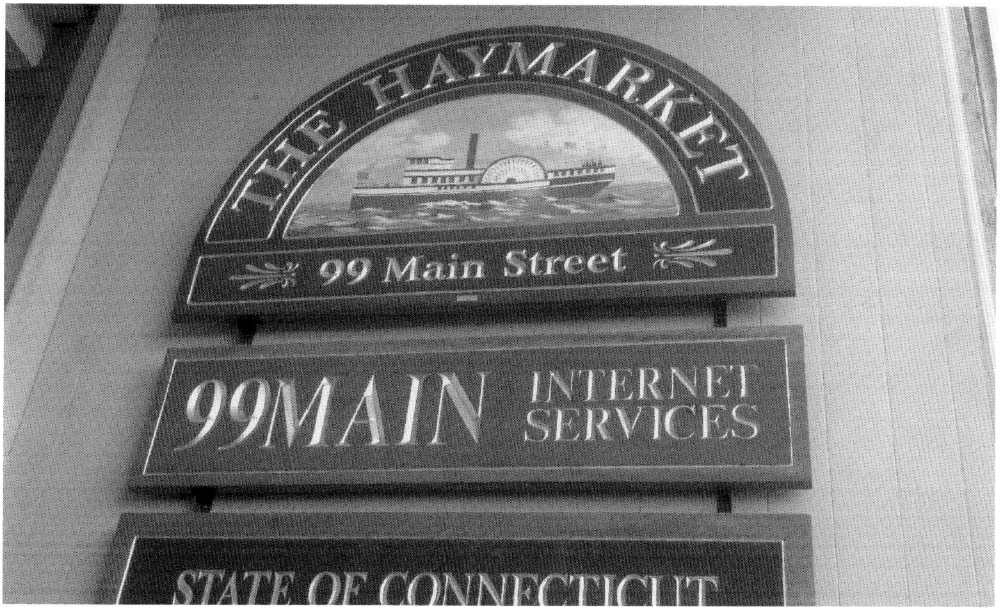

Trish Sullivan

Trish Sullivan started the local Internet business in 1996, when only dial-up service was available. Sometimes, customers had to wait for one of the 24 modems/phone lines in the network operations center to be free so they could get online. Now, the company, 99Main, is a full-service Internet firm with no waiting. Customers know Sullivan and her staff, and even the pet mice, Lenovo and Blade, by name.

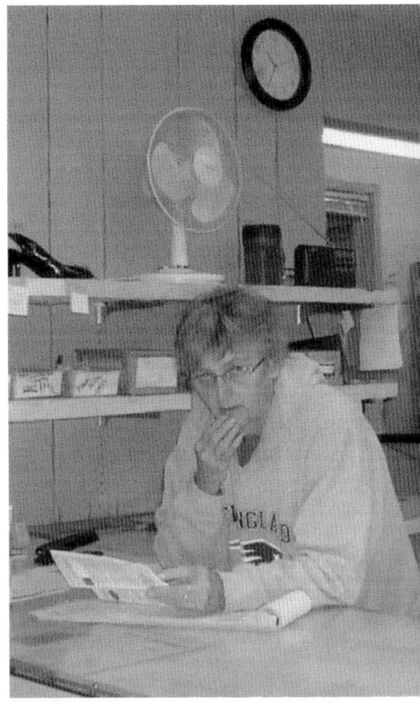

Katie Lathrop

Katie Lathrop has been an early-morning fixture at James Laundromat in Norwichtown for more than 23 years. Arriving before the sun rises, she eyes the height of the sometimes frantic Yantic River, well known for overflowing its banks from heavy rains and snow melt, scans for the familiar faces of the feral cats, and unlocks the door to greet the first customers. Each day sees a different group of customers, some bearing coffee or a homemade treat to share. When the machines are running and the chores are complete for the moment, Lathrop stands at the front door, waving to familiar drivers and school buses as they pass by. Meanwhile, Lathrop's left foot props the door slightly ajar so that she misses none of the inside activities while she smokes her cigarette.

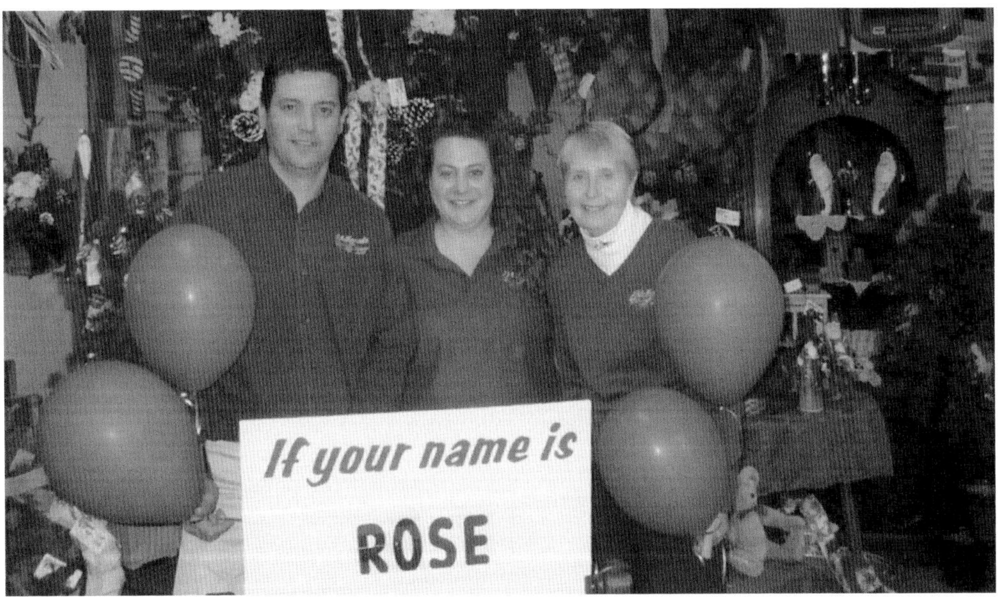

Mike Rankowitz

Mike Rankowitz proudly demonstrates his dedication to American small business by maintaining Norwich's widest selection of locally made products on the shelves of McKenna's Flowers, a tradition since 1942. Rankowitz, deciding that every day should be a celebration, chooses a name at random. Any person with that name is invited to stop by the shop to receive a free rose, the symbol of Norwich, the Rose City.

The workroom of the flower shop is familiar to many throughout southeastern Connecticut from the team-building classes Rankowitz and his staff host throughout the year for businesses, groups, and organizations. Rankowitz says, "There is no right or wrong when creating an individual arrangement."

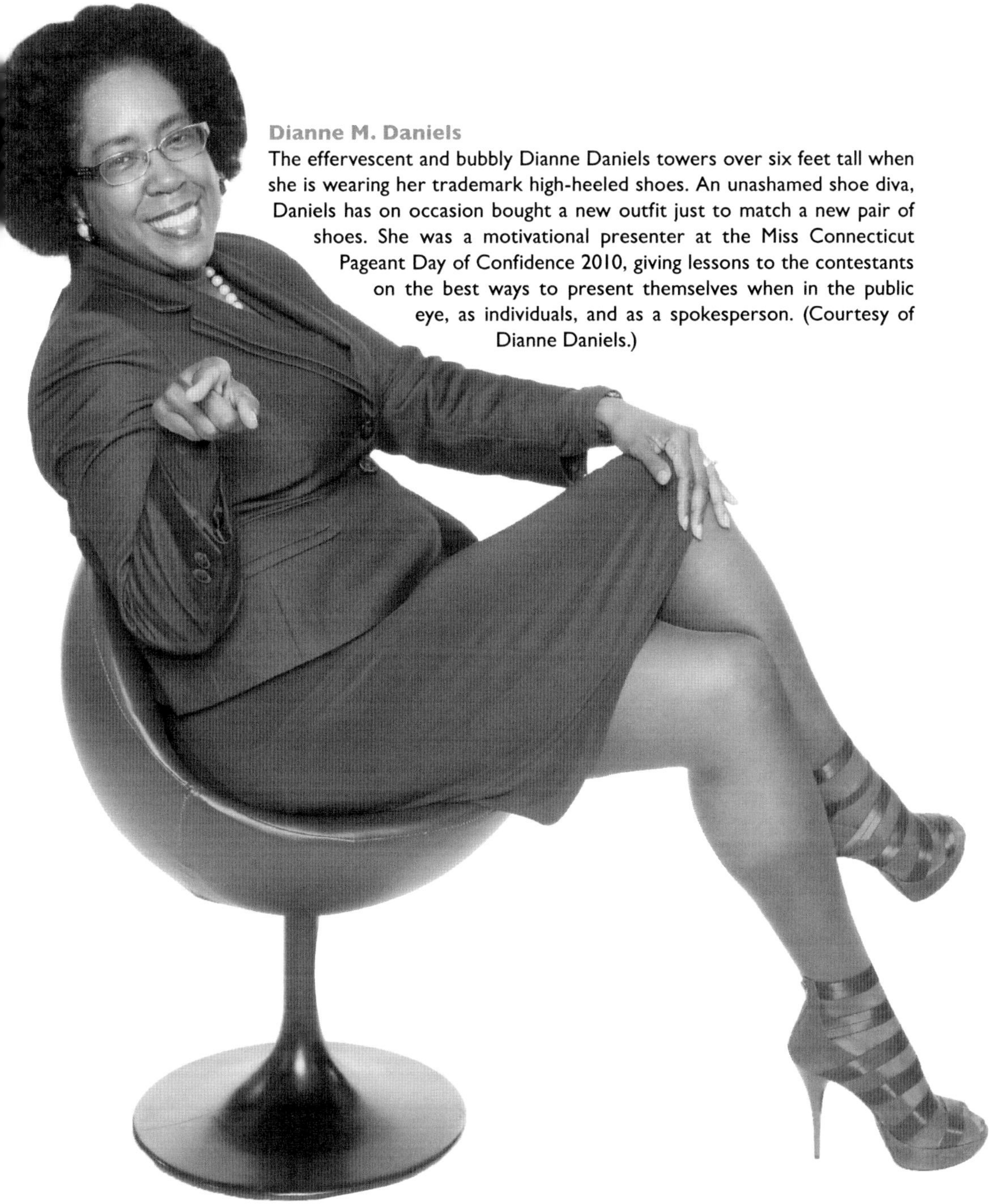

Dianne M. Daniels
The effervescent and bubbly Dianne Daniels towers over six feet tall when she is wearing her trademark high-heeled shoes. An unashamed shoe diva, Daniels has on occasion bought a new outfit just to match a new pair of shoes. She was a motivational presenter at the Miss Connecticut Pageant Day of Confidence 2010, giving lessons to the contestants on the best ways to present themselves when in the public eye, as individuals, and as a spokesperson. (Courtesy of Dianne Daniels.)

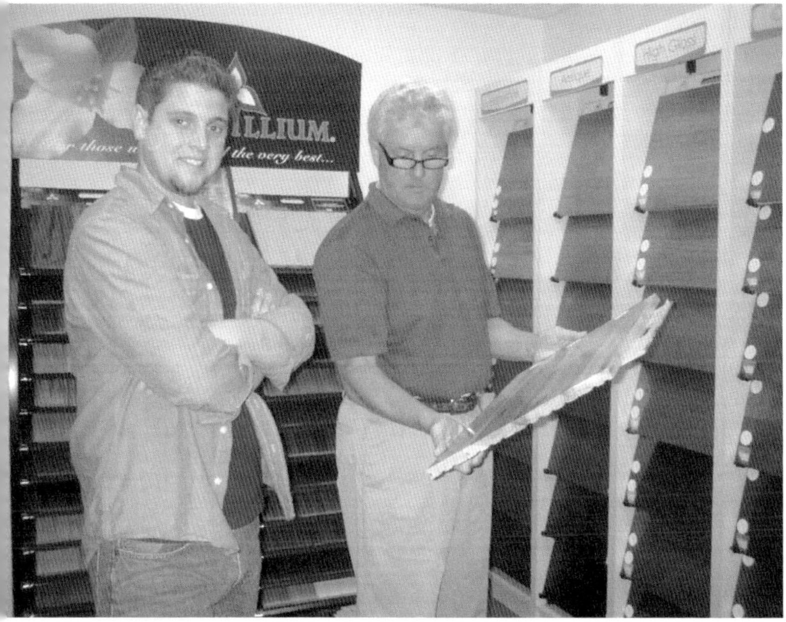

Greg and Jonathan Graf
Father and son Greg Graf (left) and Jonathan Graf (right) have laid a lot of carpet and flooring, including in houses over 200 years old. They have learned how to make the unusual work. The Grafs were excited for the opportunity to move their business into the old trolley barn, which retained the original hoists and skylights and offered room to unroll a full roll of carpeting. Visitors come to see the photographs and articles about Greenville history that decorate the walls. Some even bring an item to exhibit.

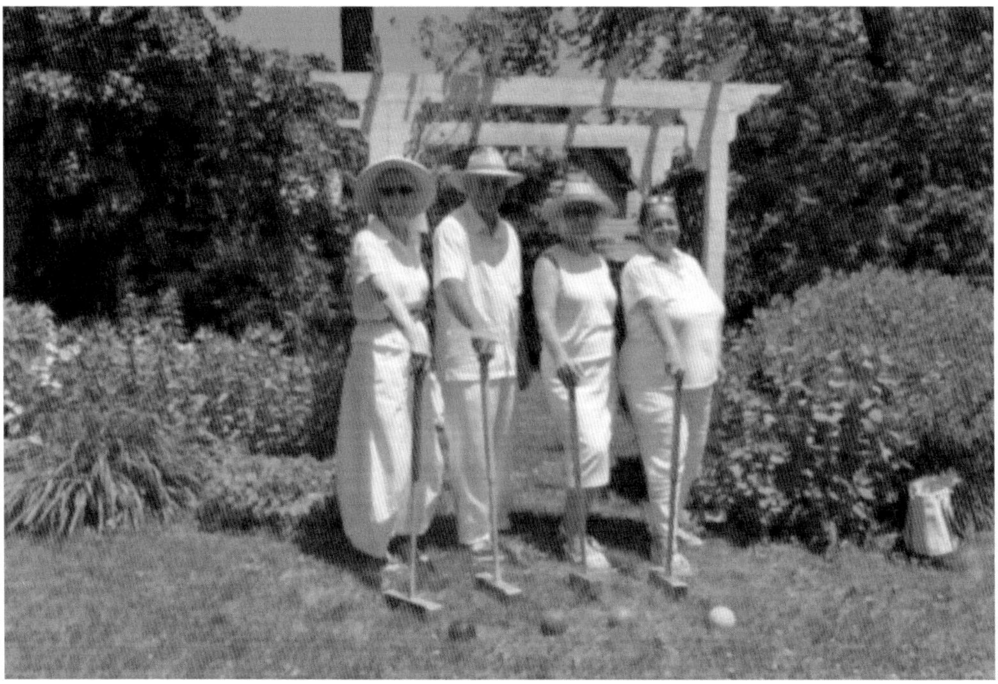

Gordon Kyle
According to Gordon Kyle, the key to business is to "be in the right place at the right time, make use of all of your resources, and use all your resources to your advantage." Kyle, who manufactures high-end wood furniture and countertops, added croquet mallets after he learned that, in 1899, Norwich hosted a major croquet convention that changed the rules of the sport forever. Then, with a little help from some friends, he organized the Norwich Croquet Club, introducing the game on Sunday afternoons to residents of all ages at the city's parks. (Courtesy of Norwich Croquet Club.)

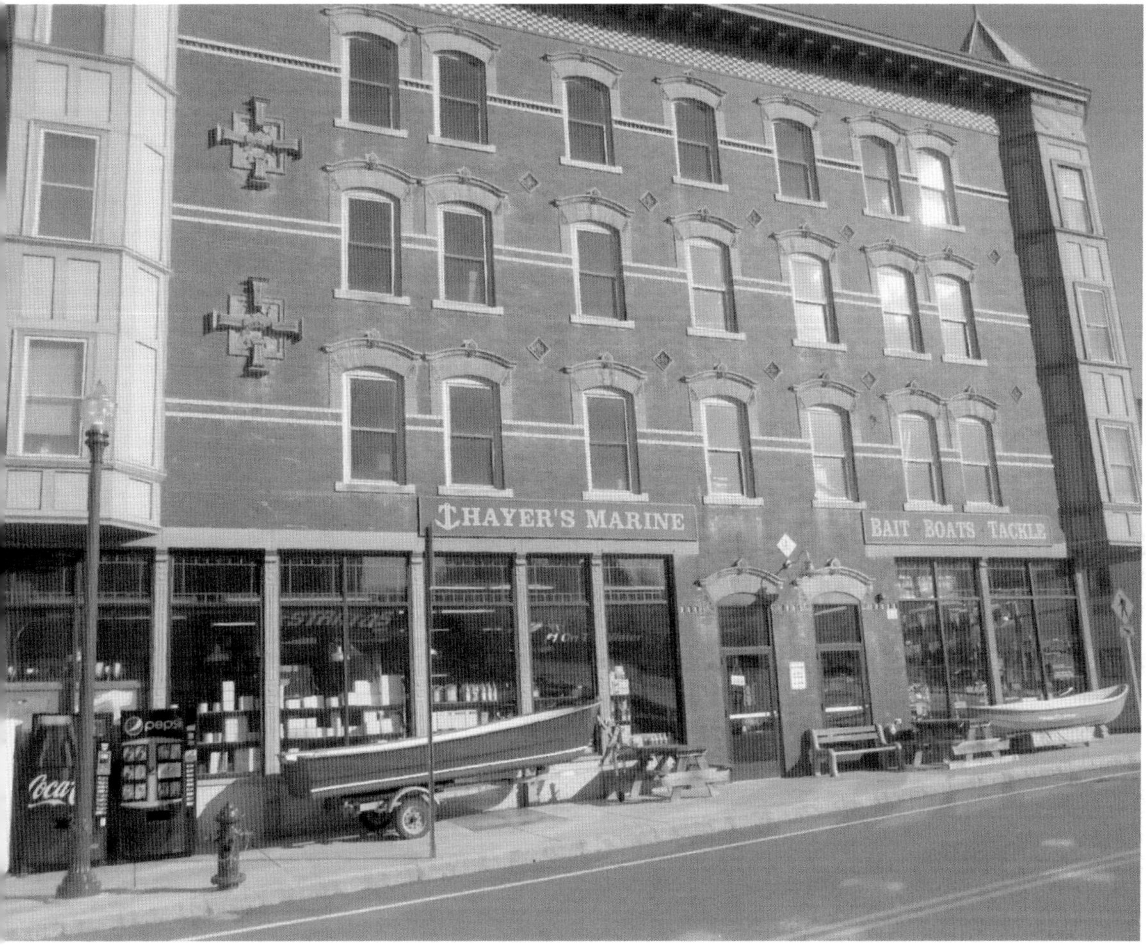

Dick and Rich Thayer

In 1966, father and son Dick and Rich Thayer began a small store called Thayer's Marine. With all sincerity and a lot of laughter, the tale of the "biggest whopper" caught at Thayer's Marine is retold time and again. The younger generations asked Dick to stop snacking from the large jar of peanuts he kept under his desk, and "Grandpa" promised that he would. He always denied that he was snacking, but the contents of the jar grew lower. One day, there was a loud yell from the office. Someone had put his hand in the peanut jar, which had somehow become partially filled with wheel-bearing grease under the layer of peanuts. There could be no denial this time.

Over the years, the Thayers have supported many environmental, water-sport, boating, and education and safety programs for children and adults. The firm has expanded into sponsorships of fishing tournaments and has often worked with the Norwich Police Department Harbor Patrol. The patrol is a specialized unit dedicated to water safety and preservation of life and property on all waters located within the City of Norwich. (Courtesy of Thayer's Marine.)

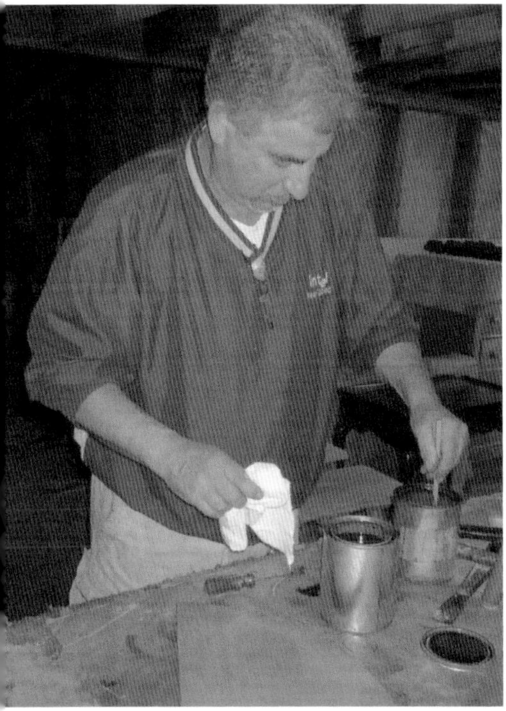

Eric Fishbone

Eric Fishbone heals the marks of life left on wood. For almost 30 years, he has mixed ingredients, stains, and colors with the precision of a chemist before dipping, wiping, swirling, and stroking. His ability to match colors, grains, and textures on antique, centuries-old pieces and rare woods, as well as new woods and colors, has made him a legend among antique dealers and moving companies. Each mark relates a tale of the item's journey and adventures and tells how it has been cared for. Repairs are made one layer at a time with the precision of a surgeon. Scars are hidden, allowing the glory and fire of the true wood beneath to show through, as it did when the piece was new.

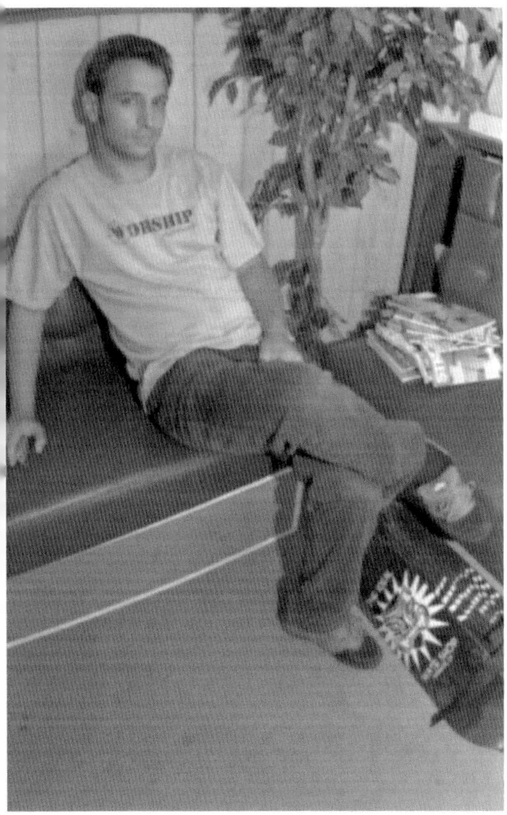

Jeff Blayman

At one time, Jeff Blayman rode his skateboard on the streets of Norwich. Now, he oversees production and distribution of Worship Skateboards, a national skateboard brand known for its unique, soulful vision and fine-art designs. After opening a local store for serious skateboarding enthusiasts, Blayman spearheaded a fundraising drive to make $40,000 worth of improvements to the local municipal skate park.

His true pride, though, is in the SOS program he created with Sensations Charitable Foundation. Every Saturday, skateboarding lessons are made available for children on the autism spectrum or with disabilities. Skateboarding, says Blayman, "is an extension of who I am creatively and empathetically, and it has certainly become a way of life." (Courtesy of Jeff Blayman.)

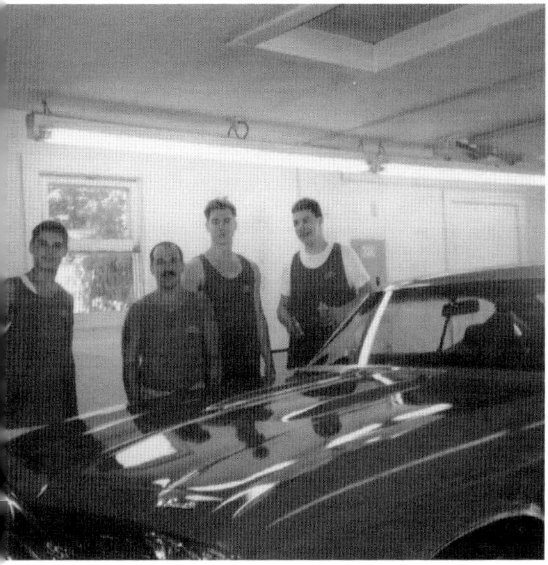

Joe DiFiore
In 1988, Joe DiFiore walked the streets of Norwich, hustling to detail cars in parking lots to make money. His first customer was Rodney Green of Olde Tymes Restaurant. Green would seek DiFiore out over and over again, and referred others to him as well. Soon, DiFiore was able to remain at home, and people brought their cars to him for detailing. Within a year, WICH/WCTY radio played the DiFiore Auto Detailing commercial, which featured the line "Old cars like new and new cars better than new!" DiFiore had men and teenagers working for him, and he filled the air in his yard with peppy music from around the world. He delights in telling his friends, "The work may be dirty, but the money is clean." (Courtesy of Joe DiFiore.)

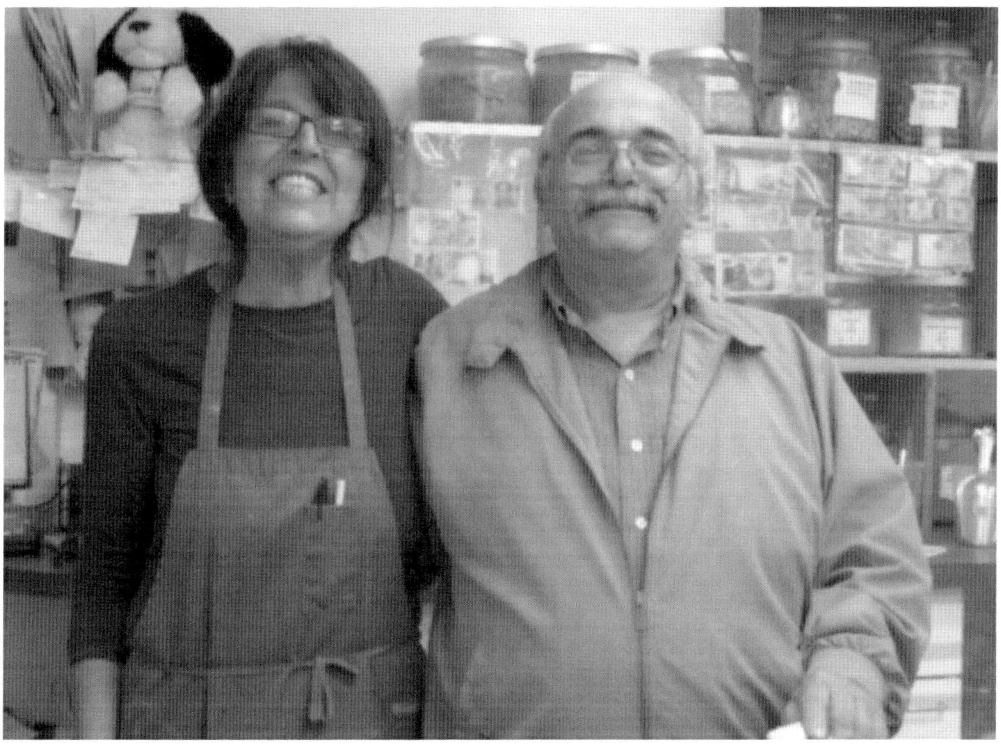

Iffat and Bassem Salahi
The Salahis are the owners of Lazizah Bakery and Market. A Middle Eastern oasis in New England, the store's name is loosely translated as "All is delicious!" Iffat speaks through her creations of eloquent, imaginative, and healthy soups and salads that delight the taste buds with unusual blends of herbs and spices from around the world. When not in the market, Bassem can be found attending events throughout the city, encouraging everyone to come to Norwich and experience the success he has found from his hard work since 2006. (Courtesy of Iffat and Bassem Salahi.)

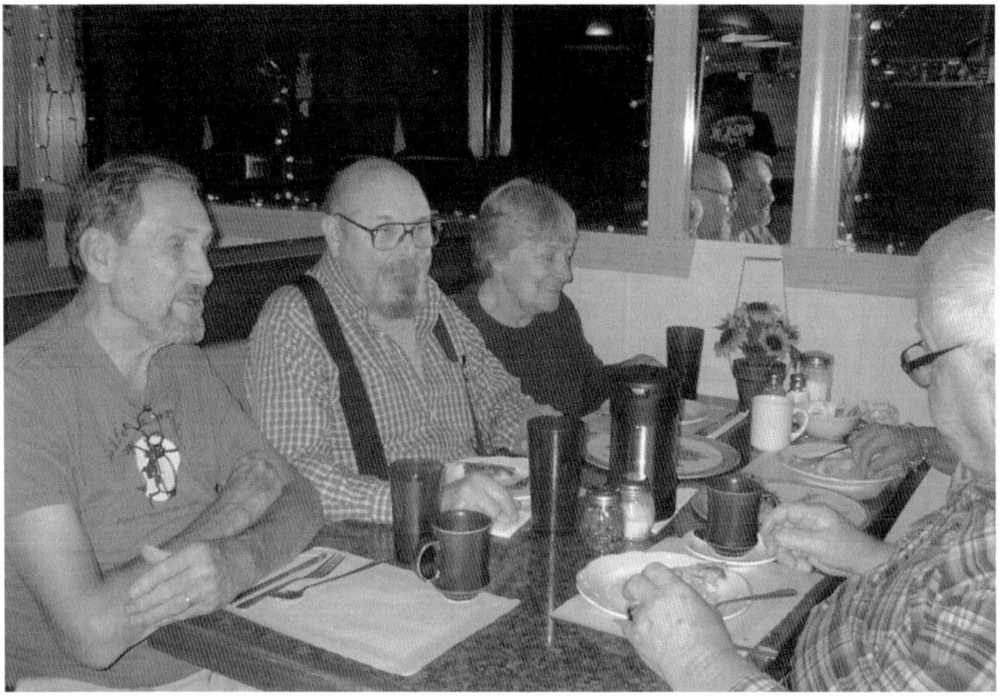

Jim Woods

Early in his career, Jim Woods (left center, wearing suspenders) discovered that he could mix two of his favorite loves, cars and electricity, "to get a charge out of life." He spent years as a mechanic and serviceman for new cars at several dealerships and was eventually the fleet manager at Simon Ford. Woods watched as more cars were being manufactured with more electric-power accessories, and he decided to focus on vehicle electrical systems when he opened Jim Woods Auto Electric in 1976.

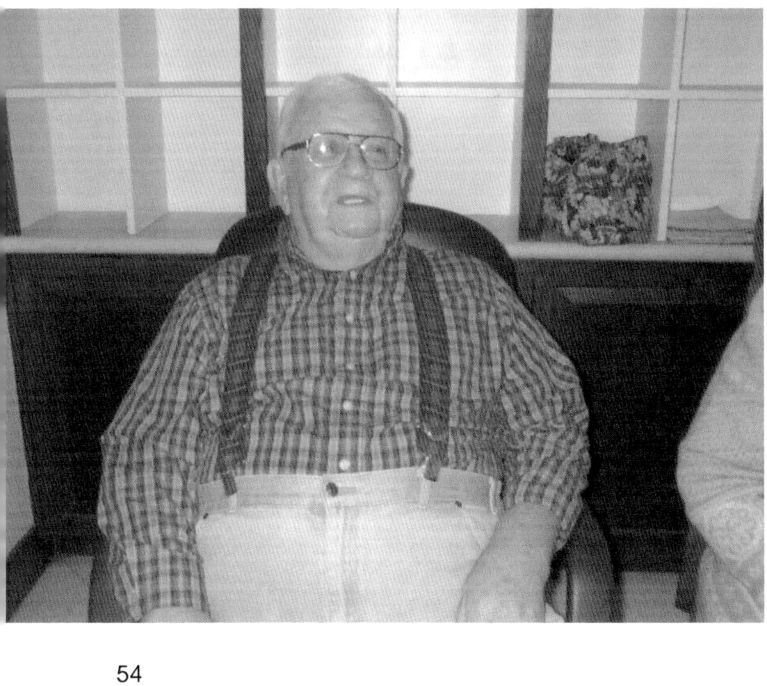

Robert Boyd

Robert Boyd always loved cars and motors. He discovered early in his life that he enjoyed knowing how they operated, and he challenged himself by making them work better than before they were broken. He made his collection of parts-only cars available to others by opening Boyd's Used Auto Parts. He matched parts, price, and personality for 54 years. Family and friends good-naturedly called him the "Automobile Undertaker."

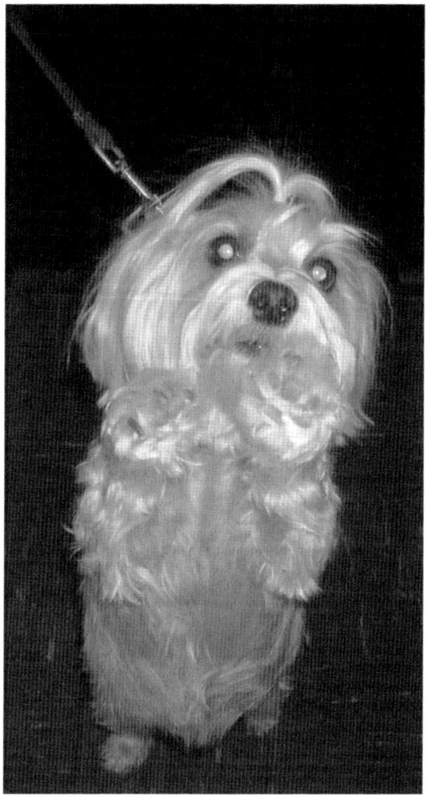

Lilly Allain

Lilly greets every customer to Jerry's Appliance with sparkling brown eyes and curly white hair, putting everyone at ease immediately. As a demonstration model, she has posed with almost every washer, stove, or refrigerator in the showroom, for one advertisement or another. Her presence allows customers to imagine the appliance in their home. Children, and especially the family pet, wearing its best collar and leash, are always welcome at Jerry's Appliance.

Robert Allain

Robert Allain of Jerry's Appliance is a proud distributor of the Crosley Corporation line of appliances from Winston-Salem, North Carolina. Running along the top of the numerous refrigerator floor models are working genuine and replica Crosley radios dating to the 1930s. A few years ago, Allain held a contest to find the oldest operating Crosley appliance in Norwich. The winning entry was a freezer being used by the Baltic Fire Department. The department won a new freezer and decided to keep the old one as a backup, since it was still working. It remains in use today. Allain is seen here at left with Deputy Chief Jerry Bastian of the Baltic Fire Department. (Courtesy of Robert Allain.)

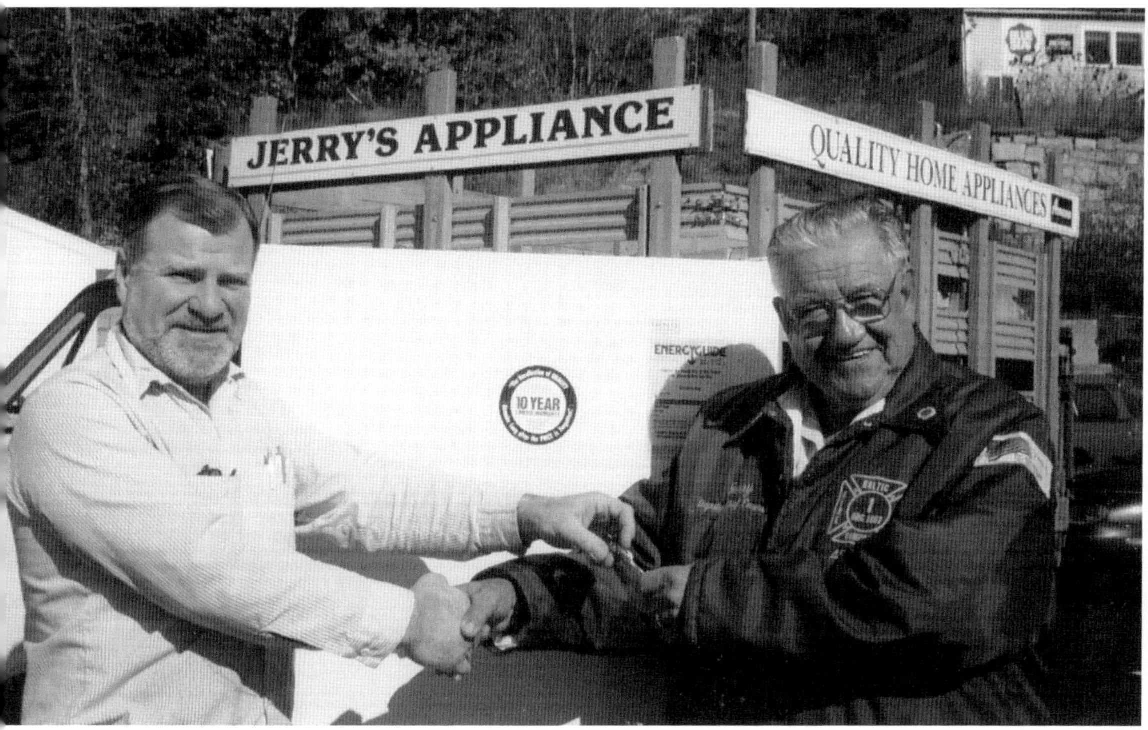

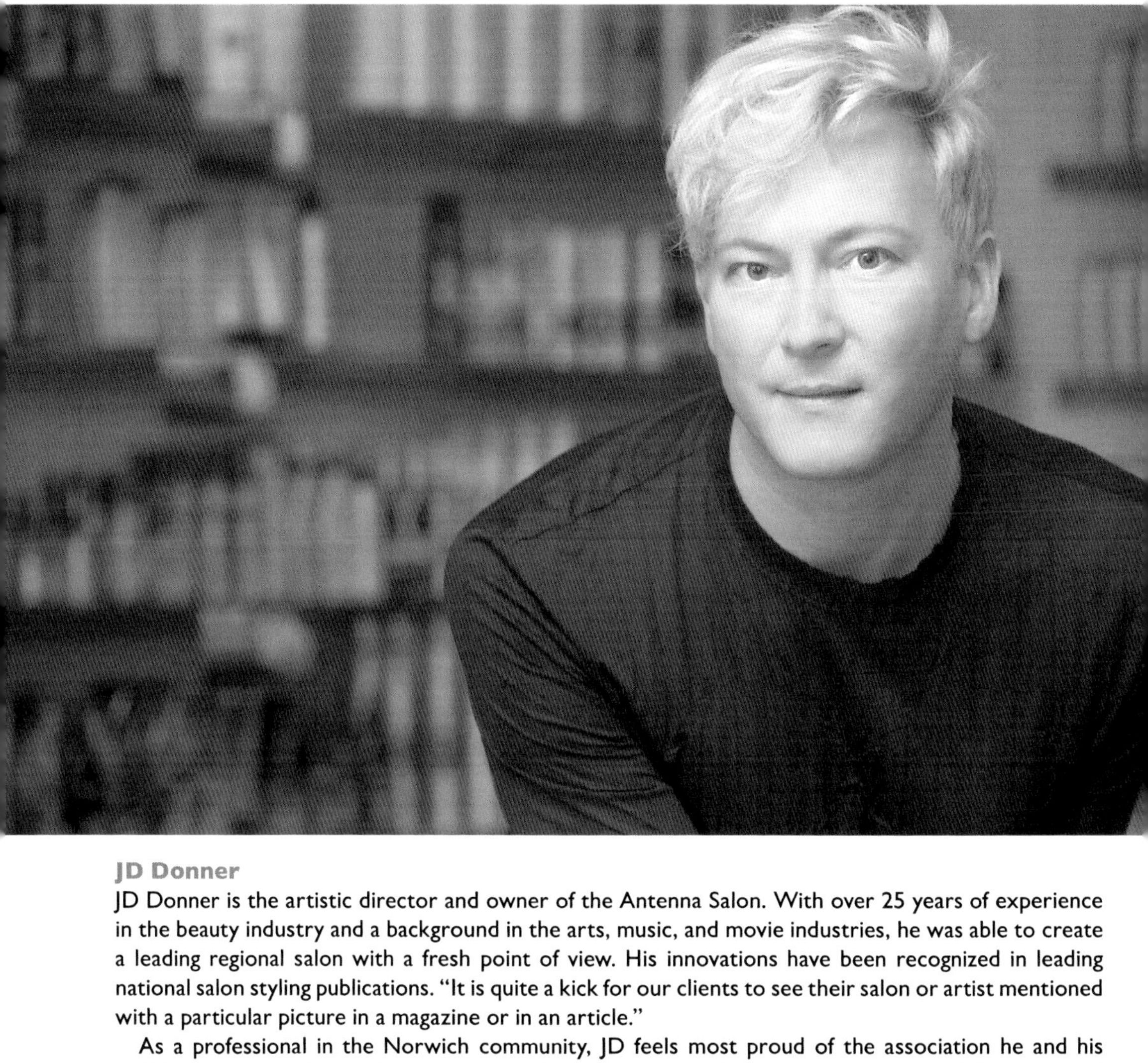

JD Donner

JD Donner is the artistic director and owner of the Antenna Salon. With over 25 years of experience in the beauty industry and a background in the arts, music, and movie industries, he was able to create a leading regional salon with a fresh point of view. His innovations have been recognized in leading national salon styling publications. "It is quite a kick for our clients to see their salon or artist mentioned with a particular picture in a magazine or in an article."

As a professional in the Norwich community, JD feels most proud of the association he and his staff have developed with the ARC of New London County. This group advocates for full inclusion of people with intellectual and developmental disabilities. In a program called "Elements of Ellen," selected individuals and clients and the Antenna Salon staff share their knowledge of and experience in the elements of style—fashion, hair care, skin care, and more—empowering the participants to feel good about themselves and the image they present to the public. (Courtesy of JD Donner.)

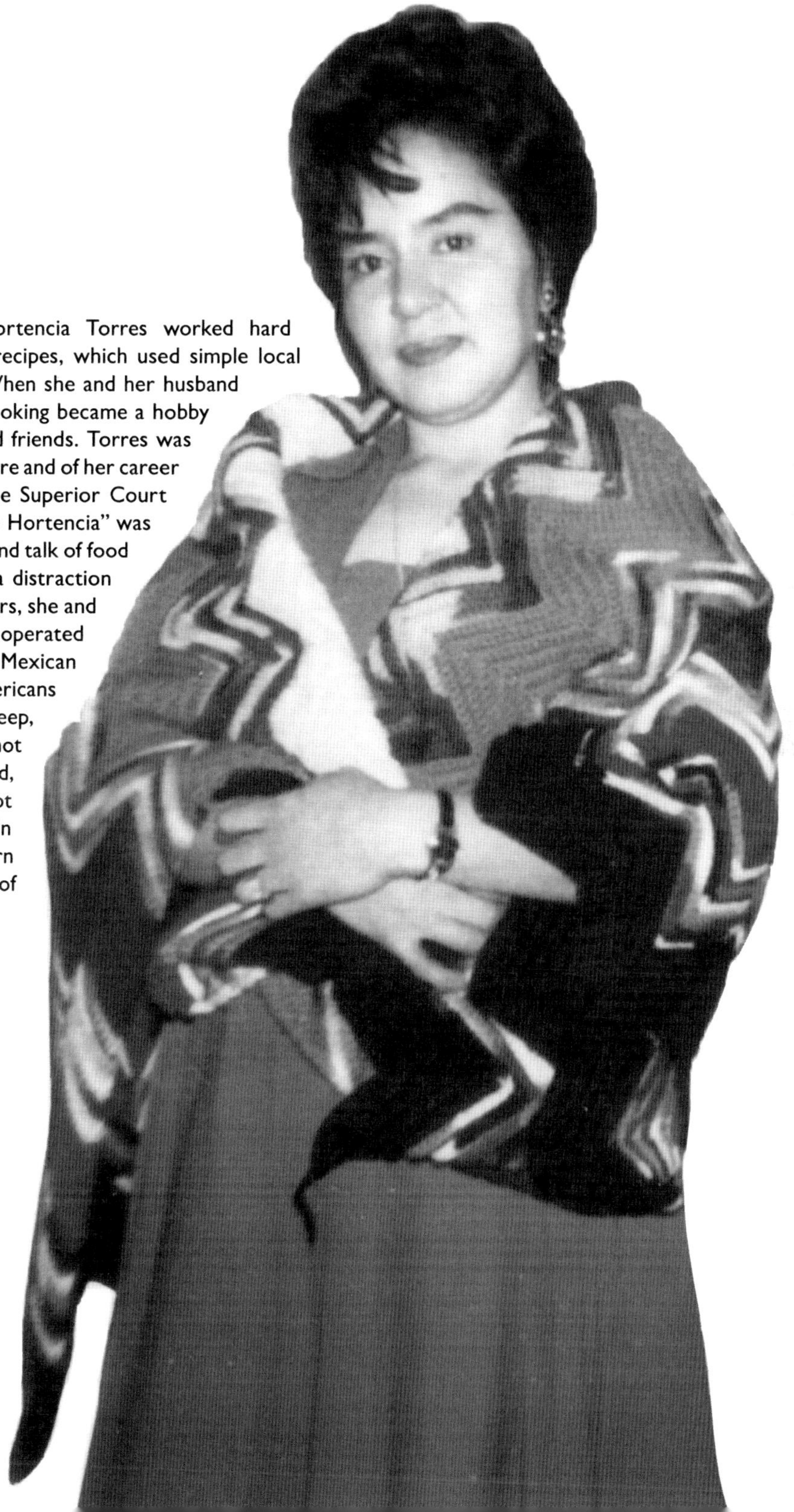

Hortencia Torres

In Durango, Mexico, Hortencia Torres worked hard and learned her family's recipes, which used simple local ingredients and flavors. When she and her husband settled in Connecticut, cooking became a hobby she shared with family and friends. Torres was proud of her Mexican culture and of her career as a judicial marshal in the Superior Court building in Norwich. "Miss Hortencia" was known for her easy smile and talk of food to soothe nerves and as a distraction for the anxious. For 43 years, she and her husband and daughter operated El Sombrero, an authentic Mexican restaurant introducing Americans to Mexican food and her deep, rich, mahogany-colored hot sauce. The restaurant closed, but "Miss Hortencia's" hot sauce is still available in stores throughout eastern Connecticut. (Courtesy of Akil Peck.)

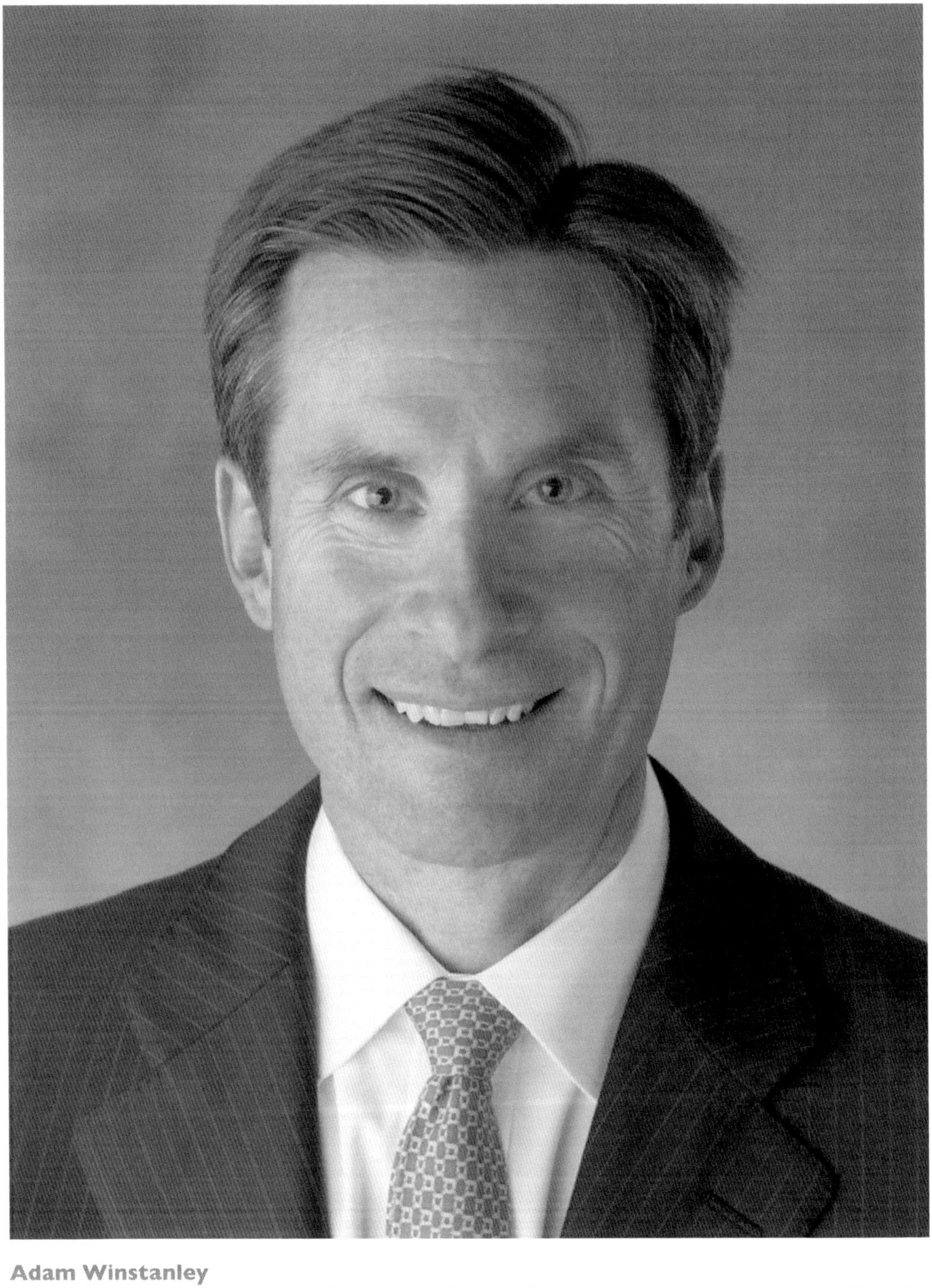

Adam Winstanley

The threat of rain on the day of the ribbon cutting for the refurbished Norwichtown Commons Shopping Center worried all but developer Adam Winstanley. He became an instant legend when, with a single phone call, he arranged for the complete ceremony, including its speakers, to be moved inside the fruit and vegetable aisle of the Stop & Shop Supermarket. The ceremony's background music was the sound of bags rustling and purchases being made. (City of Norwich Office of the Mayor.)

Frank Vocatura and Vocatura's

In 1919, two men formed a partnership in downtown Norwich. Together, they began the National Bakery. The bread they baked fresh every day brought crowds to their door. After a few years, Frank Vocatura (pictured below) bought his partner out and changed the name to Vocatura's and began a legacy that has spanned almost four generations.

Vocatura brought in family to help run the bakery and to ensure that the quality of the bread remained high. By doing this, he ensured that the demand for the fine bread never wavered. Over time, more members of the family became involved in the bakery. The family was close, and their voices could get loud; but, then, so could the teasing and the laughter. In 1941, the bakery moved to 163 Franklin Street, into a building they shared with other businesses. Some members of the family served their country in the military. Michael F. Vocatura sent a letter to the *Westerly Sun* newspaper, telling of his transfer to a new unit as the company baker and how the scenery in Wyoming was fine once "you get used to it." Vocatura men who were serving their country sent letters home, and these would be shared with the bakery's customers, who had become extended family. Photographs of men in uniform adorned the walls. The number of loyal customers continued to grow.

In 1956, Vocatura's moved to its own building, on the Taftville/Greenville line. There was some concern that the customers would not follow. But they did, and the lines for bread and sandwiches grew longer. Over the years, the steady stream of bakers included Donald Pavlak, Tony Turano, Tony Vocatura ("Uncle Tony"), and Michael F. Vocatura ("Uncle Mike"). There were packers, drivers, and deliverers like John Bohara and Lorenzo Vocatura. No one seemed to mind standing in the long line as it snaked around the building. Even in the rain or the cold, standing in line was a chance to relax and visit with neighbors and friends. In the 1970s, to earn extra money, the sisters from the Baltic Academy would come and slice cheese all day long for the sandwiches and grinders.

No matter the time of day, the air in the store is filled with the rich aroma of fresh bread. At lunch and dinnertime, tall stacks of freshly sliced meat and cheese stand ready for those waiting in an amiable line.

The same ovens are still used today, and Vocatura's is still a family affair, where the past and present meet. Uncle Joe, Blowpipe, and Pepsi are on hand, the bread is still baked in the wee hours of the morning, and Uncle Mike arrives at 4:00 a.m. to keep a watchful eye on things, seven days a week. (Courtesy of Vocatura's Bakery.)

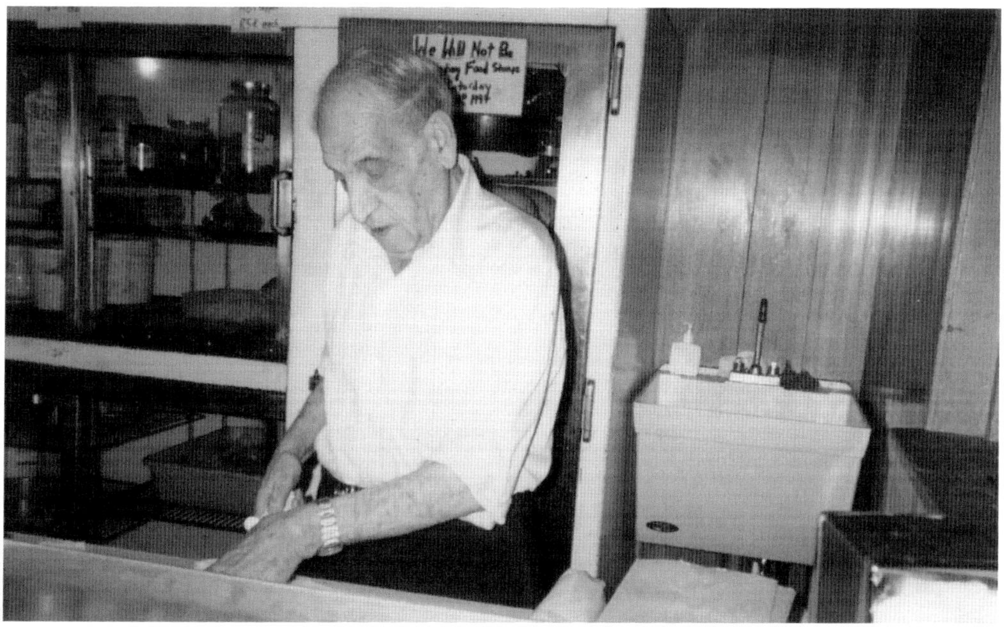

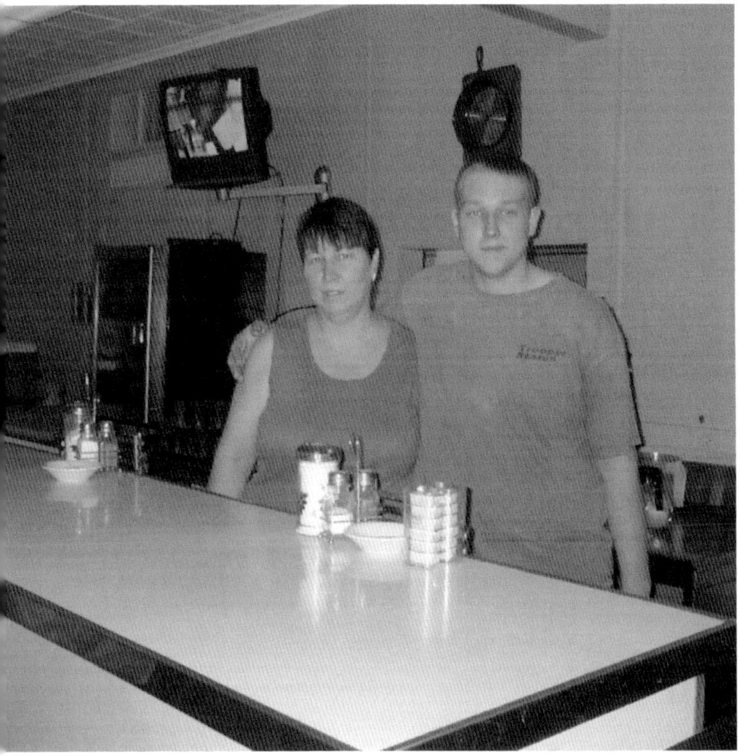

Philip and Rena Whitworth
Phillip Whitworth promises "never to serve something that does not taste good." Everything comes out of the kitchen fresh and hot, with no delays under warming lights or on warming trays. Phillip and Rena Whitworth own Taft Food, a restaurant at the far end of Taftville. At this establishment, which is open for breakfast and lunch, pots of coffee are fresh, and customers are encouraged to interact freely with neighbors and friends they have not met yet.

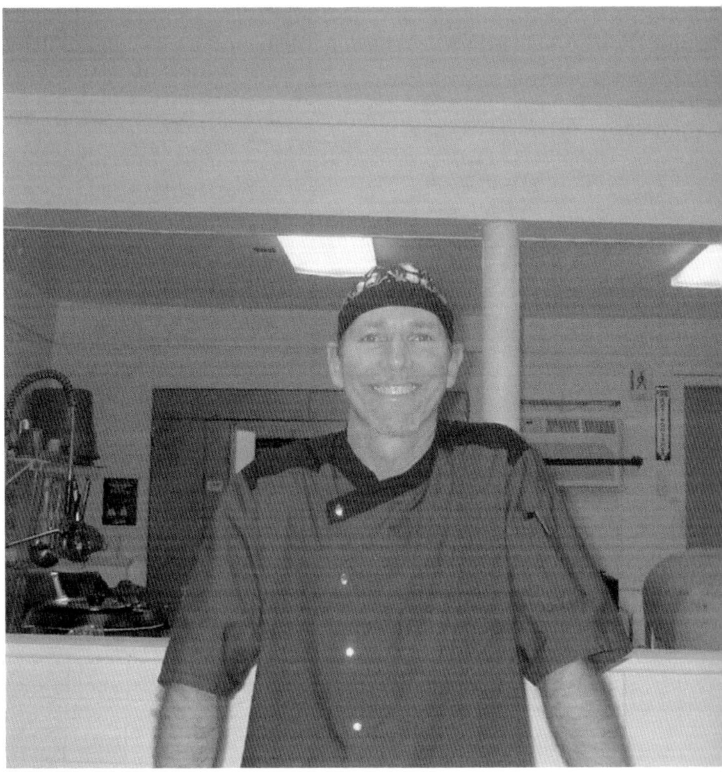

Roger Matros
While serving in the US Coast Guard, Roger Matros became accustomed to being a part of the environmental solution. So, when he opened The Jolly Roger sandwich shop, he continued his role of being a part of the solution by using locally grown products served in biodegradable containers that will not last for years or float out to sea, endangering animals and the future. Even Matros's location recycles a Greeneville landmark building from a previous business.

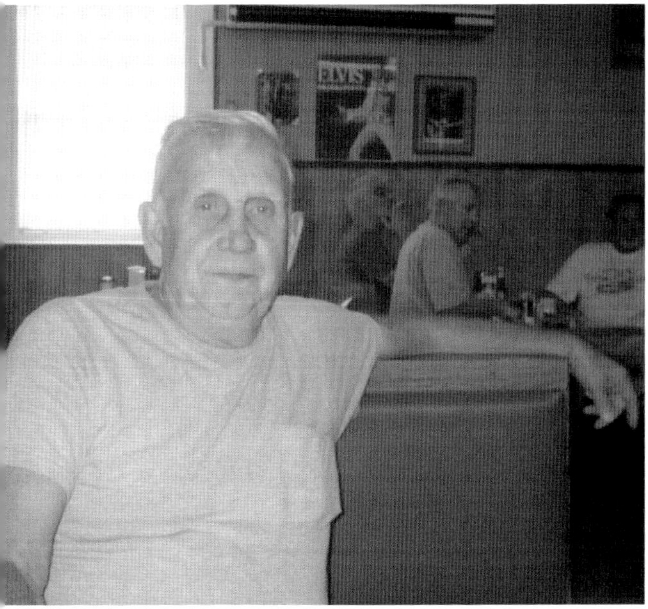

Andrew Gauthier

"Butch" Gauthier likes things as they are. Hard work and flexibility have been the key to his staying in business for over 38 years. Butch enjoys his cigarettes, so when smoking became banned in restaurants, his establishment became Butch's Breakfast Club. Here, smokers are welcome to write their name in the membership book and light up. Gauthier describes his business as follows: "We are a family operation, and everyone who comes in here becomes a part of our family. So long as the lights are on, everyone knows they are welcome to come in. In here you can smoke, linger, and visit with friends."

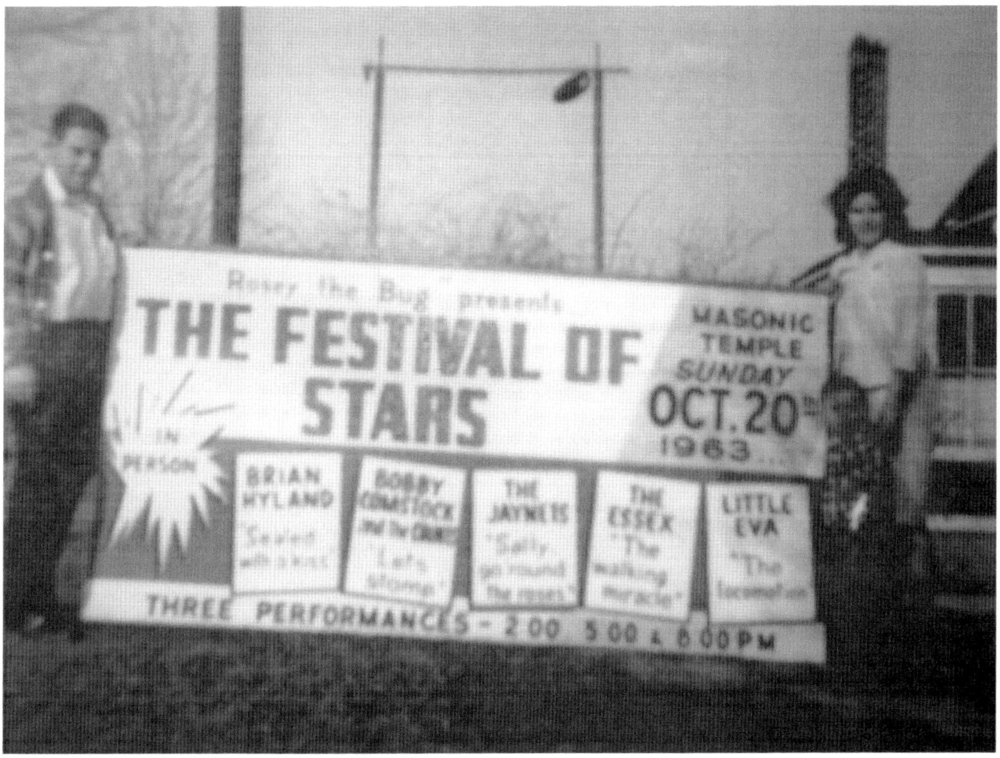

Rosario Presti

Presti is better known as "Rosey the Bug," because he has always been "buggy for music." Since the 1960s, when he opened Rosey the Bug's Dance Arena, and into the 1970s, 1980s, and to the present time, Presti has entertained every generation with popular music of the day and old-time dance hall music in "every venue that will let me set up." (Courtesy of Rosario Presti.)

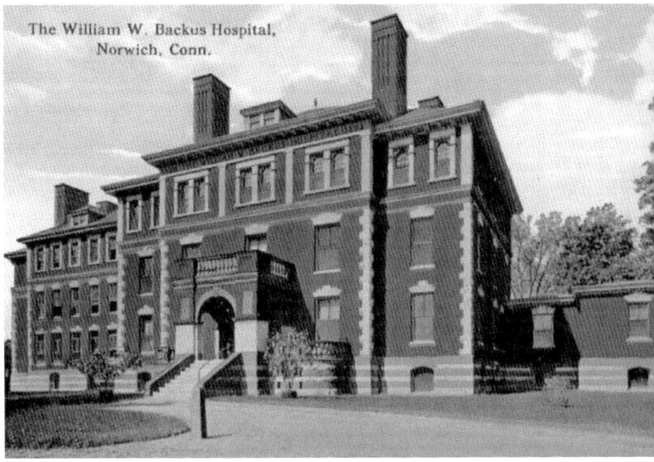

William Wolcott Backus

W.W. Backus was determined to leave a permanent mark in his community. Industrialist William Albert Slater donated 18 acres to a project on the thoroughfare between Norwichtown and the commercial area, also the site of the harbor and the railroad. Backus donated $185,000 (approximately $4 million today) to fund the building of a hospital that could serve any current and future needs.

Backus died in July 1893. On October 4 of that year, with much fanfare, the William W. Backus Hospital opened, with 63 beds, including separate male and female wards, an isolation room, an operating room, a staff of 16, and a nurses' training home. (Courtesy of W.W. Backus Hospital.)

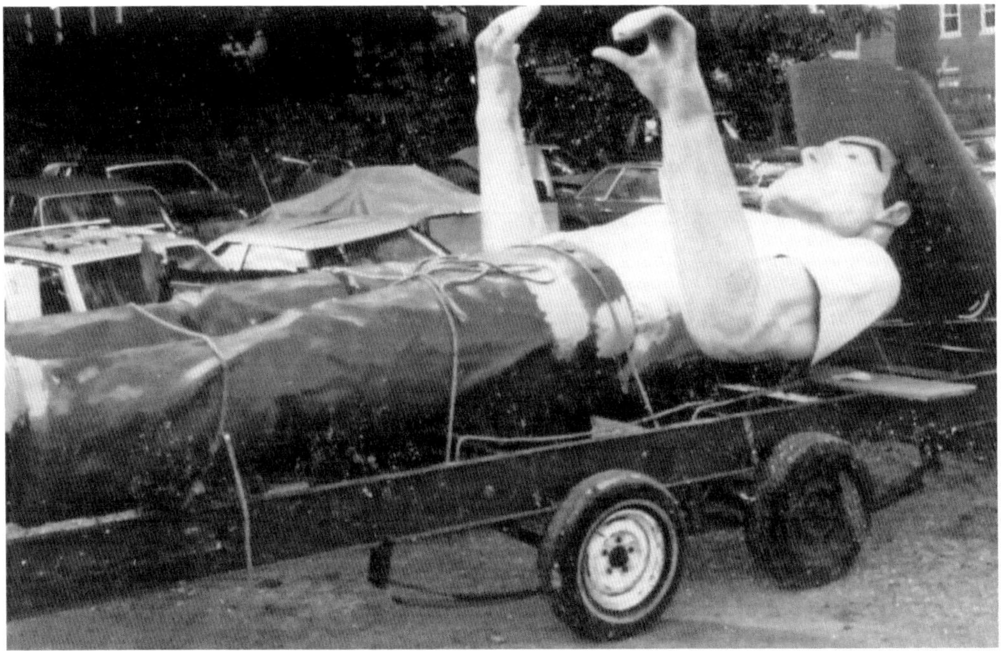

Phillips Cowboy

In the 1960s, this "cowboy," almost three stories tall, was the marketing landmark for the Phillips gas and service station on West Main Street in Norwich. Then, Alix Cohn set the cowboy up in front of his trolly barn in Taftville. For a few years, the cowboy even had a chance to lie down and rest inside the barn. But when Joe Matera moved his store to West Main Street in 1986, he remembered the cowboy.

The cowboy was repainted by Norm's Auto Body & Repair and returned to stand at the bustling Willow Tree Plaza, greeting customers by the doors of Surplus Unlimited, a discount store of household goods and business supplies, not far from where the cowboy stood in the 1960s. (Courtesy of Frank Obuchowski.)

CHAPTER FIVE

Hobbies, Entertainment, and Passion

Blaise Pascal said, "Nothing is so intolerable to man as being fully at rest, without a passion, without business, without entertainment, without care." In Norwich, it is difficult to find a green space not in use. Residents are encouraged to share their interests and their hobbies. Teaching, demonstration, and observation give citizens and visitors opportunities to share in a relaxed atmosphere.

Mohegan Park is almost 400 acres of woods, trails, gardens, and swimming and fishing spots in the center of the city. Norwich is proud to have a unique New England parade, open spaces, neighborhood parks, and athletic fields convenient to every neighborhood of the city. It also has a municipal golf course, an ice-skating rink, a minor-league baseball stadium, a dog park, multiple walking tracks, a skateboard park, a harbor, and a variety of boat launches for motorboats, canoes, and kayaks.

Small art galleries are nestled in downtown storefronts, and the Slater Museum Cast Gallery offers visitors the chance to see a plaster-cast collection of ancient monumental sculptures. Colonial life in America can be seen on self-guided walks through neighborhoods, at the Leffingwell House Colonial Museum, and at the Perkins-Rockwell House Museum, operated by the Daughters of the American Revolution, Faith Trumbull Chapter.

Evenings and weekends offer participation in, or attendance at, musical theater, outdoor band concerts, and a variety of club activities.

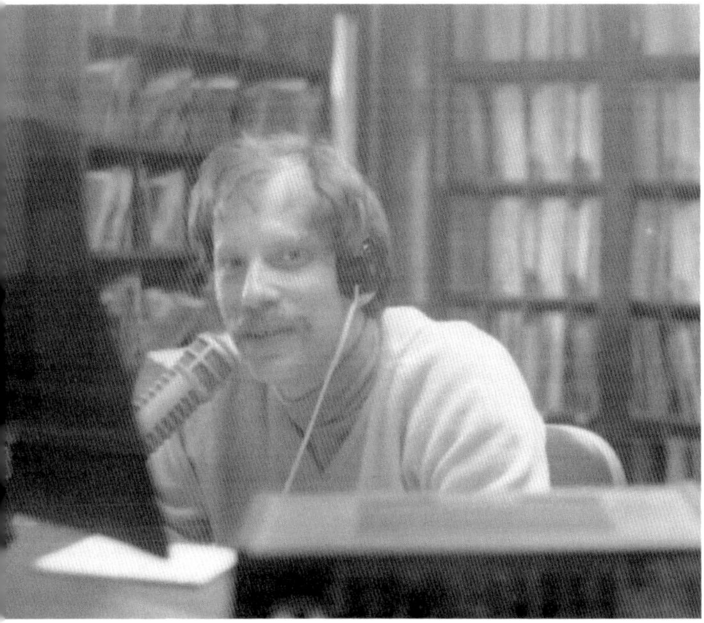

Stu Bryer

Bryer has talked his way through every event, every election, and all types of weather as the midday voice of WICH-AM radio. After 42 years, Bryer says he "still enjoys going to work" as the host of the noontime call-in talk show *Potpourri*, offering discussion of current events and topics important to his listeners. Celebrities and survivors are put at ease with his soft voice, polite ways, and reassuring stories. Smiles and trust can be heard in his interviews. Most important, Bryer has brought new and old friends into the homes, vehicles, and workplaces in Norwich and beyond. (Courtesy of Hall Communications.)

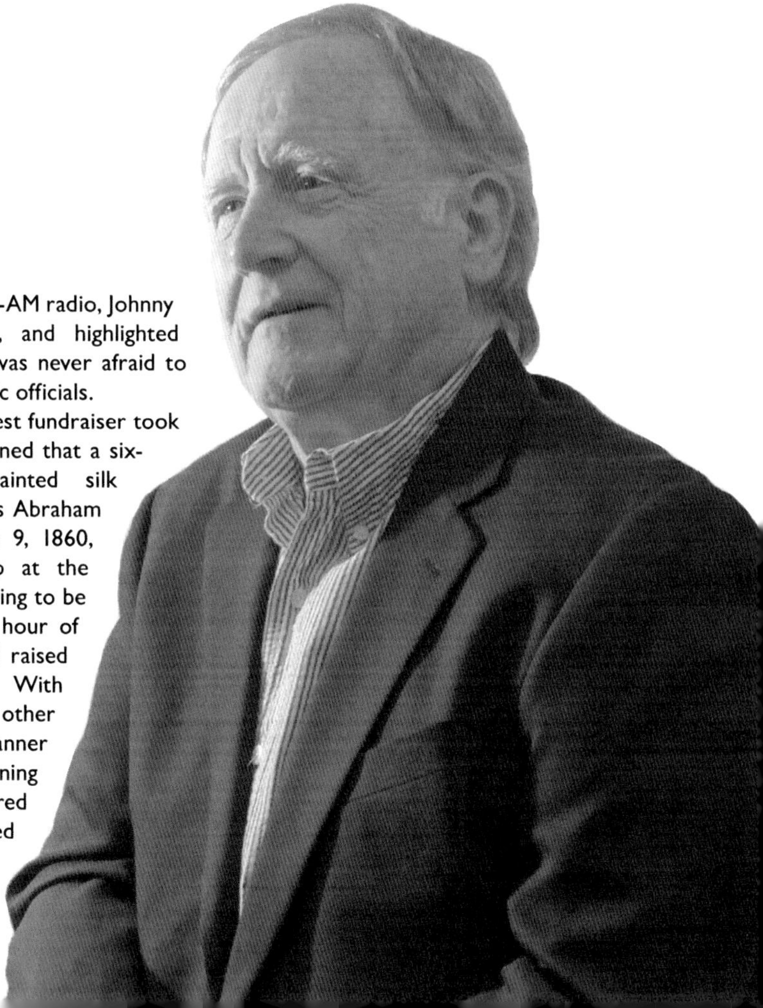

Johnny London

For over 30 years on WICH-AM radio, Johnny London addressed, raised, and highlighted community issues, and he was never afraid to question the actions of public officials.

London's biggest and fastest fundraiser took place in 1997, when he learned that a six-foot-by-seven-foot hand-painted silk banner featuring a beardless Abraham Lincoln, made for a March 9, 1860, presidential campaign stop at the Norwich Town Hall, was going to be auctioned off. Within one hour of going on the radio, he had raised $13,800 for the auction. With a final push, London and other dignitaries brought the banner back to Norwich with a winning bid of $32,500. The restored banner is proudly displayed in city hall. (Courtesy of Johnny London.)

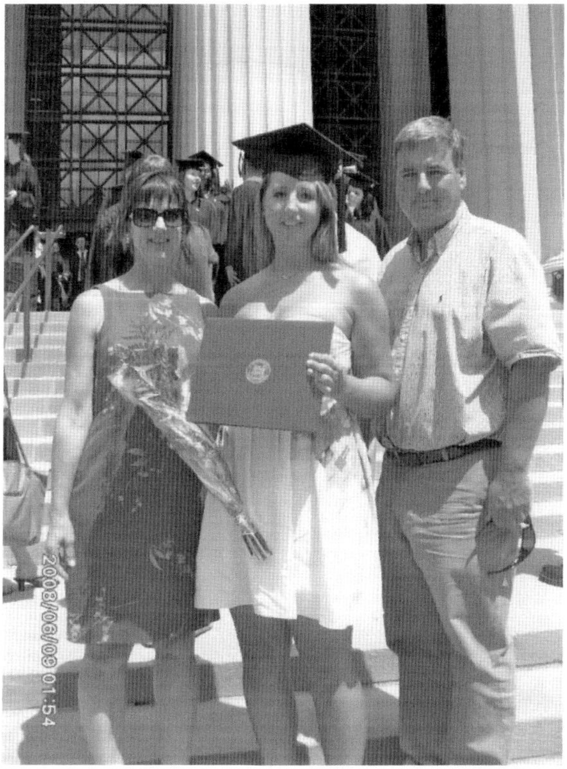

Hughie Schnip

"My Name is Hughie Schnip." "My name is Hughie Schnip." "My name is Hughie Schnip." On an episode of the television show *To Tell the Truth* in June 1974, a trio of 13-year-old boys made the claim to be the real "Hughie Schnip" of Norwich, the official WICH-AM radio weather forecaster and the youngest meteorologist on the radio in the country. He was more well known than he imagined, as the panel of celebrities quickly guessed his real identity. Going away to college in 1978 ended Schnip's broadcasts on WICH. Hugh (at right) is pictured in 2009 with his wife, Wendy, (left) and daughter (center). (Courtesy of Hugh Schnip.)

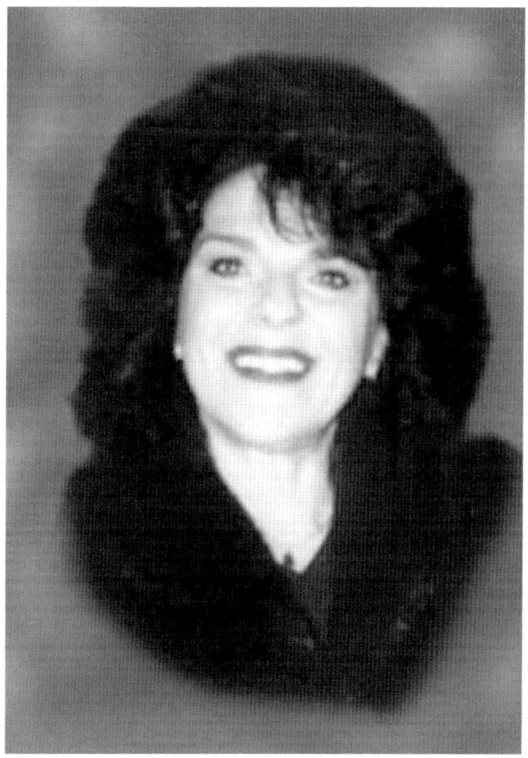

Pat Gagliardo

Pat Gagliardo acknowledged being an intuitive clairvoyant/medium in September 1978. In 1980, after an intense interview with Dennis McCarthy and Stu Breyer on WICH radio, she took a moment on the steps of the station to release any negative energy that had built up. Gagliardo immediately felt better and continued on her way.

But, just after she left the building, all of the electric typewriters suddenly stopped working. WICH's automated sister station, WCTY-FM, suddenly began playing incorrect playlists and sent incorrect information over the airways. Spontaneously, and for three full days, all the broadcasting tower lights went out, and the Federal Aviation Authority became involved, as the tall unlit towers were a hazard to air navigation. A consulting electrical engineer reported, "A huge power surge from an unknown source was the cause, and nothing could be done; it would just have to run its course." (Courtesy of Pat Gagliardo.)

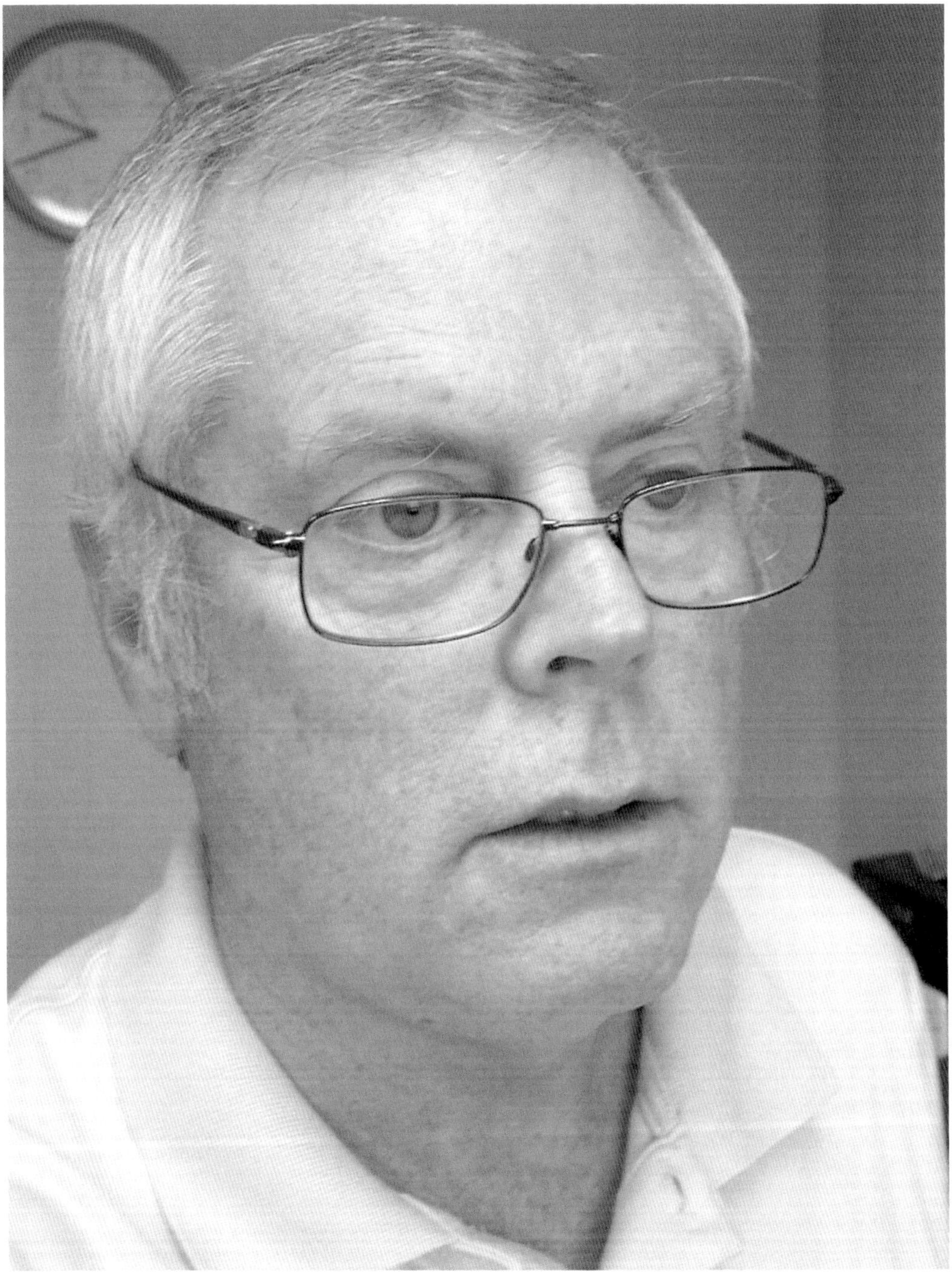

Bill Kenny

"It takes more power to be a light than a horn," said Bill Kenny, who invests his time and energy creating and maintaining a Facebook page called "Celebrating Norwich, Connecticut." He and his wife were active in their children's schools' Parent Teacher Organizations, and it was a small step to extend that involvement to the Baseball Stadium Authority, School Building and Technology Committee, Charter Review Commission, and Ethics Review Committee. (Courtesy of Bill Kenny.)

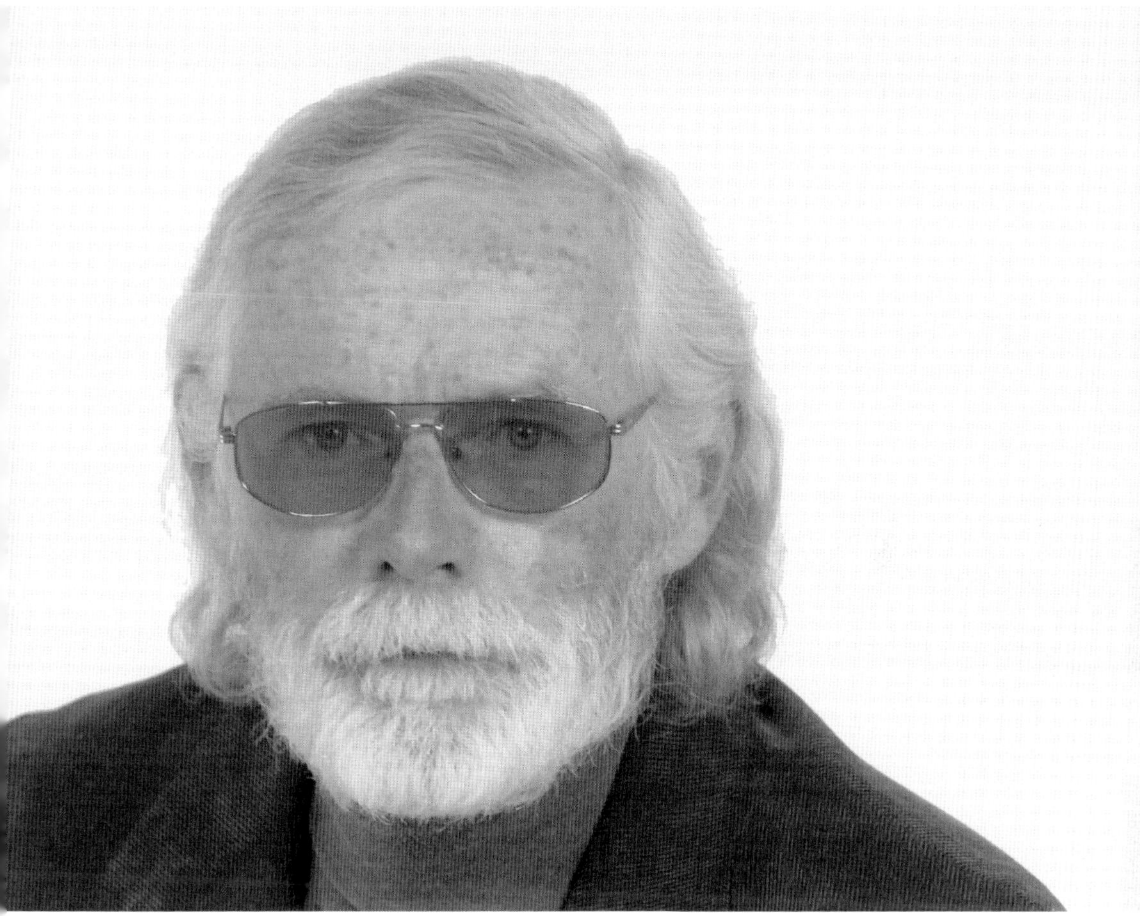

Ray Hackett

Ray Hackett took over the city hall beat for the *Norwich Bulletin* in 1988. He was city editor from 1994 to 2000, then reinvented himself as political savant and guardian of free speech, influence of the paper's editorial page, and capital reporter. Hackett is the most skilled and sought-after election debate moderator in New London County. His questions are carefully molded, ensuring that the answers remain focused and on topic. (Courtesy of Ray Hackett.)

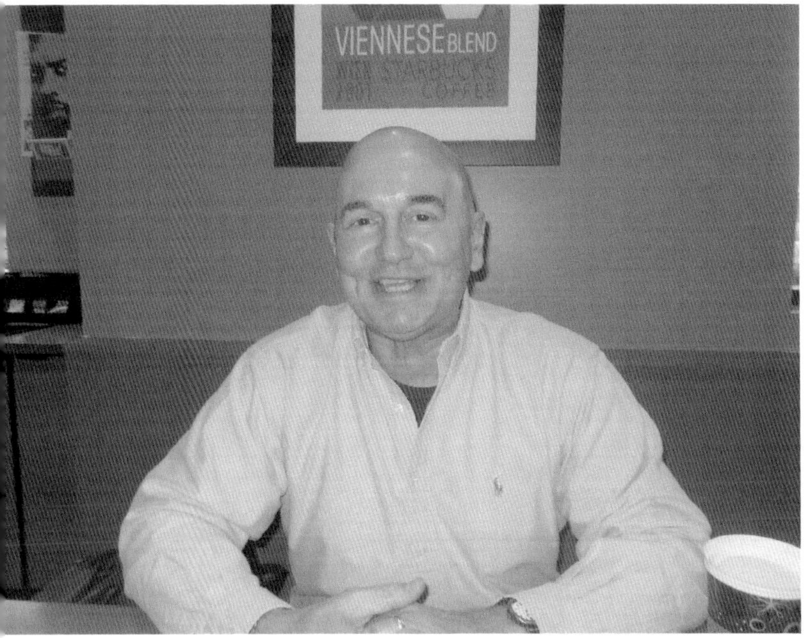

John-Manuel Andriote
Andriote is a writer who just loves to push buttons to elicit a response. His letters to the editor of the *Norwich Bulletin* newspaper led to a popular blog that regularly takes public officials to task for what they should or should not do and discusses what needs to be done. In some cases, a public official has reversed positions on an issue. Andriote regularly features the quiet good works of others. (Courtesy of John-Manuel Andriote.)

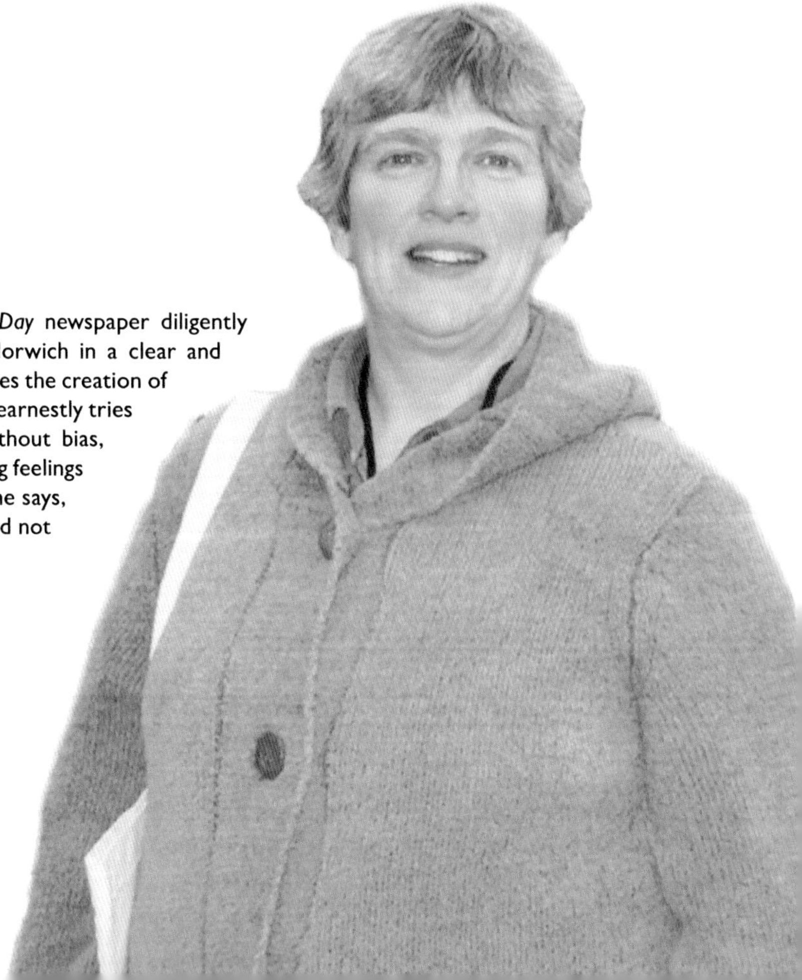

Claire Bessette
Claire Bessette of the *Day* newspaper diligently relates the events of Norwich in a clear and concise manner that leaves the creation of the news to others. She earnestly tries to report the facts, without bias, even when she has strong feelings on the topic. Her job, she says, "is to relate the news and not to create it."

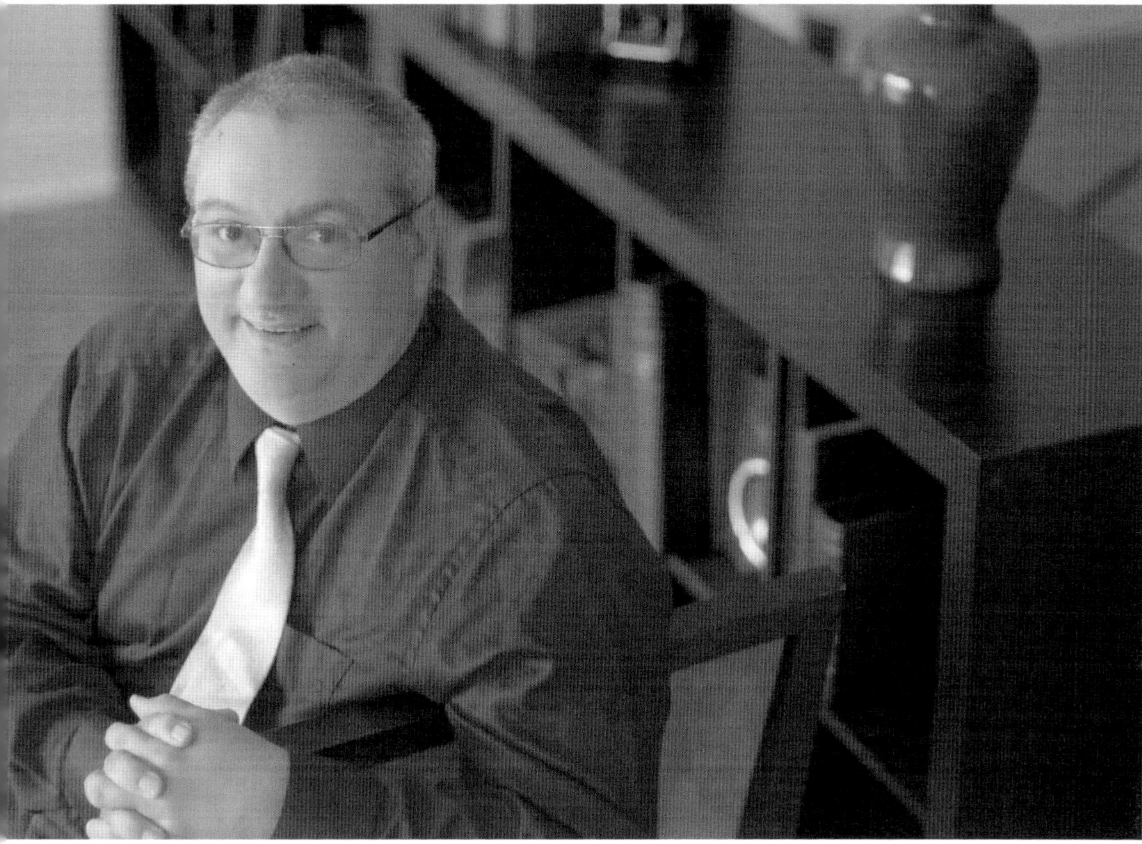

Seth Owen

Seth Owen is the owner and editor of the *Norwich Rose*, a start-up, community-based news and information website devoted to events in Norwich, Connecticut. It was designed with the smartphone user in mind. Owen mixes skills honed from his military experience, love of history, and wargaming. Owen wrote "The History of Wargaming, 1975–1990" for the July 1990 issue of *Strategy & Tactics* magazine, and he is an active contributor to websites devoted to gaming and history.

Owen reminds everyone, "Begin with telling people what you are doing while you are planning the event, tell them about the event, and do not forget to tell them after the event about what they missed." (Courtesy of Seth Owen.)

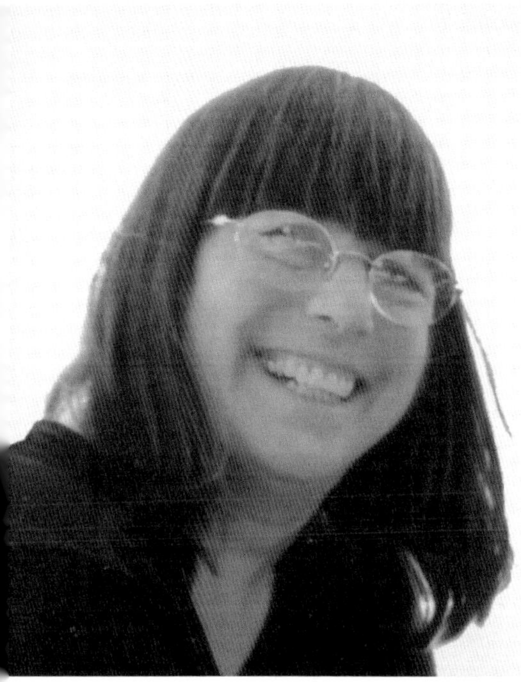

Ann Shapiro

Shapiro entertains audiences with participatory music and storytelling programs. She is recommended by the Connecticut Office of the Arts as a teaching artist, and since 1999, she has served as executive director for the Connecticut Storytelling Center. A teaching artist-in-residence in Connecticut schools, Shapiro helps students and teachers keep folk traditions alive by sharing the old stories and songs and by encouraging students to create their own. (Courtesy of Ann Shapiro.)

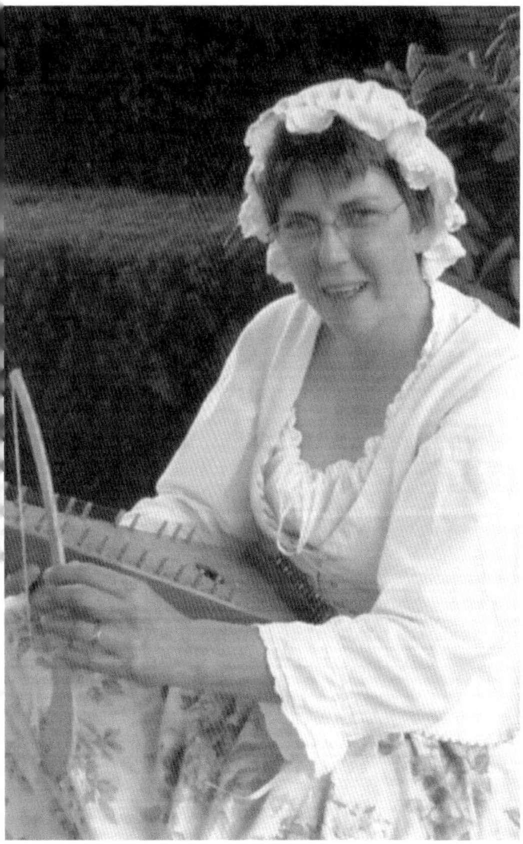

Melodye Whatley

Melodye Whatley brightens the surroundings with her light laugh, quick smile, authentic Colonial-period costumes, and her bowed psaltery (a zither-like stringed instrument played with a bow). Whatley deftly matches folk music to the place or event, whether it is a wedding, museum fundraiser, church concert, ladies' night in a garden shop, or an outing at a park. (Courtesy of Melodye Whatley.)

70

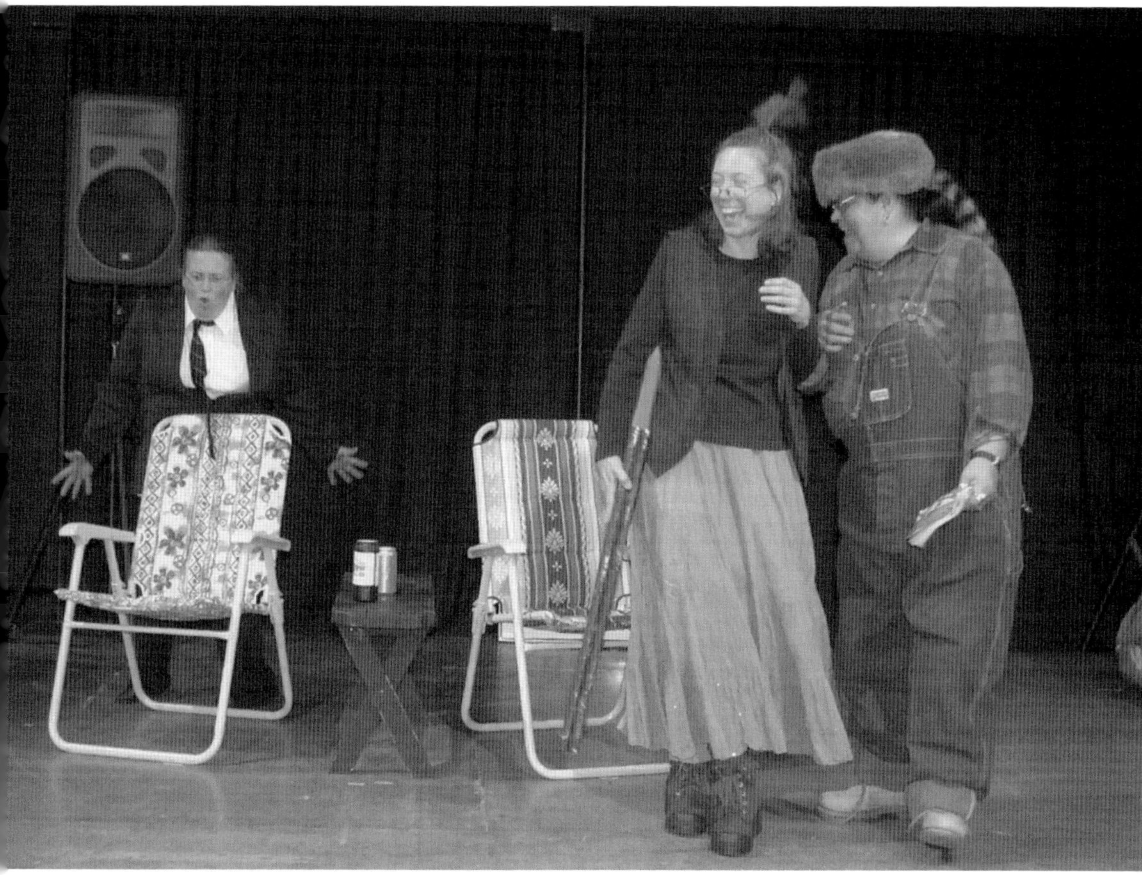

Becca Atkins
Atkins, "the Dance Lady," was invited to choreograph for The Second Step Players of Artreach, Inc., in 1992. She uses her talents as a singer/songwriter and bass and guitar player in local productions and bands, including Blue Blazes, Gypsy TimeSurf, and Shrink Rapt (Artreach's house band). In addition, she composes haikus to relax, such as this one: "Second Step Players / Recovery through the arts / Comic alchemy." She led Norwich participation in Thrill the World, a worldwide simultaneous dance of Michael Jackson's "Thriller." Since 2007, she has served as executive director of Artreach, Inc., a nonprofit mental health and arts agency. Shown here are Robin Fleming (left), Atkins (center), and Terry Alderman. (Courtesy of Becca Atkins.)

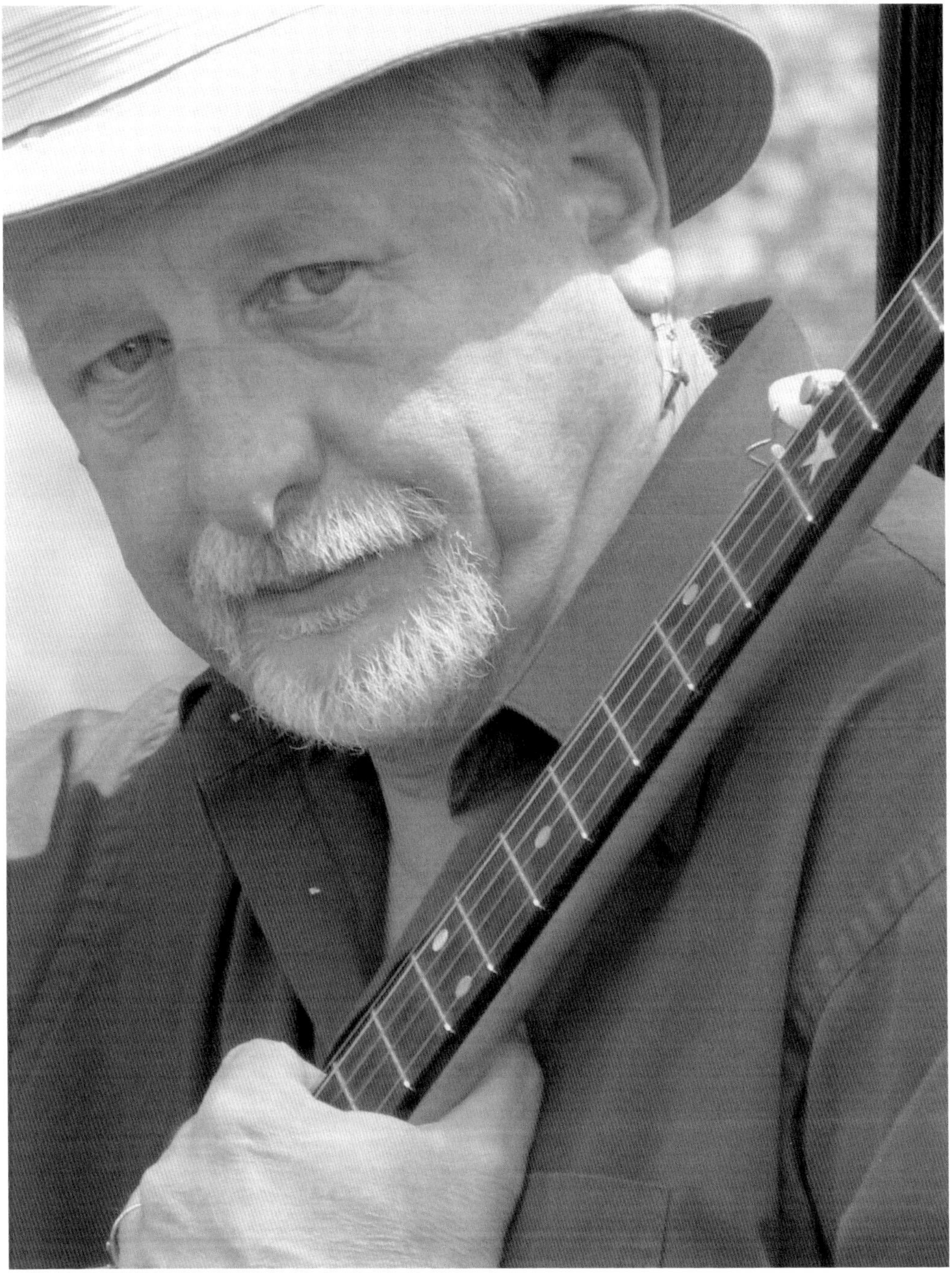

Rick Spencer
Spencer tells his tales in folk songs and in jokes, which range from delicate and sensitive to humorous and sometimes irreverent. He accompanies his oration with a variety of instruments that transport listeners to days when the wind moved the ships up the rivers and across the seas, when the work in the fields was done by hand, and when the sounds of nature were not overwhelmed by the sounds of machines. (Courtesy of Rick Spencer.)

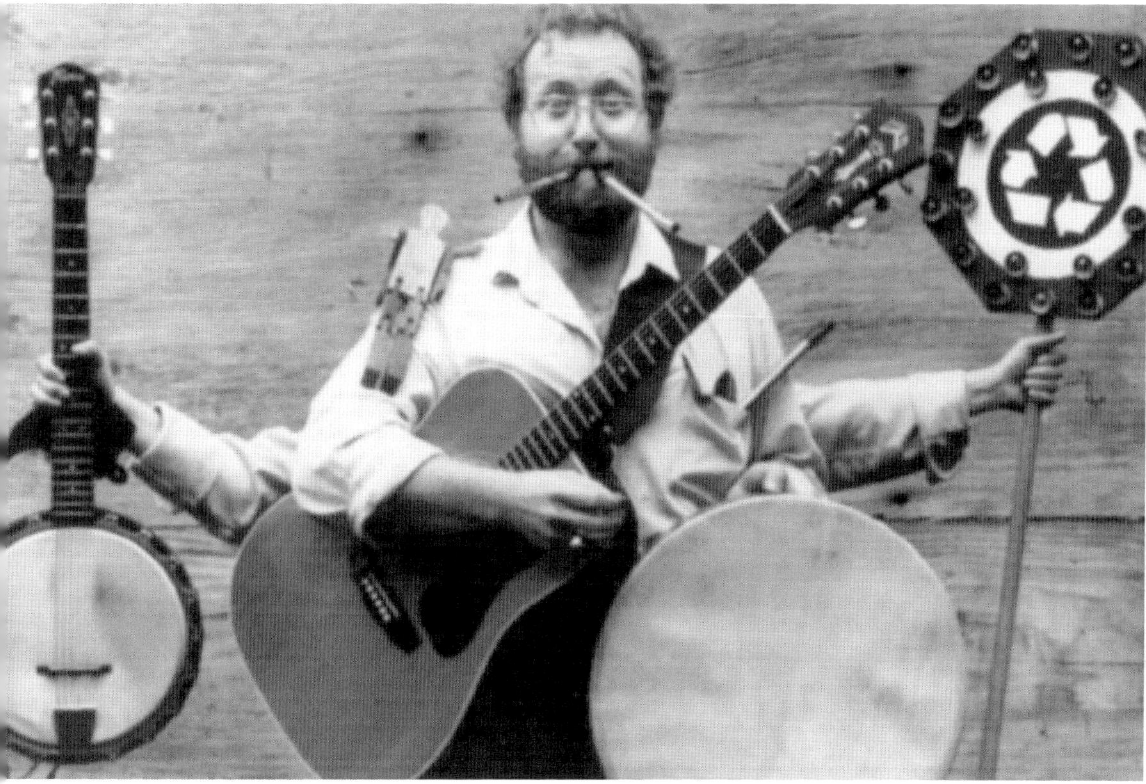

Tom Callinan

In 1991, Callinan was named the State of Connecticut's first official troubadour, for his skills as a composer of songs and as a poet who writes verses to music. He conducts thorough research and chooses the right style of music to blend with whatever story he is telling, making even the most mundane items and events memorable. Through his words, music, and voice, Callinan produced *Where Three Rivers Come Together* for the 350th anniversary of Norwich's settling. It became the best-selling CD in Norwich history. (Courtesy of Tom Callinan.)

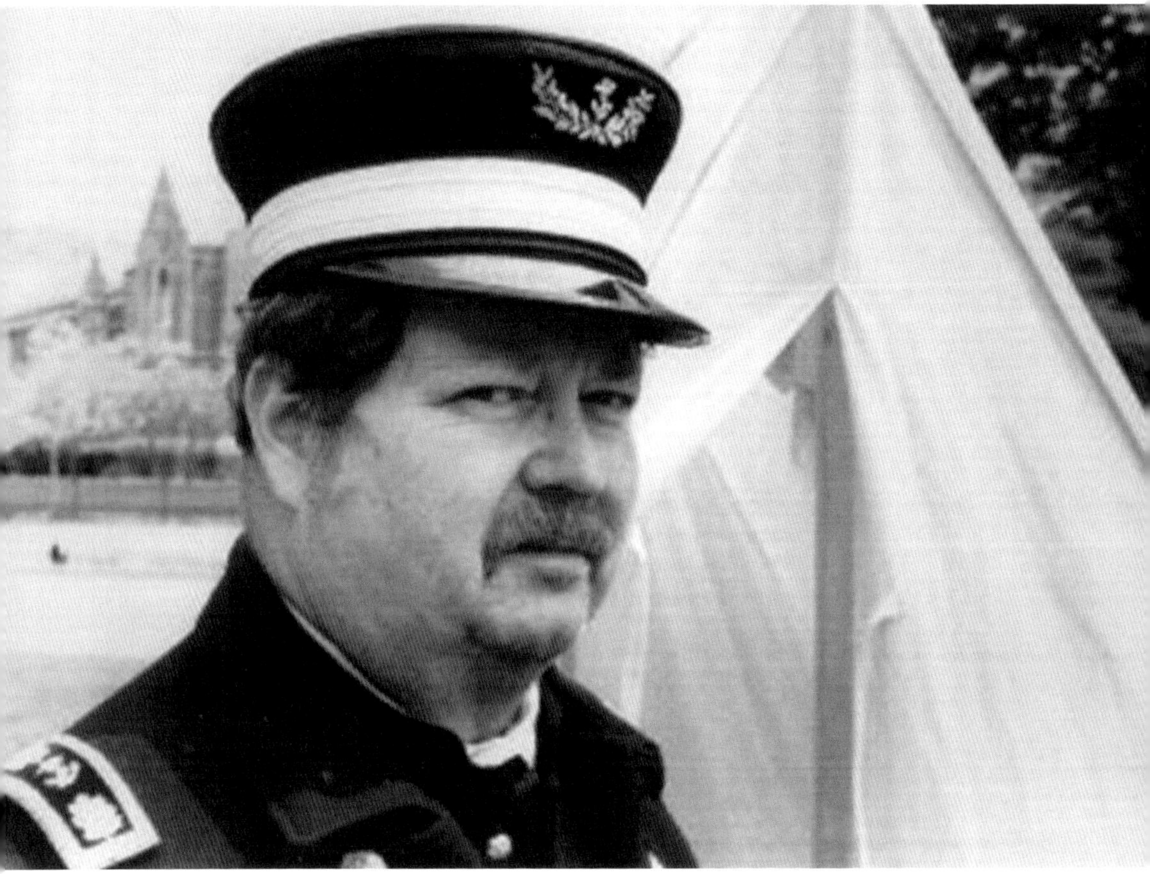

Geoff McLean
McLean portrays several personalities of the Civil War period, including US Navy lieutenant commander Ezra Seals of the first class of the Naval Academy and the salty Capt. Percival Drayton, a real-life officer who went from being a commander to Admiral Farragut's flag captain. McLean also plays the concertina and tin and wooden whistles, and he entertains at reenactments with sea chanteys. (Courtesy of Geoff McLean.)

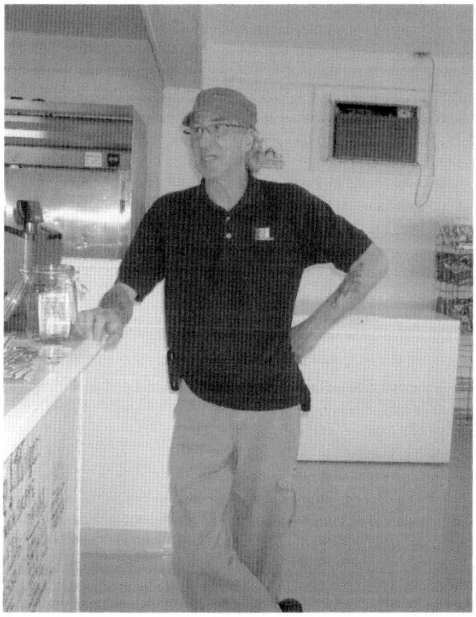

Bill Thibeault

Bill Thibeault likes being around people and playing the blues in nightclubs and bars. But he also speaks of how he was and forever will be Sn. William F. Thibeault, a sailor aboard the USS *Frank E. Evans* (DD-754). The Allen M. Sumner–class destroyer was cut in two by an Australian aircraft carrier in the South China Sea at 3:00 a.m. on June 3, 1969, resulting in the loss of 74 souls. It was a night and a memory that Thibeault carries with him every day.

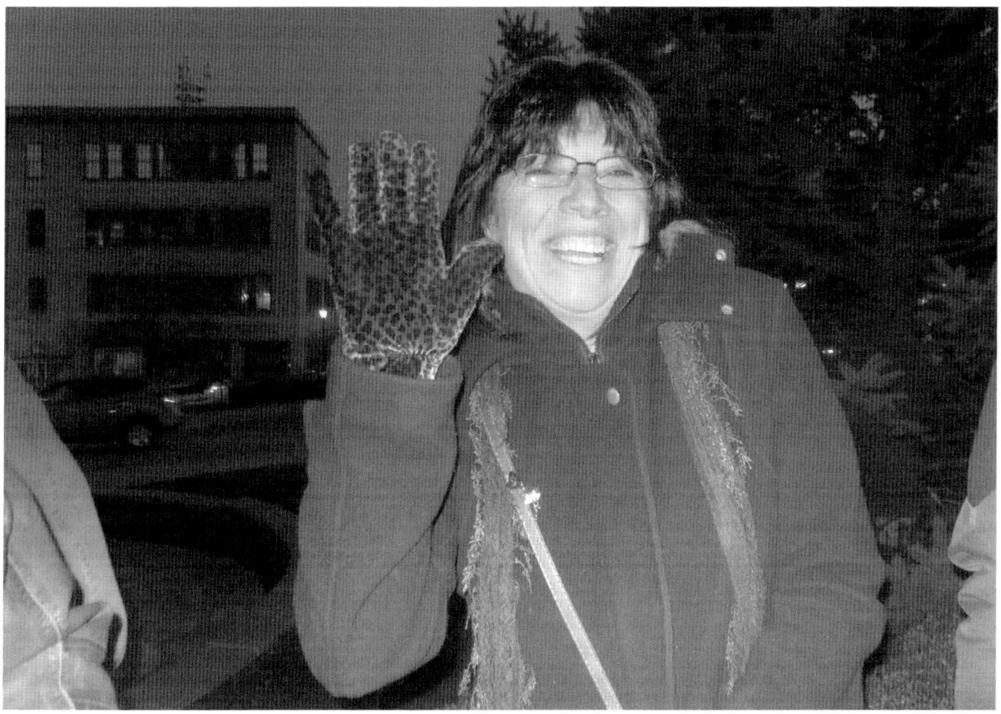

Sofee Noblick

"I am not a resident just of Greenville, I am a resident of Norwich," says Norwich alderwoman, Greenville resident, and landlord Sofee Noblick. "What is good for a community is good for our city. Telling people something is good for them is not as good as getting it done." Fueled by her favorite Starbucks coffee, Noblick is in constant motion, tending to rental properties throughout the city and attending civic meetings. She freely volunteers to meet with various state office representatives and write letters suggesting what actions would be appropriate for state agencies to take for the improvement of Norwich.

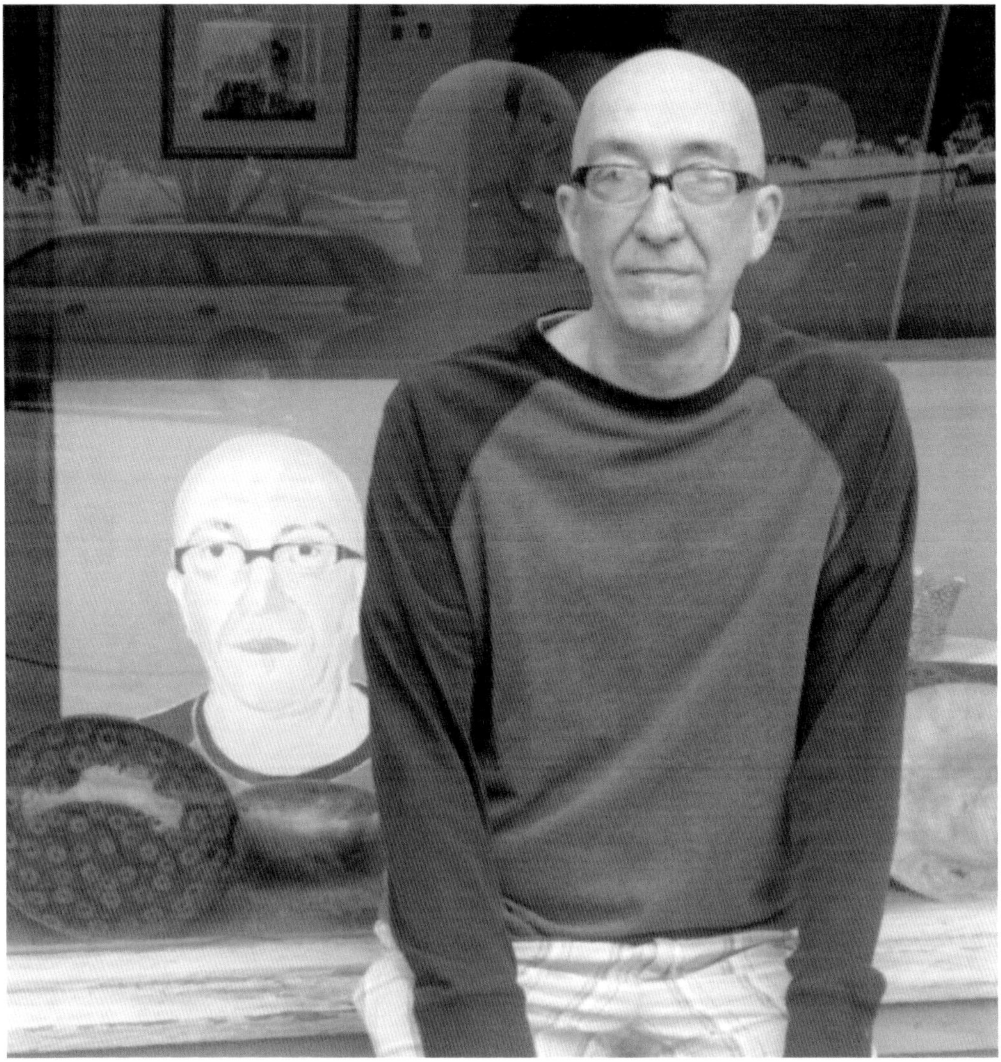

Dan Topalis

Dan Topalis believes that art should be seen. In 1994, a 19th-century portrait of Abraham Lincoln painted by Norwich native John Denison Crocker to commemorate Lincoln's 1860 visit to Norwich was stolen from its frame in city hall. In 2011, the Norwich Arts Council held a contest for local artists to recreate the stolen portrait for a prize and the opportunity for their painting to replace the stolen one.

The Converse Gallery of the Slater Museum at Norwich Free Academy was inaccessible, due to a large construction project, so the show was moved to the Norwich Art Center, with space for fewer than half of the entries—only those paintings that were the closest duplicates of the one that was stolen.

Topalis quickly organized two additional shows at his galleries, The Lincoln Portrait Show that Tells Artists: Do What You Want! and the Lincoln Orphans Exhibit: Giving a Home to the Excluded Portraits! Topalis had managed to find a way to display every painting that had been submitted to the contest and to live up to his own code that art is in the hand of its creator. (Courtesy of Dan Topalis.)

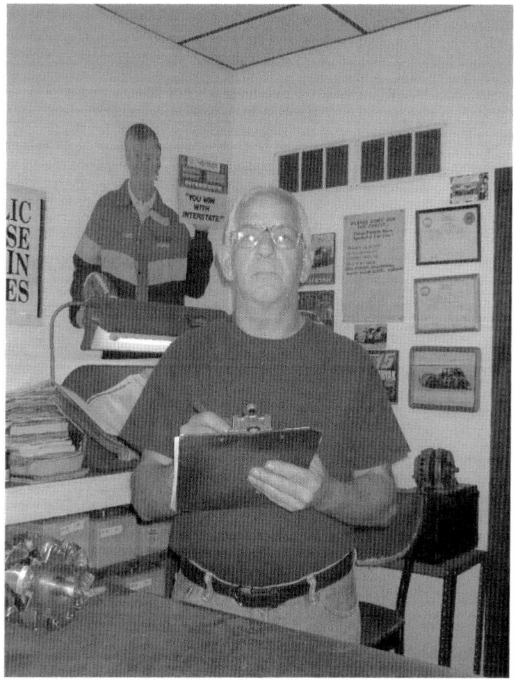

Doug Sogolow

Sogolow satisfies his need for speed when he drives his "Flying 70" in Vintage Modified car races throughout New England. The Flying 70 is based on a car and style he saw at the Waterford Speedbowl in the 1960s. Everyone built their own cars back then. His car is not a replica or a duplicate of the Sal Dee cars, but he hopes that it conveys the spirit and character of their era. (Courtesy of Doug Sogolow.)

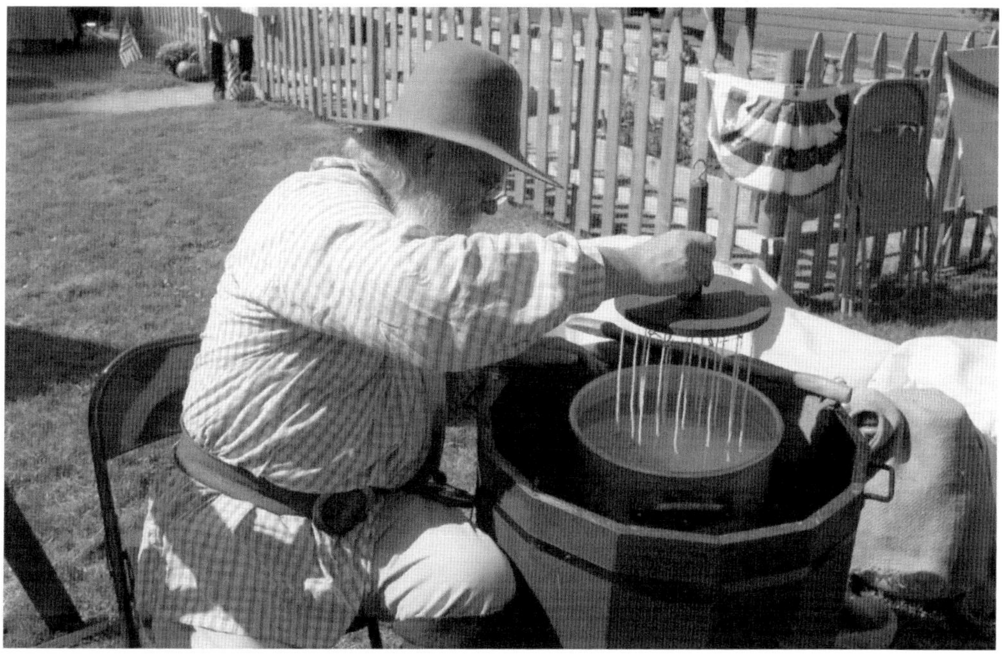

"Chili Bob" Whatley

In "Chili Bob" Whatley's large pot is the wax he melts for his hand-dipped candles. Whatley's arms move as he talks and dips in repeated graceful movements, much like a symphony conductor. He tells the history of wicks, the different types of wax, and how they have changed. Whatley easily slips into the persona of a Colonial character, giving vivid descriptions of how Norwich looked 300 years ago in the glow of flickering light.

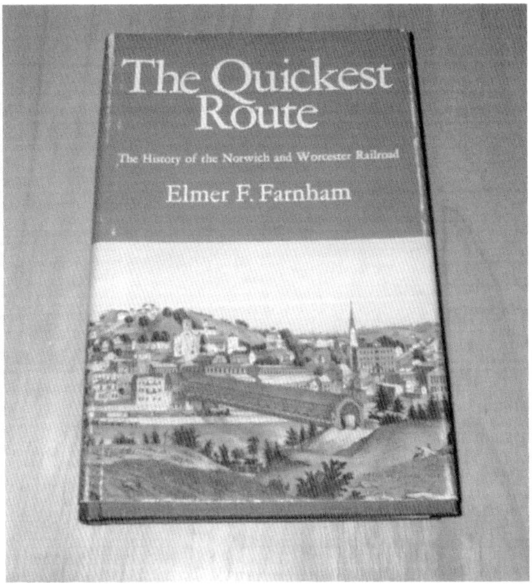

Elmer F. Farnham

Elmer Farnham wanted to write a feature for the *Norwich Bulletin* newspaper based on a scrapbook of railroad superintendent P. St. Marie Andrews. Farnham estimated that the article would be perhaps three typewritten pages in length. But, he quickly wrote 35 pages and felt he had just begun to tell the story of the railroads of Norwich. In 1973, Pequot Press published his 205-page book, *The Quickest Route: A History of the Norwich and Worcester Railroad.* Farnham died in November 1974. His collection can be seen at the Dodd Center of the University of Connecticut.

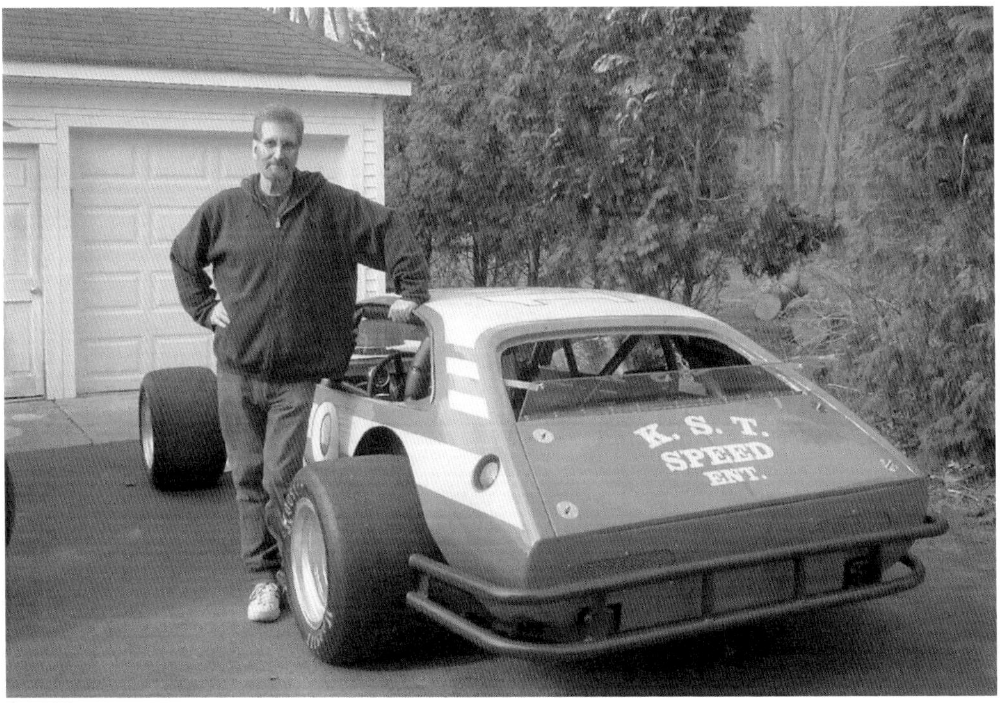

George Fratoni

George Fratoni likes the challenge of building cars that have a memory associated with them. His current car is one he watched race in Waterford when he was a teenager. By chance, he still had the newspaper clipping he possessed when he admired the driver, George "Moose" Hewitt, and the car when No. 19 won the 1975 Winston 100. After years spent sitting in a field, every inch of the handcrafted chassis has been restored, a 350-cubic inch motor was built with a four-speed transmission, and the car was fitted with 14-inch-wide wheels to ready the vehicle for the spirit of "Moose" to guide the car to leads and wins in a circuit of tribute races throughout New England.

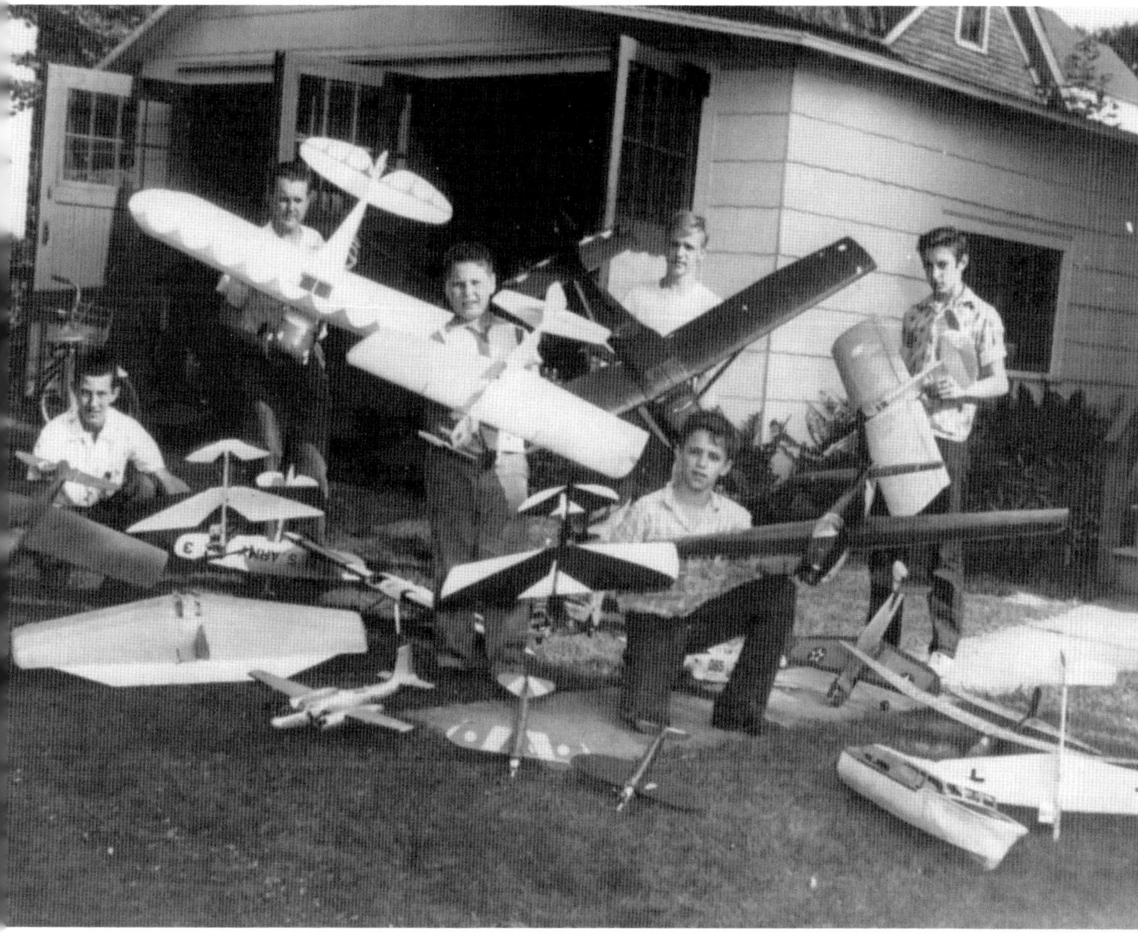

David Adelman

When David Adelman is in the park, joggers go a little slower and walkers have been known to stop when they hear the drone or catch sight of a plane looping and weaving in the sky above them. Seeing Adelman fly his plane is, for some, their only exposure to flying models. For others, it is the beginning of their obsession. Adelman says, "It is fun to take the planes to Mohegan Park or the beach and watch the expressions of the adults and the children as they see the planes fly through a series of practiced stunts. I am partial to my pretty 1957 Nobler; it is a nice size and a classic."

People pepper Adelman with questions and ask if they can try their hands at the controls. Adults, but especially teenagers, are surprised that the controller is not similar to that of a video game. Wind, weather, and humidity can all make a difference in how the plane responds.

Adelman is a walking encyclopedia of model aircraft information, design, and technique, and he likes to share it through stories and demonstrations with friends and strangers.

When Adelman flies his plane with other enthusiasts, they know they are creating a lasting memory for even the youngest observers. Says Adelman, "My dad would take some of my friends and me to New London to fly his planes when I was young. We still talk about some of the flights, the stunts and the crashes."

Pictured from left to right are Al Williams, Bud Doerr, Dave Adelman, "Sonny" Robert Caisse, Jimmy Caisse (kneeling), and Roland Marsh. (Courtesy of David Adelman.)

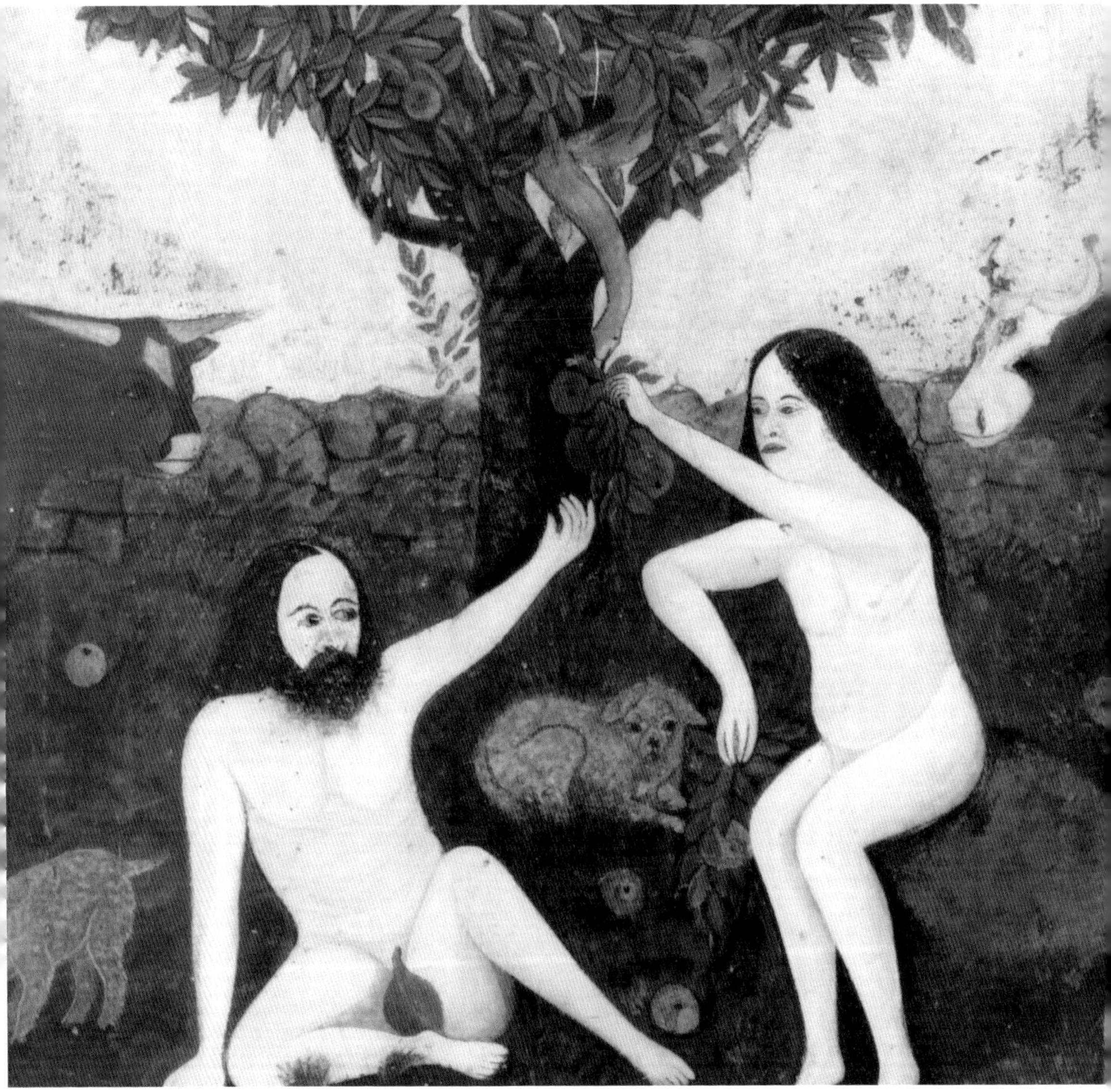

Ellis Walter Ruley (OPPOSITE PAGE)
Ruley (1882–1959) was the first of six children born to slave Joshua Ruley, who "jumped" a coal boat "that was just heading north" in Wilmington, Delaware, just after the Civil War. He once again jumped vessel upon arriving at the picturesque Thames River near Bridgeport, Connecticut. Joshua settled in Norwich after "commandeering" a rowboat heading upriver. Available brides were scarce in the region, but Joshua luckily met Eudora Robinson, a charming daughter of the Narragansett Indian tribe in South Kingstown, Rhode Island. Born in Norwich on December 3, 1882, Ellis developed a talent for masonry, working for the Sweeney Construction Company. However, he severly injured his head in an accident. After being awarded a handsome insurance settlement in 1932, Ellis married a white woman, Wilhelmina Fox, of Norwich. She was the divorced wife of his brother Amos.

Ellis and "Tootsie" purchased their home in the bucolic section known as Fox Hill. Living the bohemian lifestyle on a diet mostly of his wife's homegrown vegetables, Ellis soon took up "paintin'." Utilizing nuances of house-paint colors applied to a neighbor's window and door screens, posterboard, and Masonite board, his works today are sold for many thousands of dollars. Unfortunately, one cold morning in 1959, his frozen body, with a fractured left temple, was found on the dirt road leading to his shack, which was later found burned to the ground. Local authorities dismissed these incidents as a heart attack and spontaneous combustion, respectively.

A few years earlier, his son-in-law, Douglas Harris, had been found dead, stuffed headfirst in the small family well on Ruley's property. Harris was found to have suffered from three severe skull fractures on the left temple.

In his book *Discovering Ellis Ruley*, Glenn Smith makes a compelling case of foul play regarding the two deaths and the mysterious house burning. Currently, a cold-case investigation is being performed by the Norwich Police Department and a local attorney. In addition, a film is in the works for PBS, for which author and director Smith is seeking completion funds. Today, Ruley's art hangs in the Smithsonian, the Wadsworth Athenaeum, the Museum of American Folk Art, and in many important private collections, foremost among them that of Bill and Camille Cosby. (Courtesy of Glenn Palmedo-Smith.)

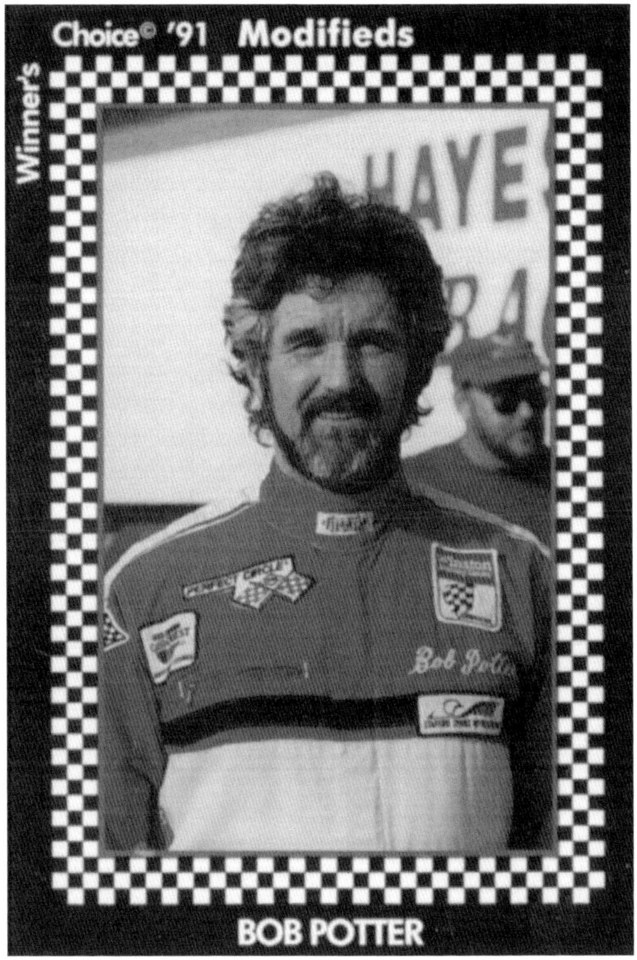

Bob Potter

Bob Potter listened for the words "Gentlemen, start your engines!" for over 35 years at racetracks across New England. He drove Modified cars from 1965 to 2001. Modified racing began as drivers modified their production cars to gain a competitive advantage over their competitors. Potter has an impressive record, including being a five-time Stafford Speedway SK Modified Champion. He has 24 career SK Modified wins at Stafford Speedway, 97 career Modified wins at Waterford Speedbowl, 6 career Modified championships at Waterford, and 30 Modified wins at Thompson Speedway.

He is currently one of the drivers allowed to take passengers for a ride on the track at Stafford Speedway between races, in a two-seater Modified car. But his current joy is racing for his favorite charity, Compassion for Cats of New London, Inc., a 501(c)(3) organization dedicated to saving the lives of abandoned, abused, and neglected animals, getting them necessary medical care, and adopting them into responsible, loving homes.

"I've always been a cat person, and this is a great organization," said Potter. "Carrie Nylen spends all her time and money taking in stray and abandoned cats. They give them shots, they spay and neuter the cats, and they provide a home for the cats until they can find an owner to adopt the cats out to. She does it all for charity, so she isn't making any money, and that's why I want to help her out. There aren't a lot of people like Carrie out there today."

Potter is a newcomer to the Senior Outlaw Wild Thing Karts, which the CARQUEST Champions for Charities drivers use. "It's fun to race those karts," said Potter. "It's a bit of a bumpy ride because the karts don't have any suspension, but it's a lot of fun to race against championship winning drivers, and this race is all about helping out. I like to help out when I can, because I believe if you help out enough, someday when you need help yourself, someone will be there to help you out." (Courtesy of Bob Potter.)

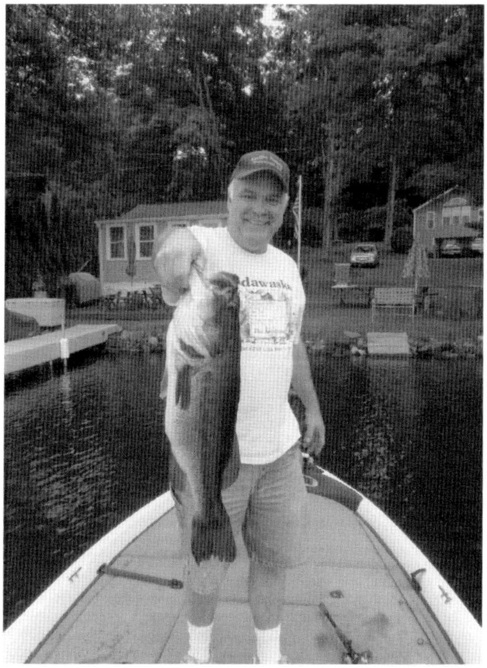

Jerry Martin
"When you enjoy something, invite a friend," says Jerry Martin with a broad grin. So, in 2009, with Norwich city alderman Robert Zarnetske, he organized the first fishing derby, sponsored by the Norwich Harbor Commission, as a part of the 350th anniversary of the city's settling. The derby continues to grow in participation each year, as more children and adults take advantage of the lakes, ponds, and rivers of Norwich. (Courtesy of Gerald Martin.)

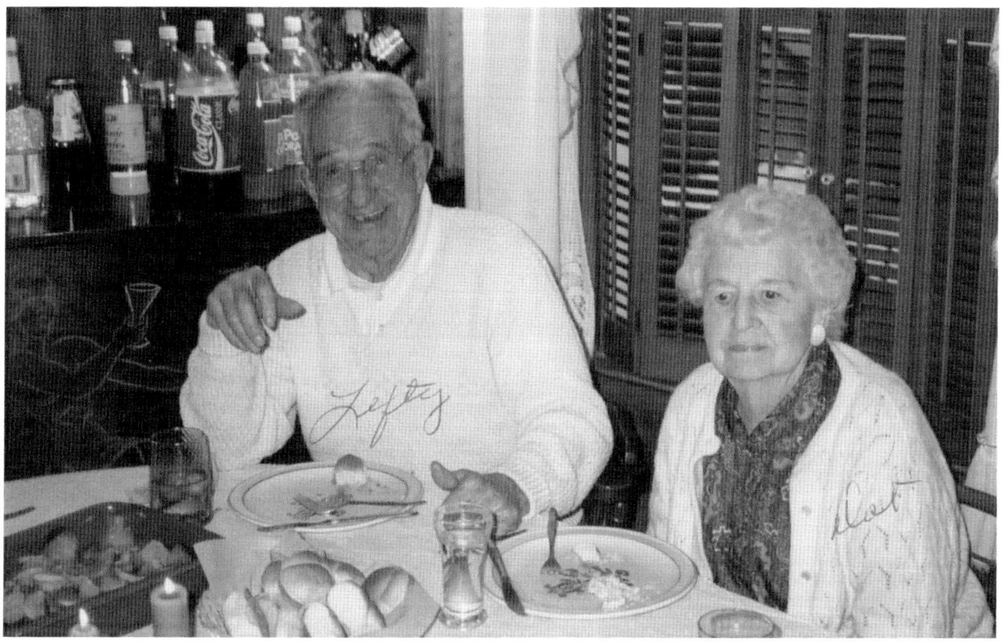

Augustine J. "Lefty" Dugas
"Lefty" Dugas of Taftville was the first Quebec, Canada, native to play in the major leagues. Dugas enjoyed telling wonderful anecdotes of his playing days and was thrilled when Dodd Stadium was built in Norwich. He attended many of the games of the AA Norwich Navigators and always tried to sit in the same seat. While Dugas was recovering in the hospital from a stroke, a Navigators ball landed on the seat and was brought to him in the hospital by a relative. He clutched the ball throughout his remaining days. (Courtesy of Jerry Olson.)

Burchard W. Marshall (OPPOSITE PAGE)
Burchard Marshall shared his dream, and a precocious eight-year-old boy with brain cancer was instrumental in making it come true. One day in 2008, at the age of 94, Marshall was introduced to Ben Goldman. They struck up a great friendship, sharing stories and the obstacles of life each of them faced. Marshall enthralled Ben with tales of adventures in baseball as a player, coach, and umpire; his time on the City of Norwich Board of Recreation; and how he played other sports whenever he had a chance. Marshall told Ben that some of the children he helped as the crossing guard at Bishop School were the grandchildren of former ballplayers he once coached or umpired. He said that some of his friends called him "Duke" off the ball field, because of the care he took in his style of dress. His trimmed mustache and beard were trademarks of his appearance. Marshall spoke of how he made friends for a lifetime in sports, and that this spilled over into his other great joy, singing. He told stories of how, in the early 1950s, he was a member of The Four Notes, along with well-known piano player Tommie Simmons and the late Danny Jenkins and Arthur Lacey, both of who were former baseball players.

Marshall shared how he began at the age of 15, playing on the Werman Shoe City League team until it disbanded. Then he moved on to the Greenville Athletic Club squad in the City League, the Decatur Athletic Club, and the New London Colored Elks. Most of his playing time was spent as a catcher, travelling the state of Connecticut playing independent baseball. While playing for the Norwich Yellow Jackets one day, major-league scouts there to watch Gene DeSautels (who later played for the Boston Red Sox) were overheard to say, "the colored fellow was better." Unfortunately, because of the era's practice of segregation, "Burch" was never given an opportunity to play in the major leagues.

Ben could not understand why, if Marshall was so good in baseball, he never made the big leagues. Ben did not accept the color difference as a valid reason. Larry Lucchino, the owner of the Boston Red Sox, was a family friend. When Ben had an opportunity, he told Lucchino at length about his new friend and asked, "Couldn't something be done?"

Within a month, Marshall was invited to Fenway Park for a day and made an honorary member of the Red Sox. He and Ben were driven to Boston in a limo. Marshall was given a red jacket and cap and was invited to sign the "retired players" wall at the Green Monster. He was also featured on a Red Sox segment on Boston television. His involvement in sports through coaching and umpiring three generations of players earned him a place in the Norwich Sports Hall of Fame and in having skybox seats at the Dodd Baseball Stadium named in his honor.

Ben Goldman is a cancer survivor attending high school. Every Thursday, during the FoxCT 4:00 p.m. news, he hosts features about charity events taking place in Connecticut to raise awareness, because he knows firsthand the positive impact they can have on a person's life. (Courtesy of Ann Valazco.)

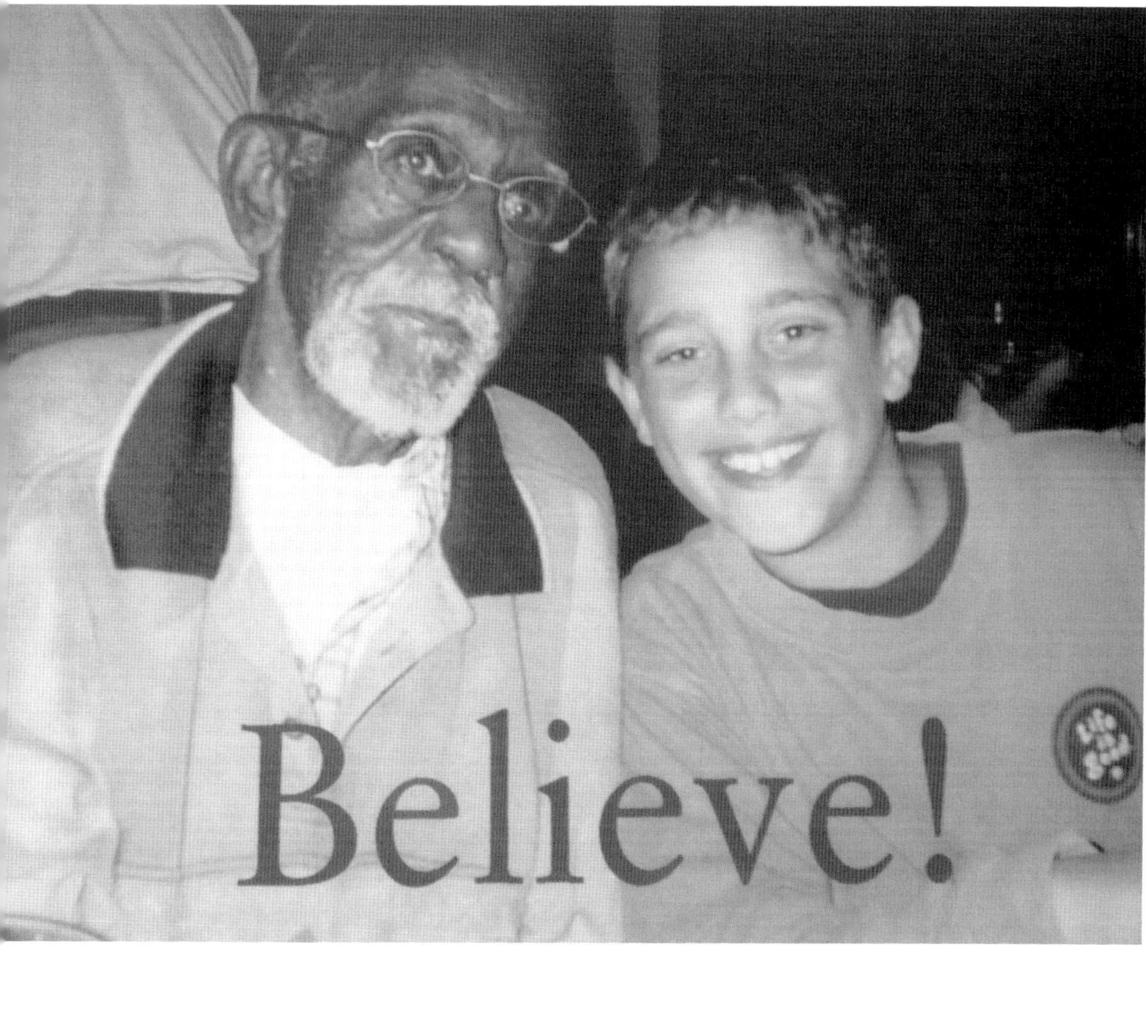
Believe!

Lisa Marien

Marien is a music educator, vocalist, worship leader, arts consultant, and producer/arranger, connecting with students in Norwich and New London public and magnet schools and the Wildwood Christian Schools. She and the students perform in traditional and nonconformist locations to fill the world with music. Alone, in pairs, and in groups, the residents of Norwich work to enrich their neighborhoods and lives with pride in their past and an eye toward the future. This continuation of traditions forever improves the present for tomorrow. (Courtesy of Lisa Marien.)

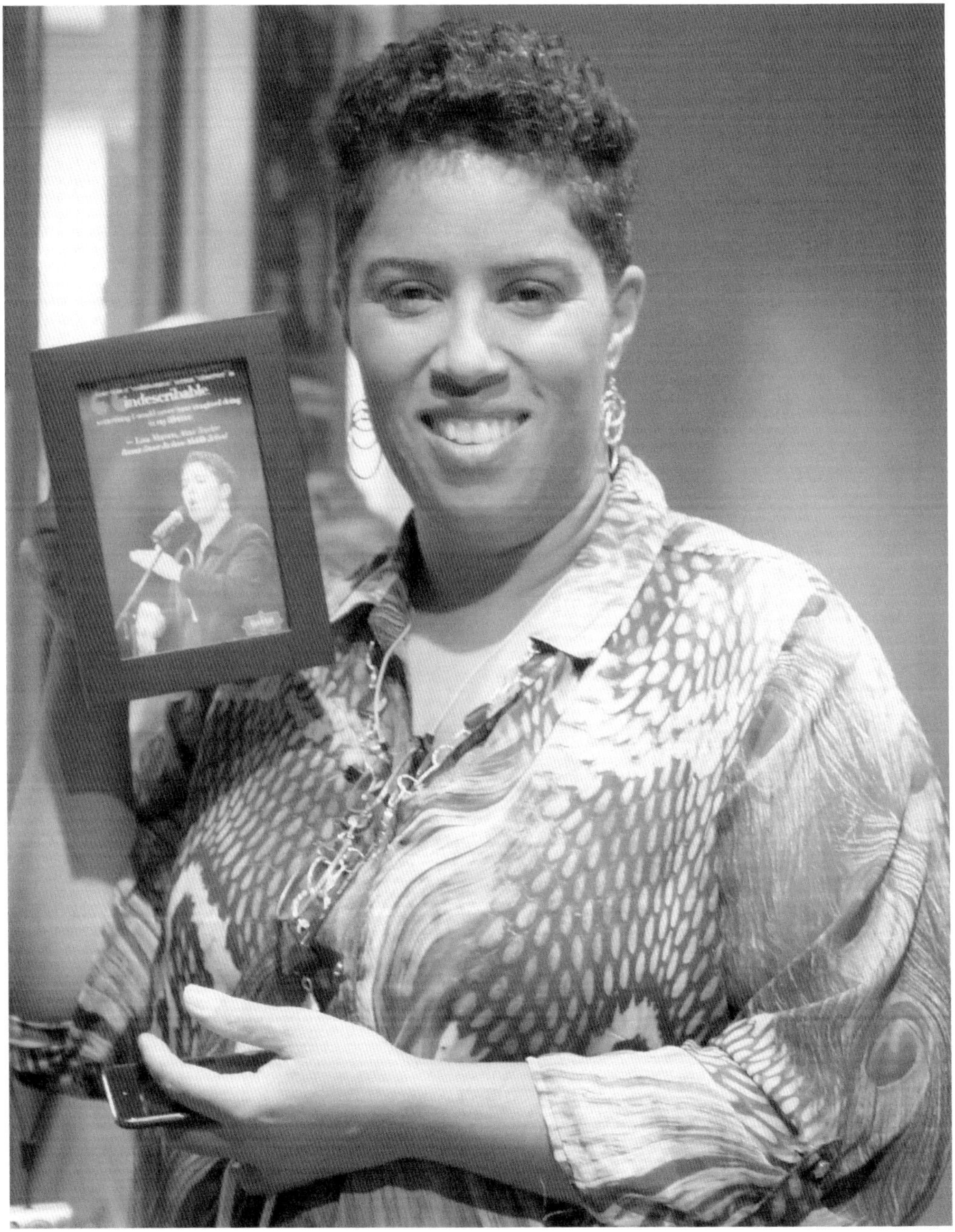

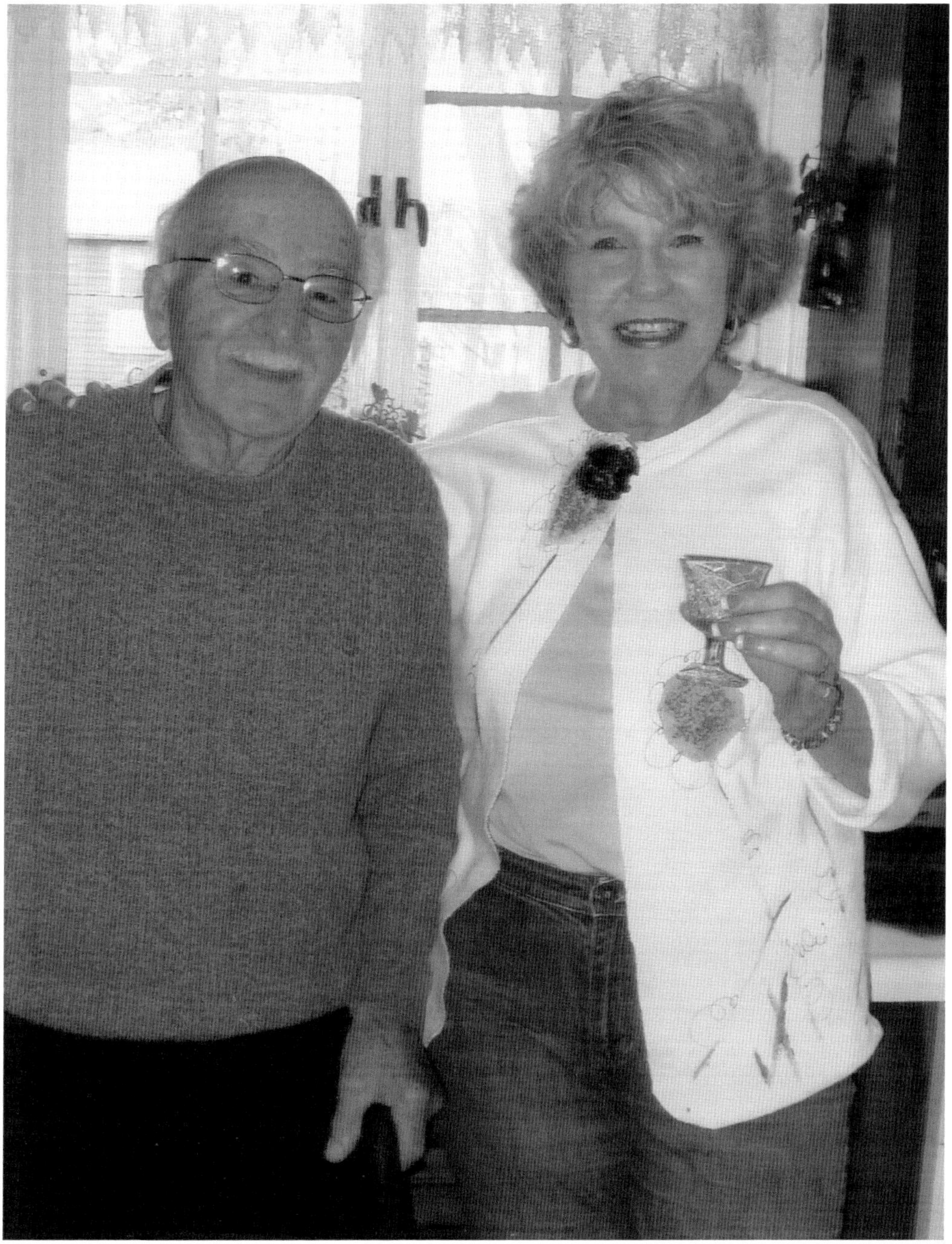

Jackie and Peter Quercia

Jackie and Peter Quercia were instrumental in organizing Downtown Oldie's Nights in the 1990s. The event featured bands, antique cars on display, dancing in the streets, and fundraising for the purchase and installation of large outside speakers. Jackie and Peter find adventure in traveling the world through local restaurants and "talking with others about the displays in the different art galleries, library events, the new musical at the Spirit of Broadway playhouse or the new business opening down the street." (Courtesy of Jackie Quercia.)

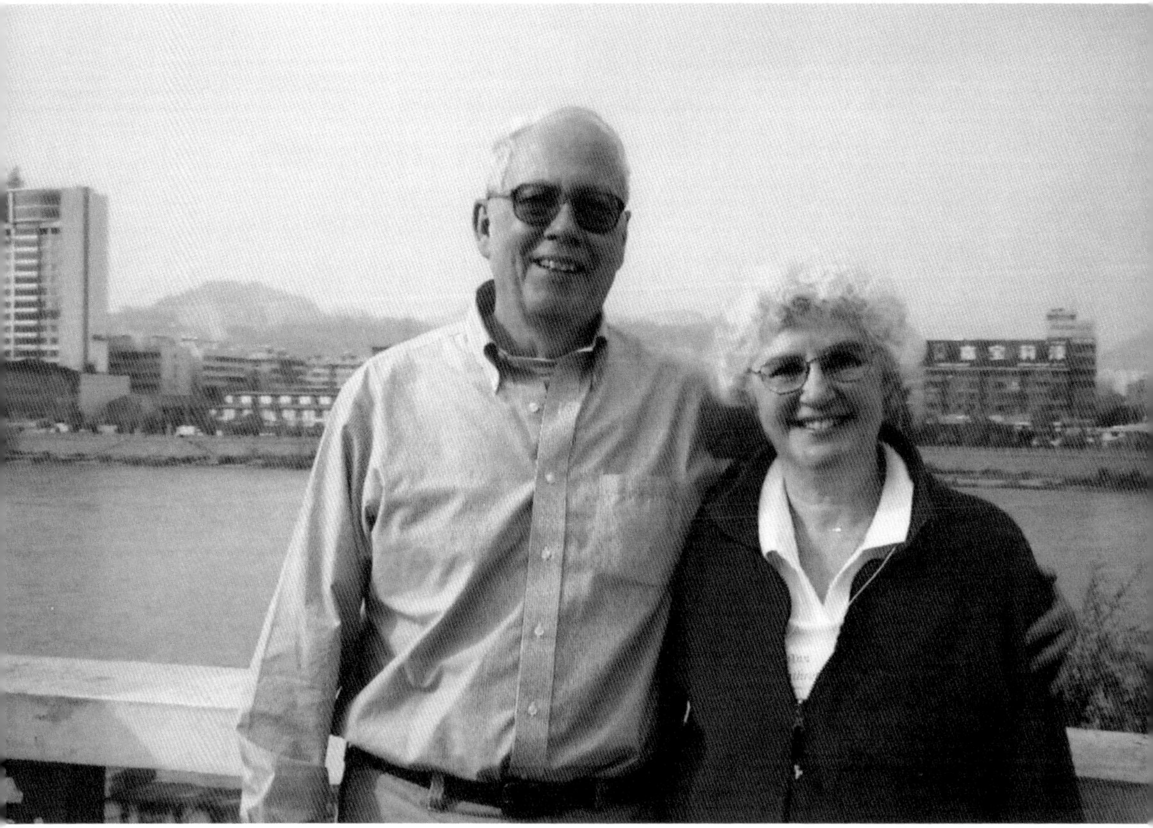

Ann and Art Lathrop

The Lathrops are leading forces in the maintenance of the history of Norwich. Ann can frequently be found in the Lowthorpe Meadow as a volunteer, mowing paths, uprooting invasive plants, and caring for wild flowers in the mix of wet meadow and dry grassland in the heart of Norwich. Art often leads tours through the streets of the old city, discussing its lanes and architecture with authority and a soft, firm voice. (Courtesy of Art Lathrop.)

Bob and Betty Schmidt

Bob and Betty Schmidt have been a team for over 60 years. Each has always been there to support the other while volunteering for a church, sports, or school event and, now, as active grandparents. Together, they remodeled 12 Norwich homes. For 39 years, Bob used his experience to help others while working at the Cash Home Center. (Courtesy of Bob and Betty Schmidt.)

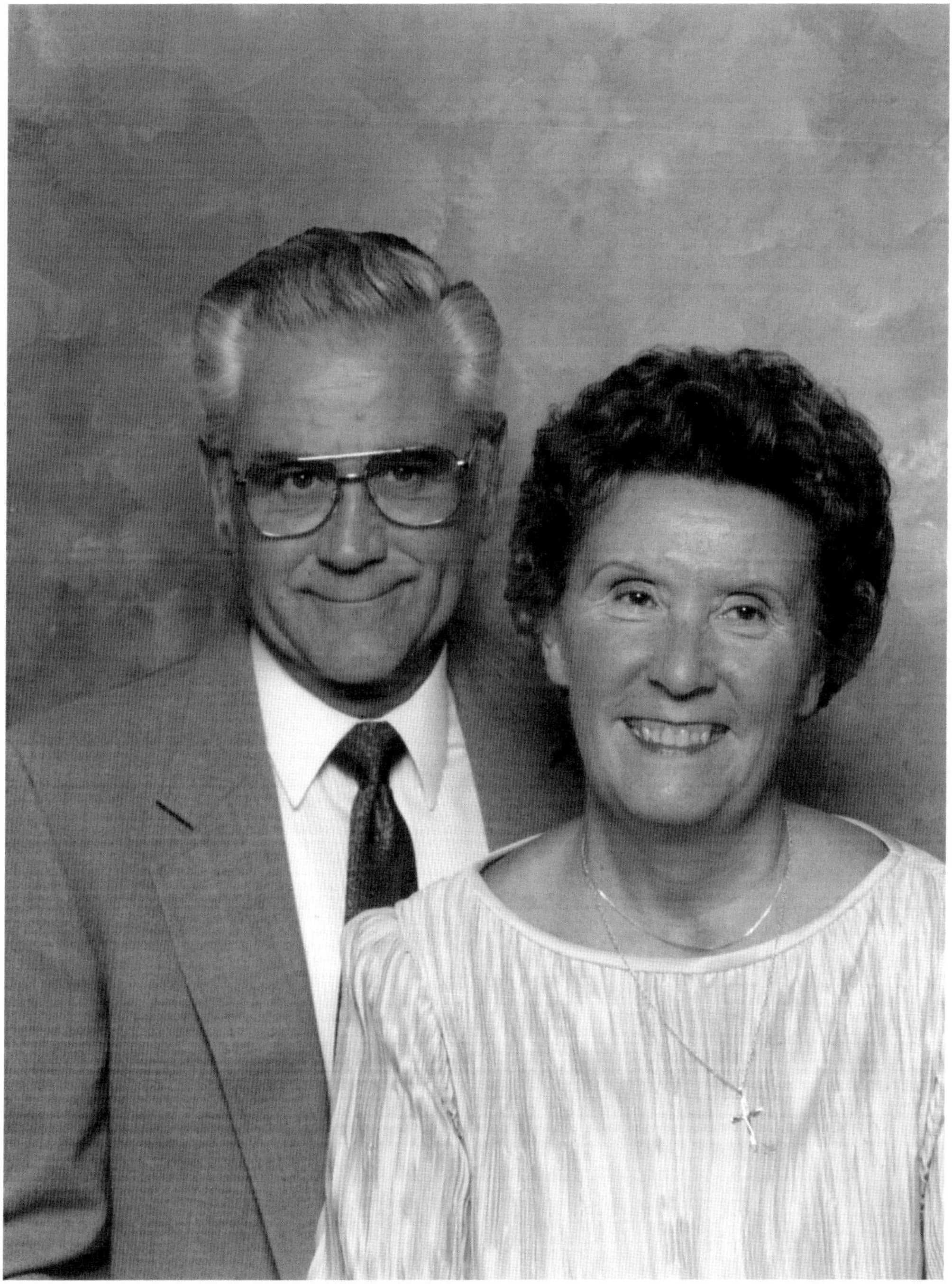

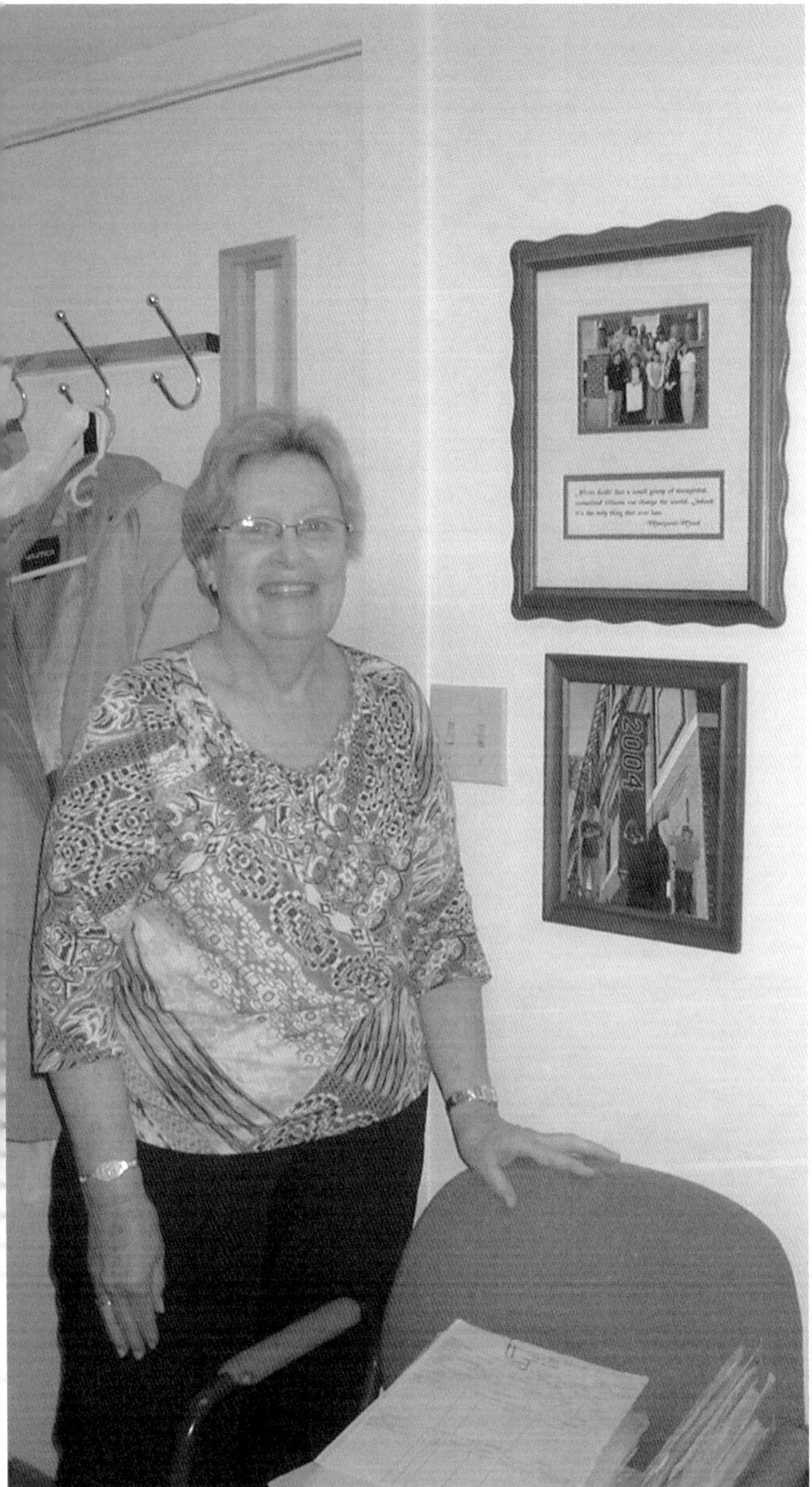

Beverly Goulet
Beverly Goulet played basketball for the University of Connecticut Huskies during the 1960s, and she never stopped being a team player. For more than 25 years, as director of human services for the City of Norwich, Goulet and her team respond to every imaginable need during times of trial and crisis with an indomitable spirit to "do the right thing." Goulet has convinced philanthropic organizations to support the labors of her small department and, in this way, has created the only city department that has expanded its budget without increasing its allotment from the city.

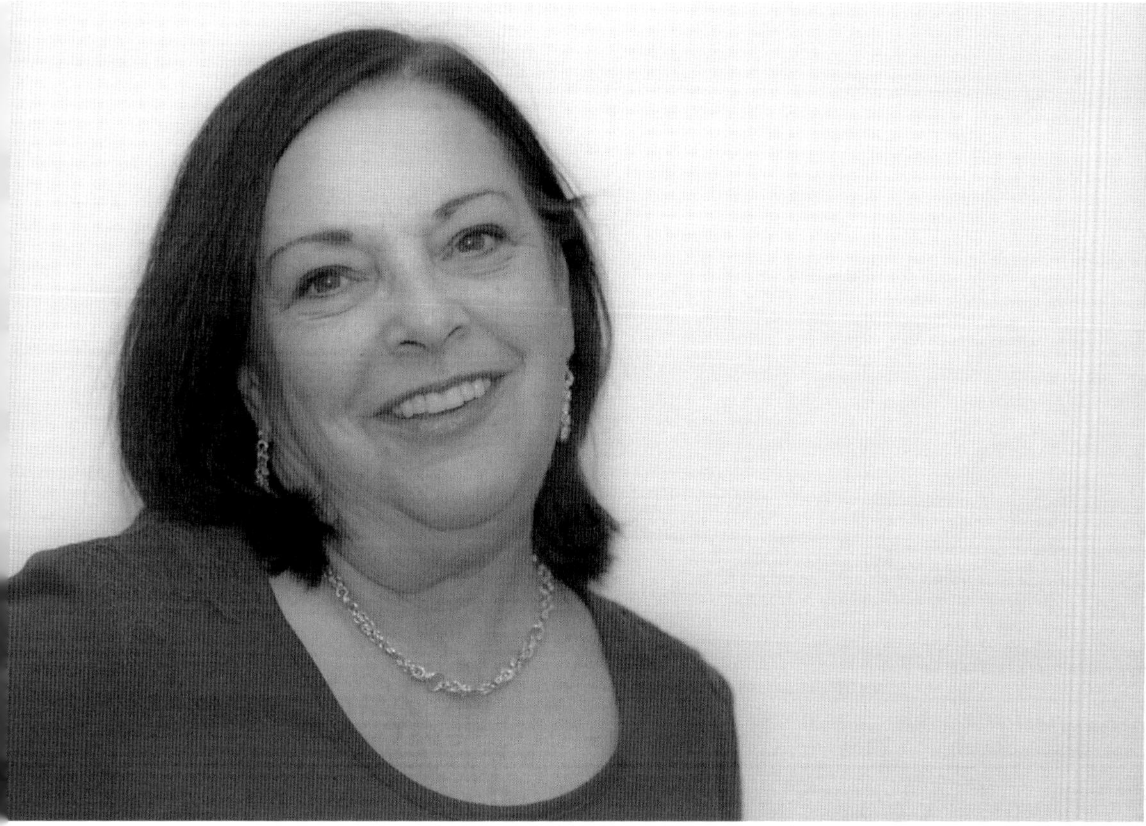

Bonnie Hong
As one project ends, Bonnie Hong will be found already on step two or three of her next project to make Norwich a better place to live. While standing in the rain coordinating the rubber duck race fundraiser on the Yantic River, she was also arranging the donation of a used ambulance chassis to create the prototype of a modern battery-powered trolley for tourism promotion. That project coincided with the creation of Green Energy Technologies, a new company that creates electric trolleys for the national tourism industry. (Courtesy of Bonnie Hong.)

Anna and Donald Alfiero (OPPOSITE PAGE)
"There is more than one route to the correct answer. "Anna Alfiero has said this to her Waterford middle-school students, to fellow Norwich Board of Education members, and to her husband, Donald. So, it is no wonder that Anna was chosen to be the first Connecticut teacher inducted into the National Teachers Hall of Fame in Emporia, Kansas, and to be an honored guest of Pres. Bill Clinton at the White House.

The *New York Times* called Donald Alfiero the "Ambassador of Norwich" for his indefatigable energy to make the community brighter and better in the eyes of its residents and visitors. He fought for the installation of "Welcome to Norwich" signs at each of the nine gateways to the city. Then, in over 90-degree weather, he planted flowers beneath the signs so they would look more welcoming. But even this was not enough, so he delivered dozens of planters filled with dirt and more plants around the downtown area, driving his old truck and with his rescue dog by his side. (Courtesy of Anna Alfiero.)

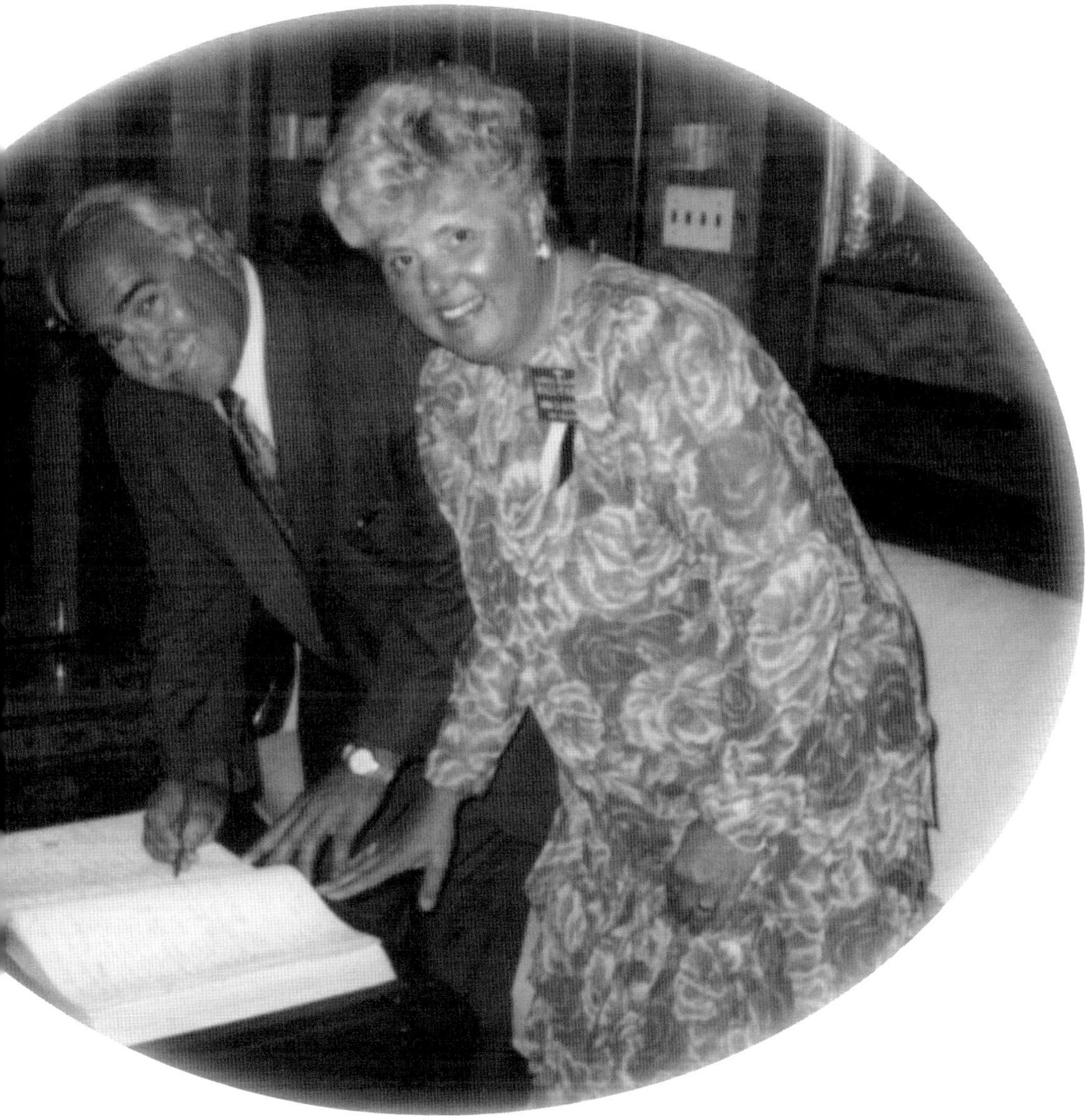

Benjamin P. Lathrop

As a father and grandfather, Benjamin Lathrop did more than just worry that not enough children were exercising their minds and bodies. He called people he knew to form a committee to organize Read to Ride, Inc., a 501(c)(3) nonprofit organization designed to award children in the Norwich and Montville school systems with a bicycle, helmet, and bike lock for their participation in a reading incentive program.

In the organization's first year, it awarded 160 bikes, and the program continues to grow every year. Participating young readers and bike donations are always increasing. "Reading and riding are good health habits that can last a lifetime," says Ben with a smile.

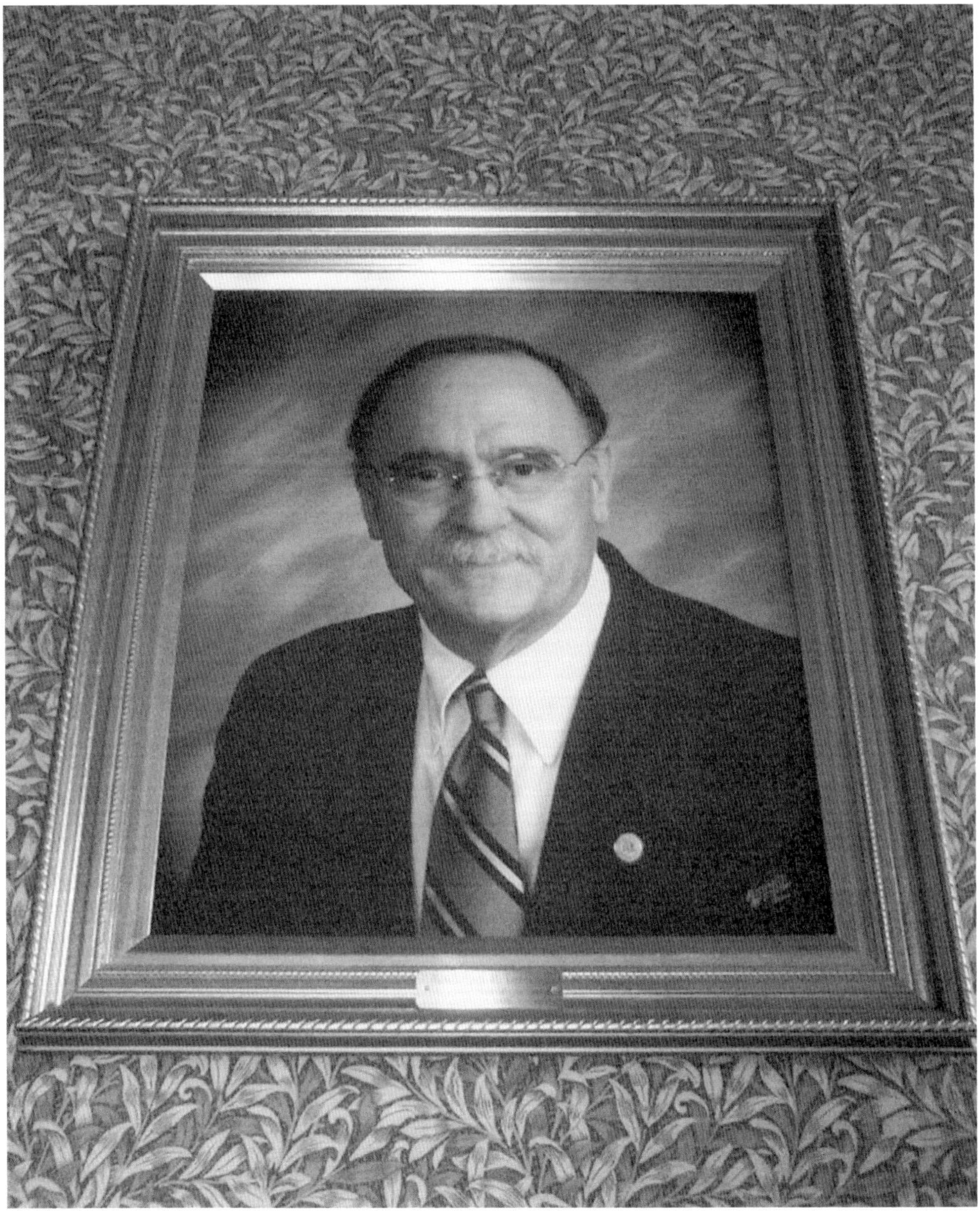

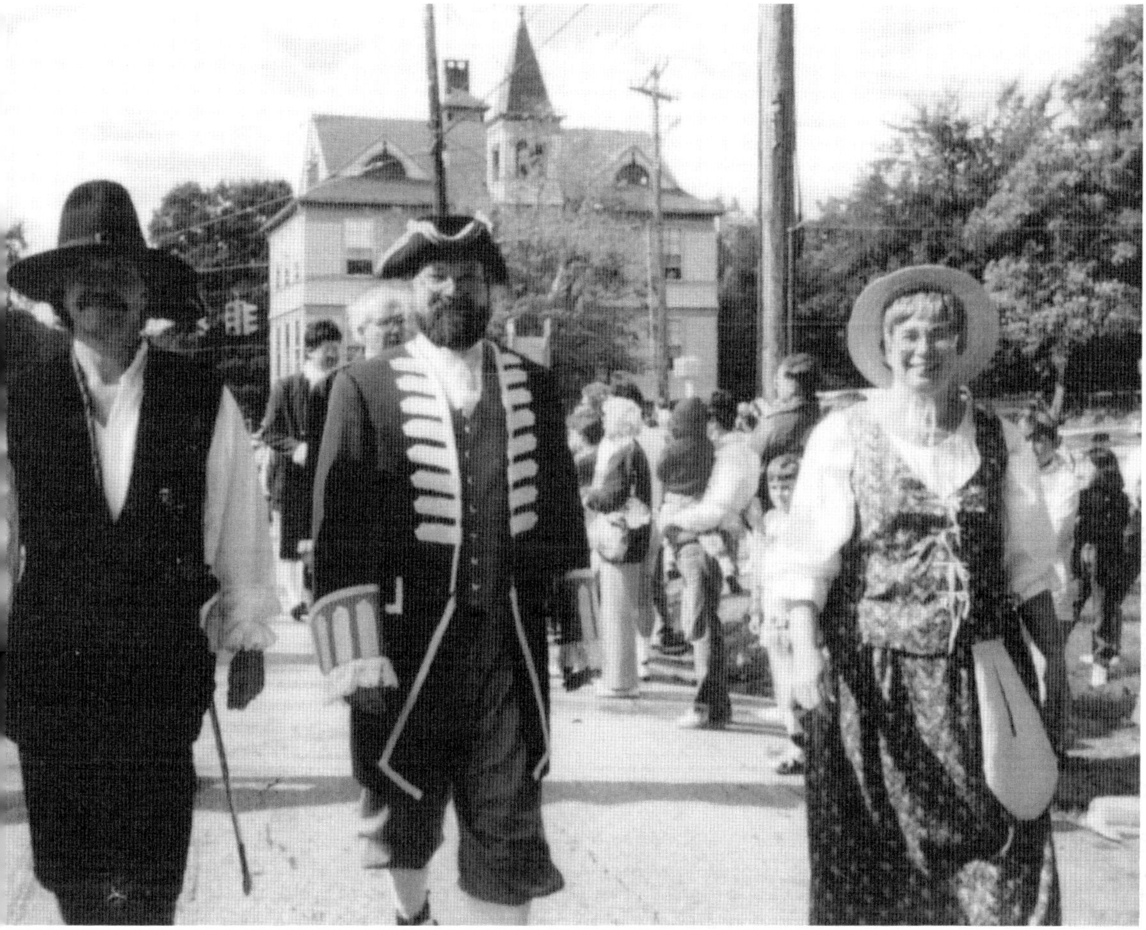

Dianne Slopak

Dianne Slopak arranged the Norwichtown Days, in which visitors in modern dress and people in period costumes sit beside crackling campfires on the Norwichtown Green and celebrate the settling of Norwich in 1659. As children in costumes of short pants and billowy shirts chase each other and play with dogs and the occasional loose goat, women sit in circles with needlework, exchanging stories, remedies, and recipes. Men gather in groups, telling tall tales of their adventures and share news of the past and present. (Courtesy of Dianne Slopak.)

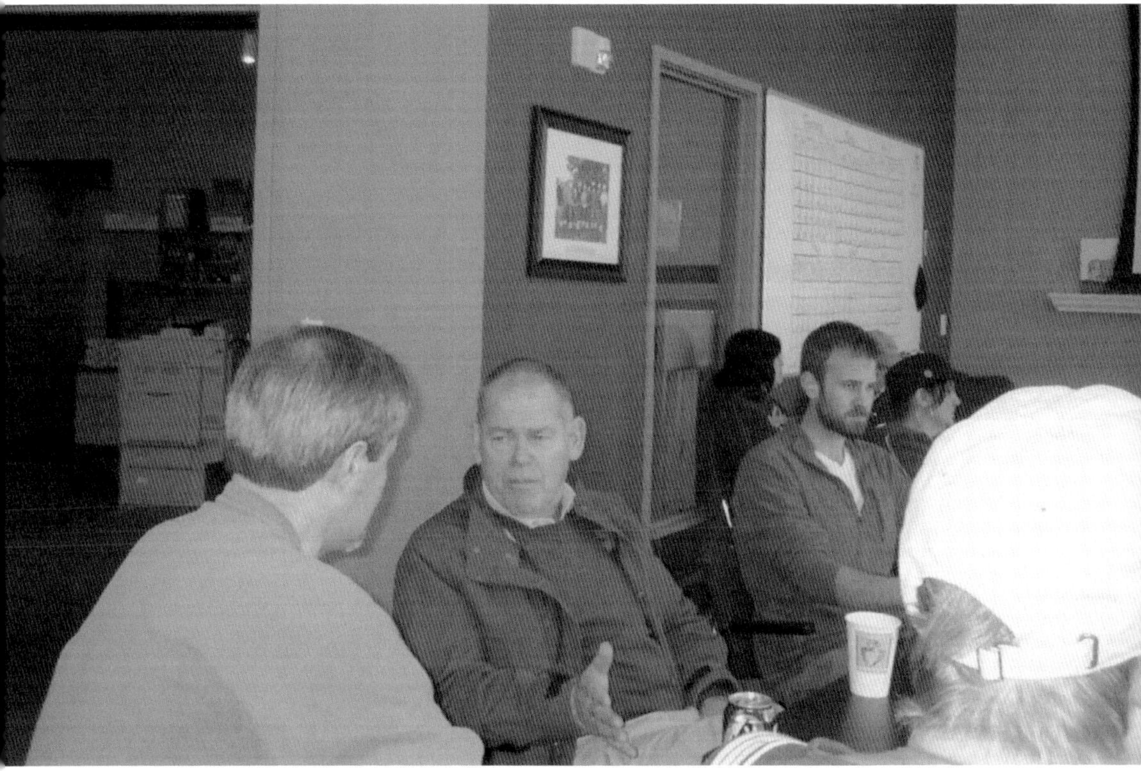

H. Tucker Braddock
For over 23 years, H. Tucker Braddock greeted everyone who entered A.P. Savage Supply hardware store with a handshake and a direct look in the eye. When Braddock retired from business, he brought his personal touch to service on the Norwich City Council from 2010 to December 2013. He walks the streets daily, greeting people he knows and those friends that he has not met yet.

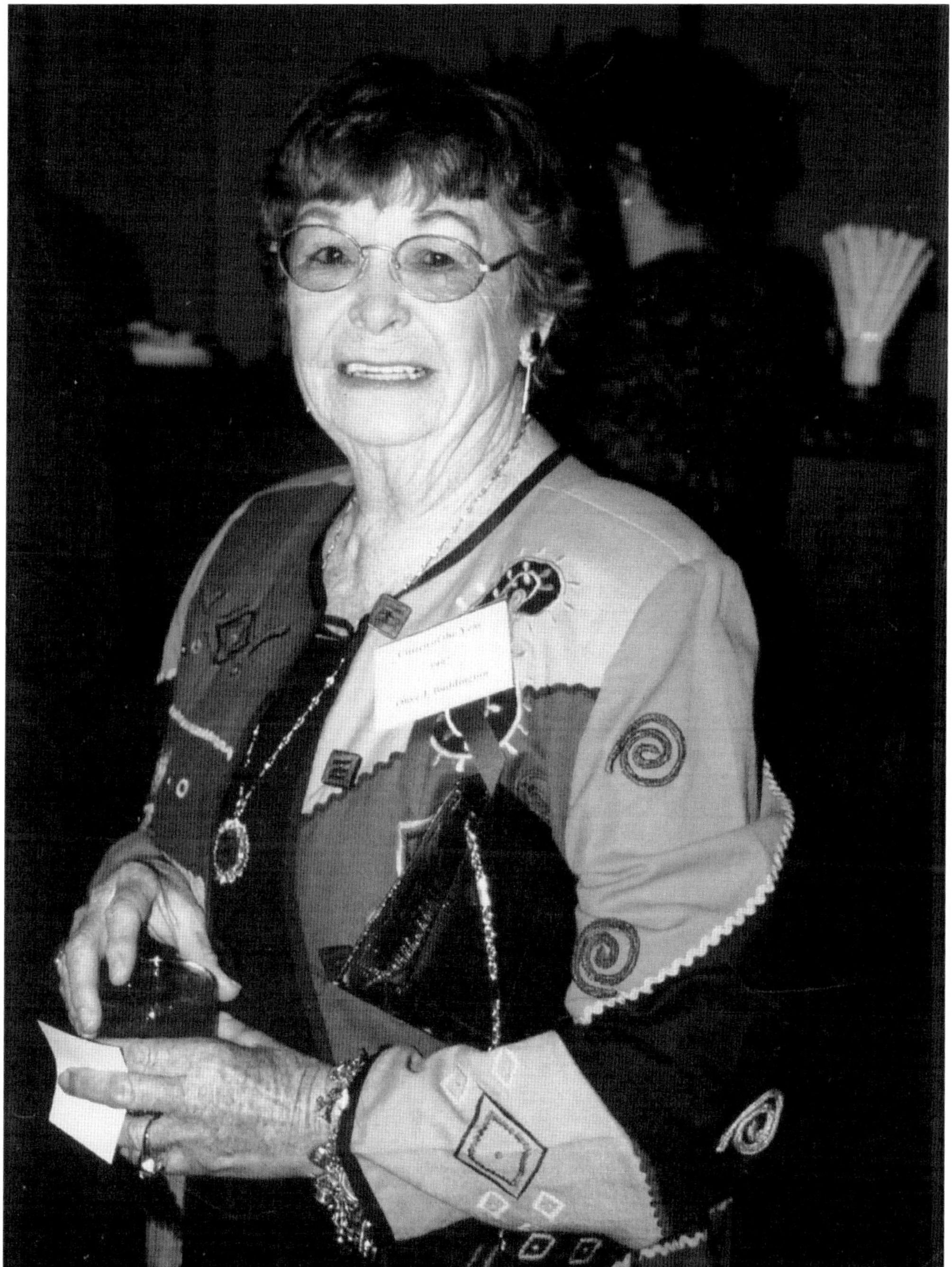

Olive Buddington

A woman accustomed to being in charge, Olive Buddington taught school in Greenwich for 37 years. She then returned home to Norwich to put her skills to work for several social service agencies and on the city council, as a leader and resource for current and future programs affecting adult health, education, and tourism promotion. (Courtesy of Olive Buddington.)

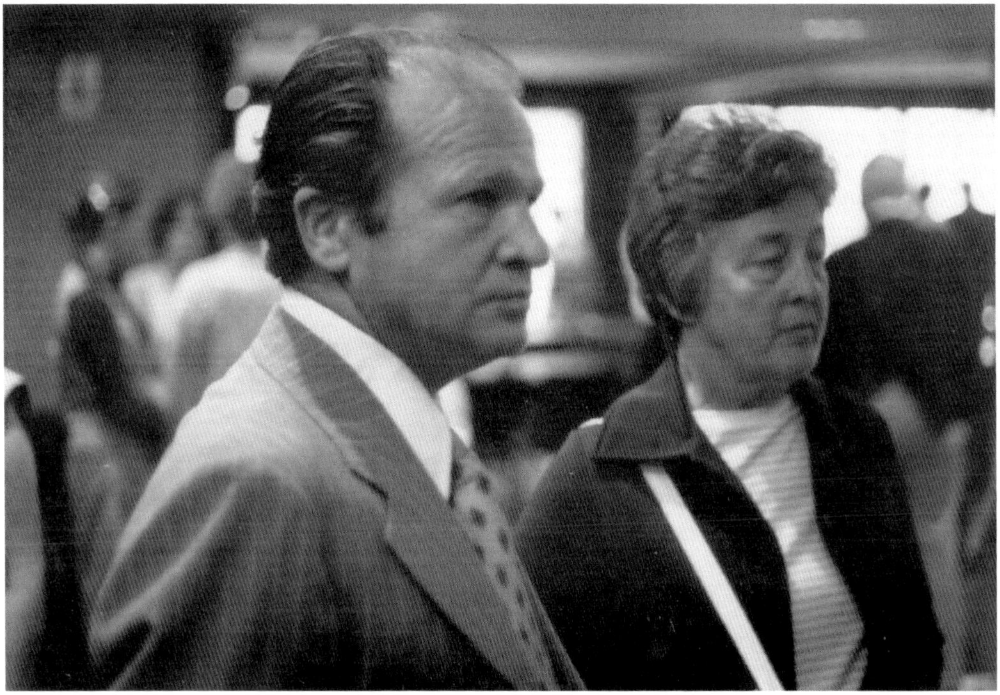

Walter Nelson Way

An avant-garde hometown boy and champion of tourism as an industry, Walter Nelson Way's visions included rehabilitating buildings, creating a museum, and establishing a marina. It was his suggestion for the marina that motivated the *Norwich Bulletin* cartoon contributor, McGreggor, to draw the image below, "If Walter Has His Way." Way is proud to reconcile the fights he has undertaken with a ready grin and an easy "You win some, you lose some." (Courtesy of John Way.)

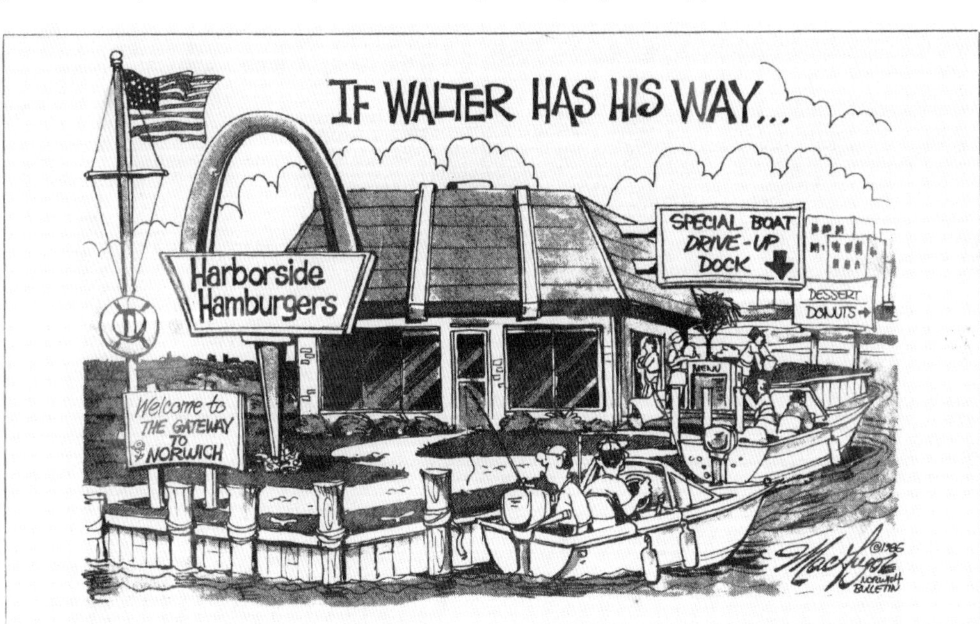

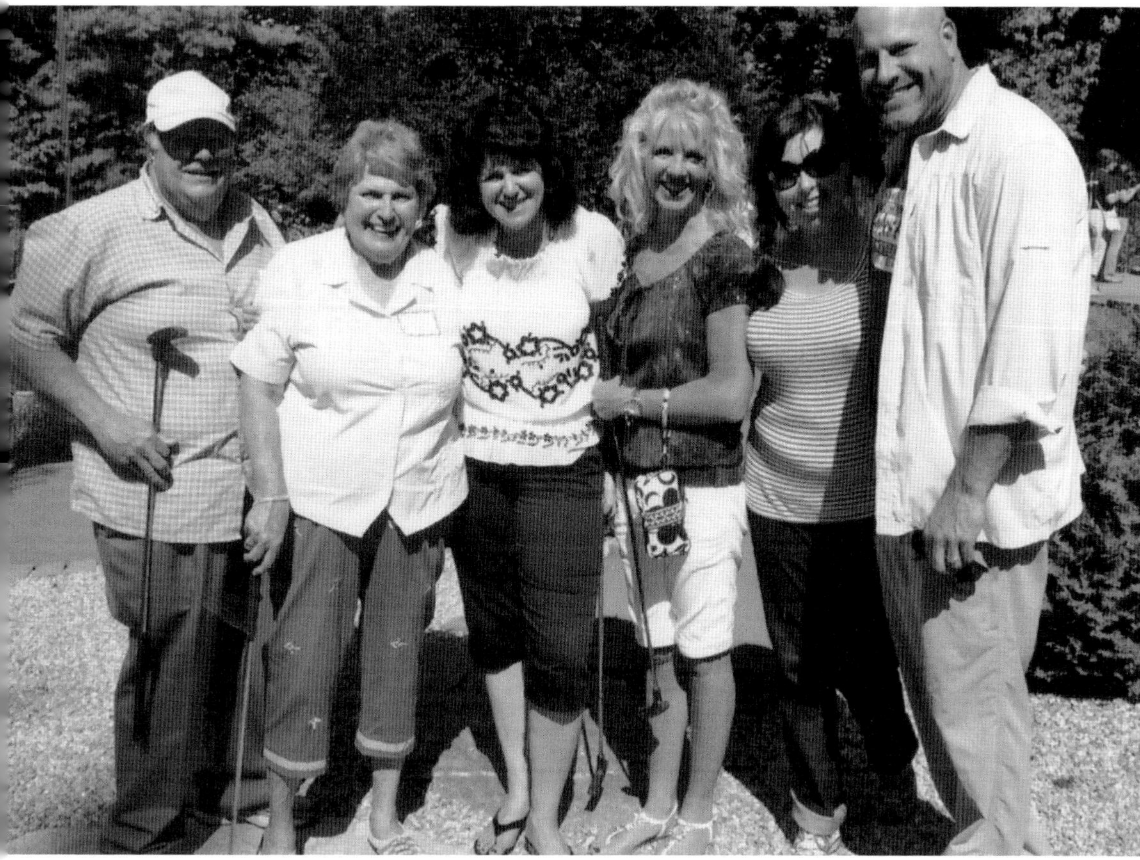

Yvette Jacaruso

Only Yvette Jacaruso (pictured second from left) would opt to sing a song of welcome to her replacement as president of the W.W. Backus Hospital Auxiliary instead of giving a speech. She said, "No one person can do it alone," while offering her seemingly limitless enthusiasm and dedication to her successor's list of events and activities, which raise funds for the hospital's community service programs. From left to right are Frank Jacaruso, Yvette Jacaruso, Maria Hamel, Sue Habeeb, Corie Jacaruso, and Jon Jacaruso. (Courtesy of Yvette Jacaruso.)

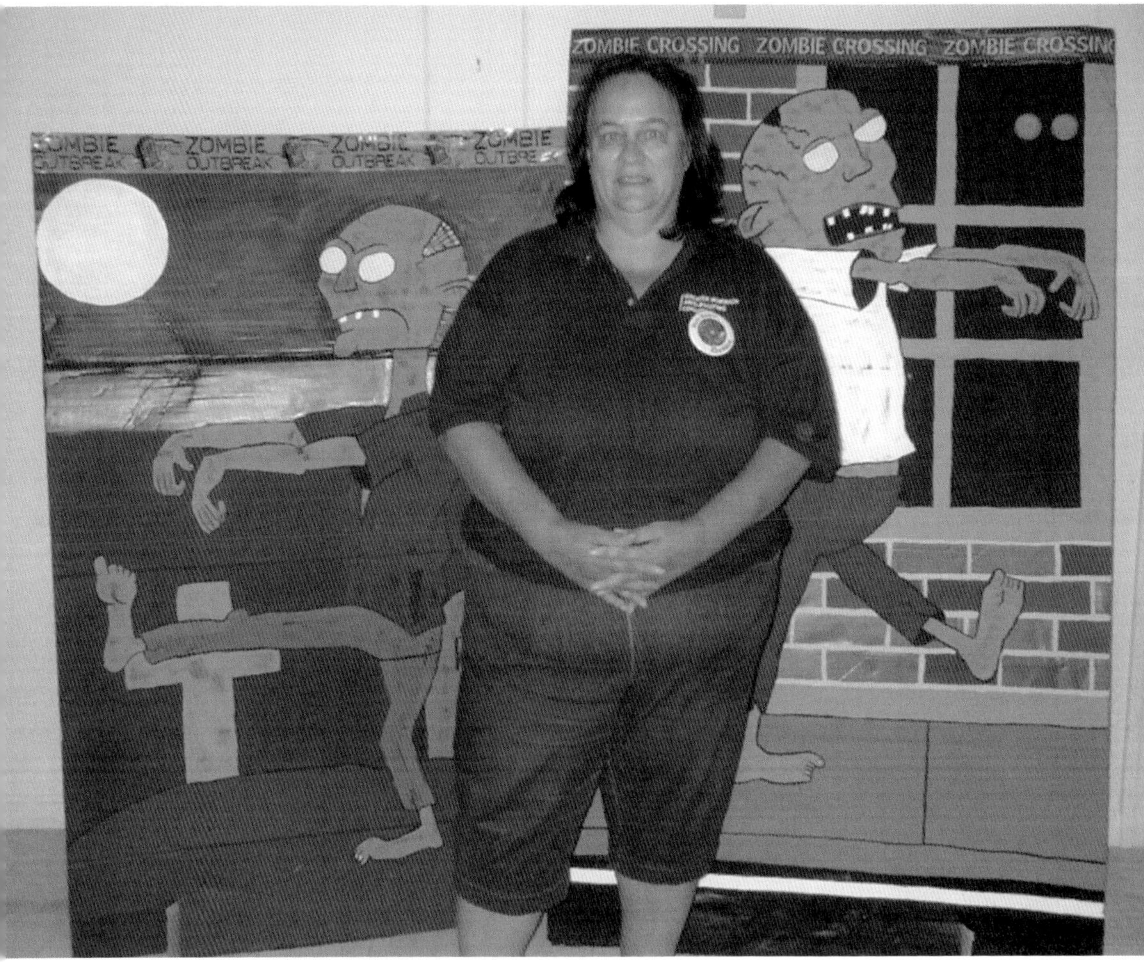

Debbie Kievits
Debbie Kievits got tired of waiting for administrators to put an end to bullying in the schools. She rallied parents at a kitchen table to form Bully Busters. The group sponsors dance programs, drum circles, poetry clubs, and a variety of other events for children and teens to have fun in a safe place with their peers. "Our biggest success is when the kids take the leadership role and bring their friends down," says Kievits.

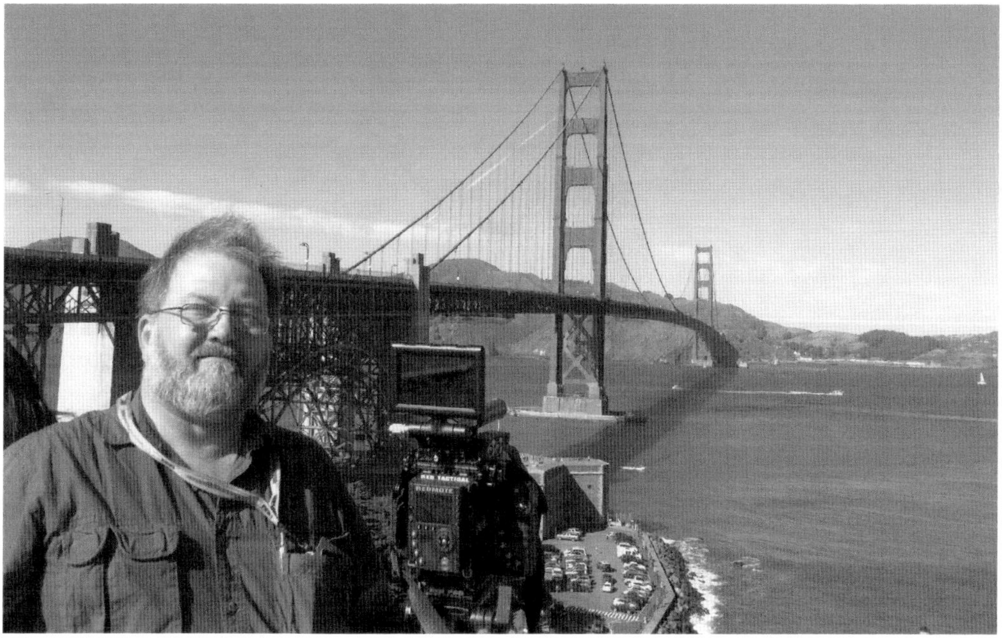

Brian Kobylarz
Kobylarz used his business and leadership skills to bring new life and creativity to the Downtown Neighborhood Revitalization Zone. Among the attractions are a multicultural festival with music, food, and dance from around the world, dragon boat races in the harbor, holiday decorating contests, and political debates that encouraged various sides of an issue to be heard. (Courtesy of Brian Kobylarz.)

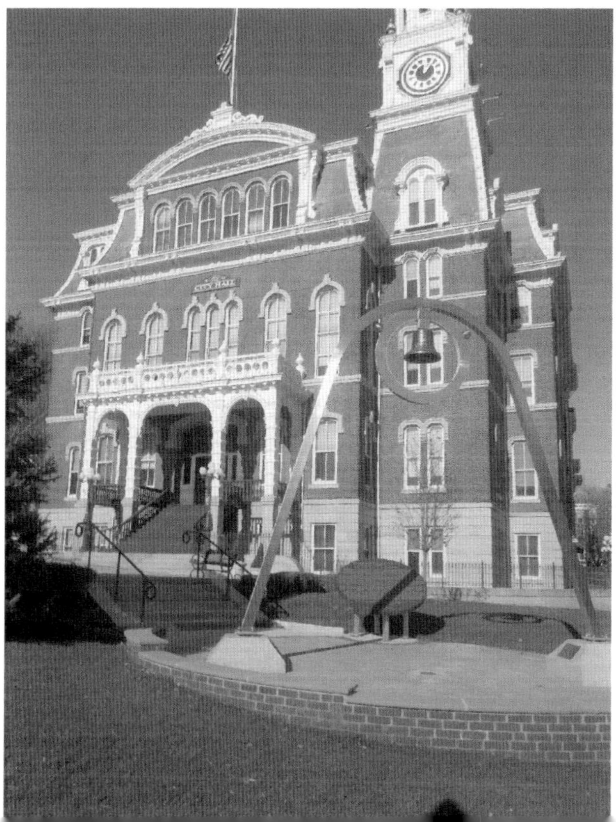

H. Kevin Harkins
Harkins became intrigued by the number and variety of bells that he heard being rung at various times around the city. Help from friends led to a mapping out of the many bells and the creation of a CD to share the beautiful sounds and to raise money for the repair and maintenance of the bells. (Courtesy of the Bells of Norwich.)

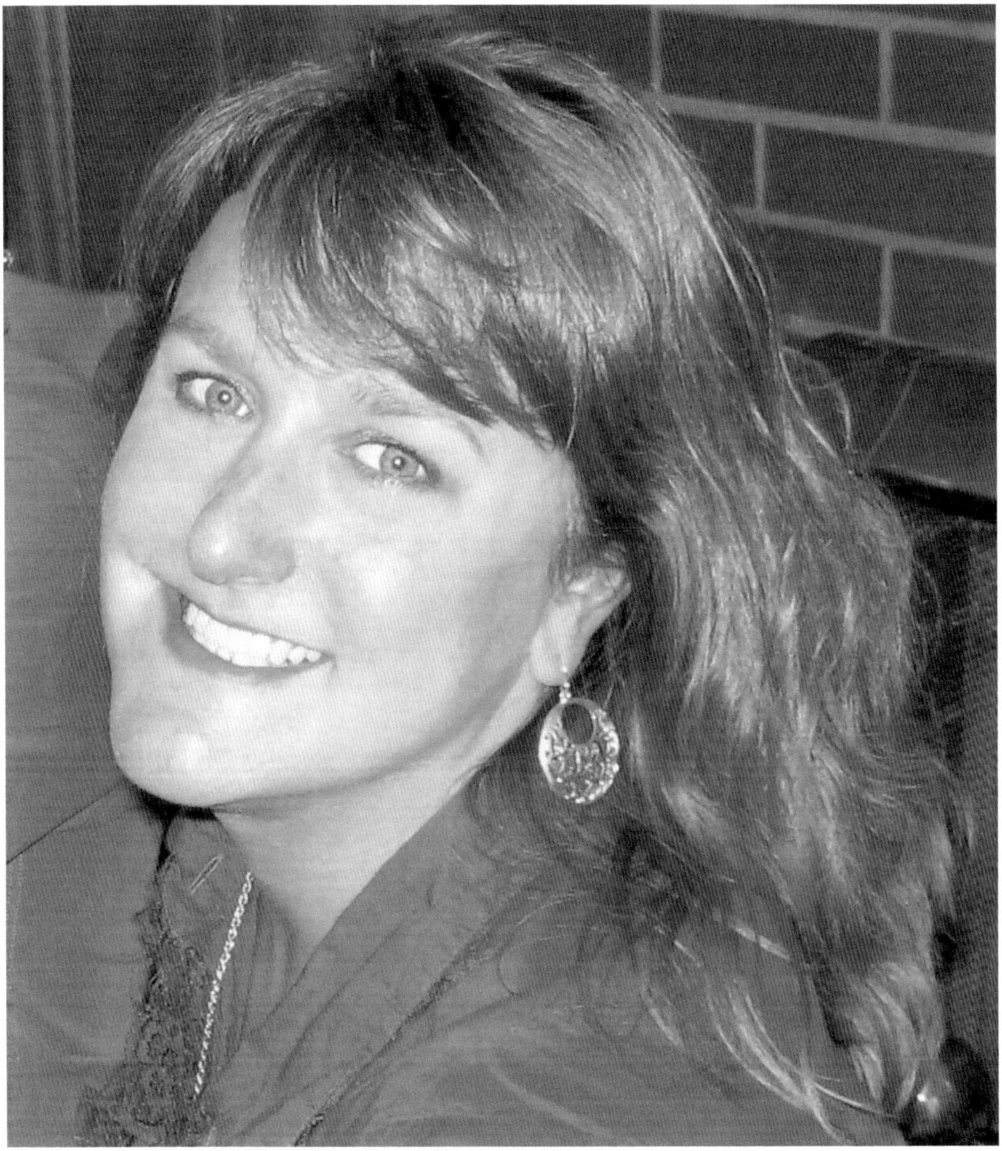

Dianne Brown

Dianne Brown fell in love with the "mansions" of Broadway in Norwich and, eventually, convinced her husband to move to a 4,000-square-foot Greek Revival home near Broadway in the historic district of Little Plain Green. She became the volunteer secretary, membership chair, program coordinator, and "Jill of all trades" for the Norwich Historical Society after volunteering on the Norwich Semiseptcentennial celebration history subcommittee. (Courtesy of Dianne Brown.)

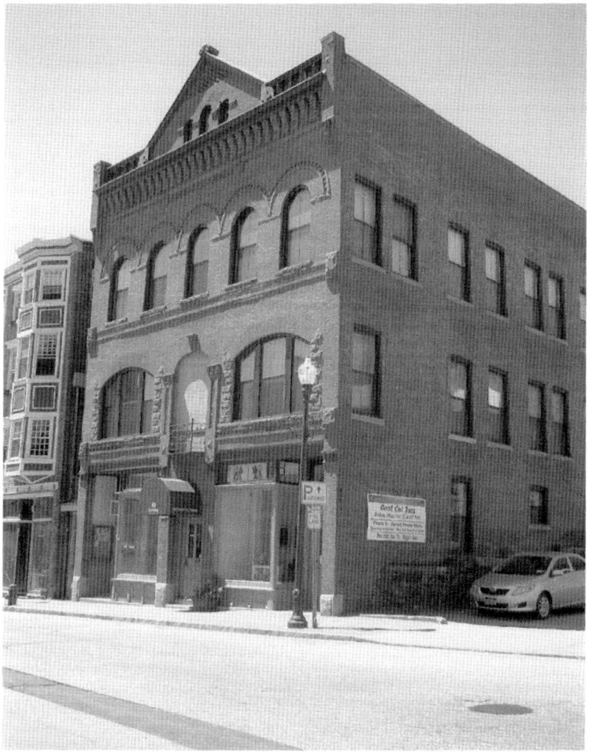

Thom Keaney
Thom Keaney never forgets to call out a friendly greeting when he volunteers at the Norwich Arts Center, located in the 1876 St. Mary's Total Abstinence and Benevolence Building. A curious but friendly presence is so strong that, when it came time for the very first play to be performed on the third-floor stage, it was unanimously decided that it should be the play *The Face on the Barroom Floor*, based on a ballad by John Henry Titus in 1872 about a skilled artist turned drunk and the lost love of his life.

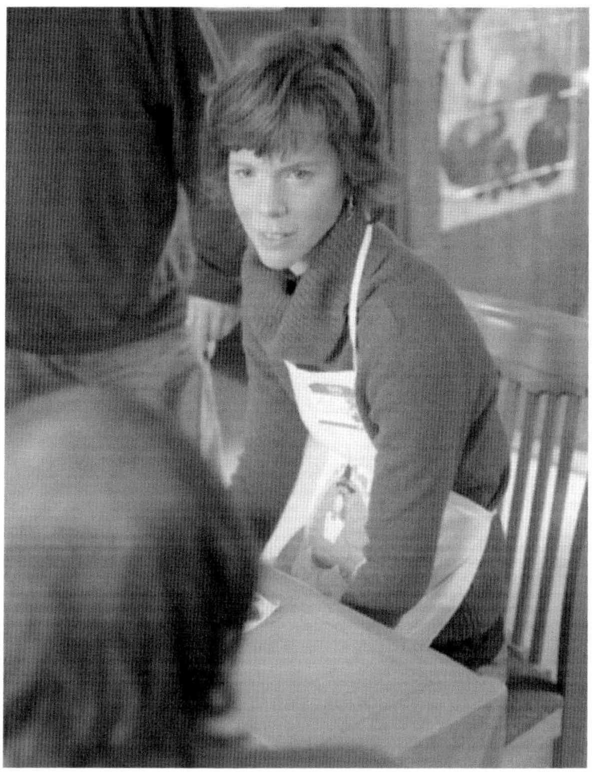

Jillian Corbin
Corbin is the spirit behind St. Vincent de Paul Place, an agency operated by the Catholic Diocese of Norwich that strives to meet the needs of the homeless and those with limited income in the Norwich area. Under the direction of Corbin, the agency has expanded to include instruction in a wide variety of employment skills, community gardens filled with vegetables and herbs, a winter sleeping-bag program, and other community service programs that have stretched local resources in new directions to meet ever-increasing needs. Corbin exemplifies dedication, resolve, and creativity in her role. (Courtesy of Chris Hetzer.)

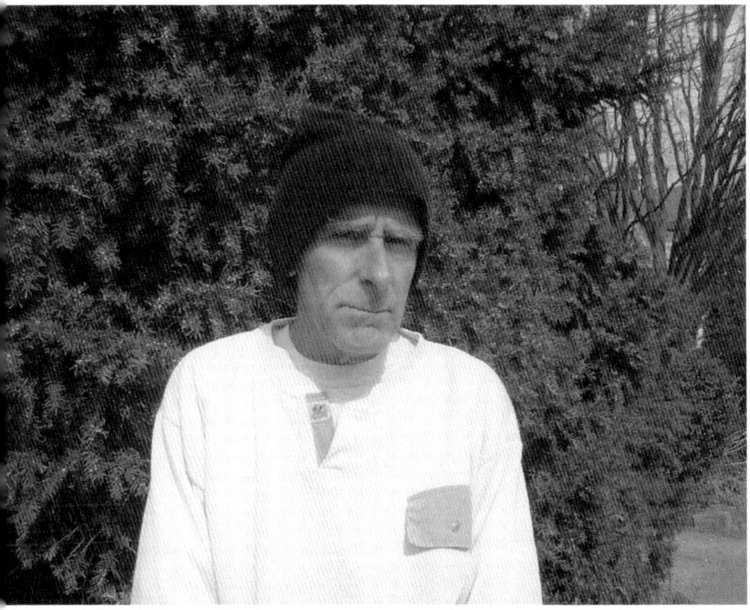

Dr. Geoffrey R. Akers
A year-round runner, Dr. Akers, PE, MBA, is a familiar figure on the streets of Norwich. He has earned 76 medals in US marathons (1985–2011) and a listing in the USA Track & Field Directory (1998). Akers helps keep his city safe and clean by reporting his observations of road and sidewalk hazards to appropriate city departments. Dr. Akers has not owned a car since 1983.

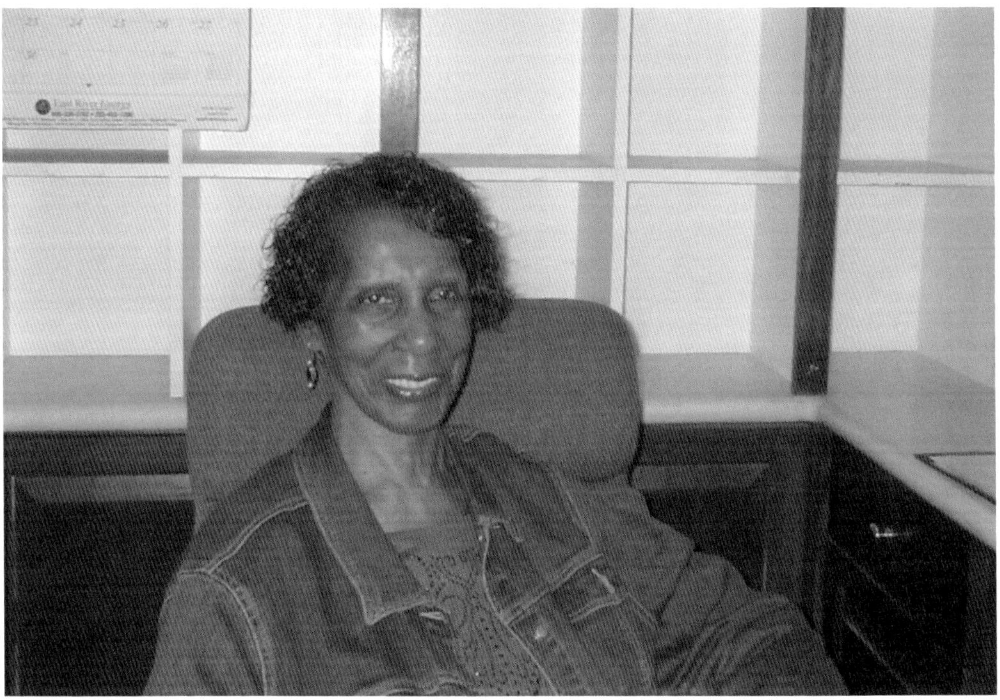

Carol Maranda
Carol Maranda is one of a group of volunteers at the information counter on the first floor of city hall. She is trained to meet and greet visitors to the Empire-style building and to answer their questions. The most whispered request is for the location of the public bathrooms (third floor). The most brusquely asked request is for the tax collector's office. (It is located behind them. They walked by it.) All volunteers are prepared to act as an escort to an office if necessary. And, by the way, the elevator for the four-story structure is just on the other side of the booth.

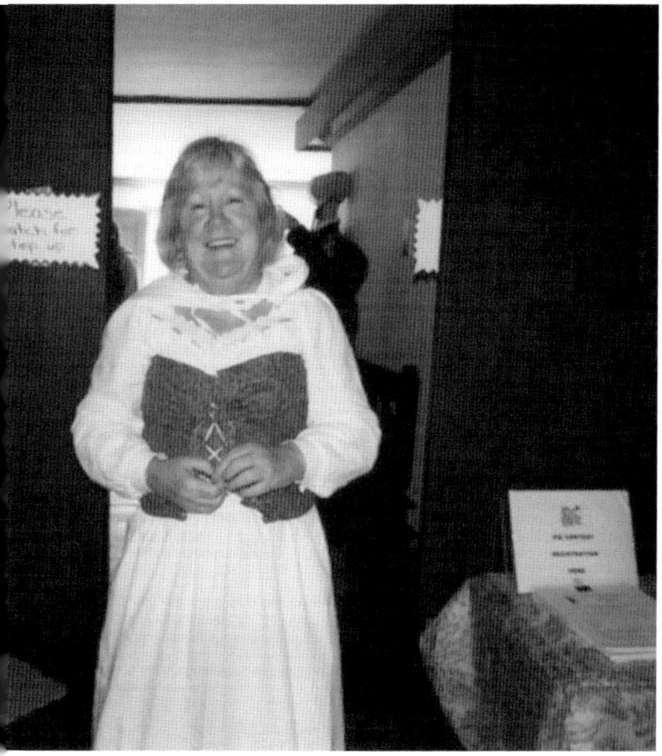

Kate Clark

Kate Clark has been a volunteer guide at the Leffingwell House Colonial Museum for more than five years. While taking visitors through the garden, she looks for her favorite insect, the praying mantis. Clark enjoys demonstrating how a praying mantis will delicately sip water from a convenient leaf or her hand.

Clark uses her love of nature to create unique pieces of jewelry and figurines from plants, stones, and branches to sell at area craft sales. Occasionally, she has helped a figurine find a home on a branch or on the stem of a plant in the garden. These items are used as an example of how important it is to examine plants closely, to discover the unexpected.

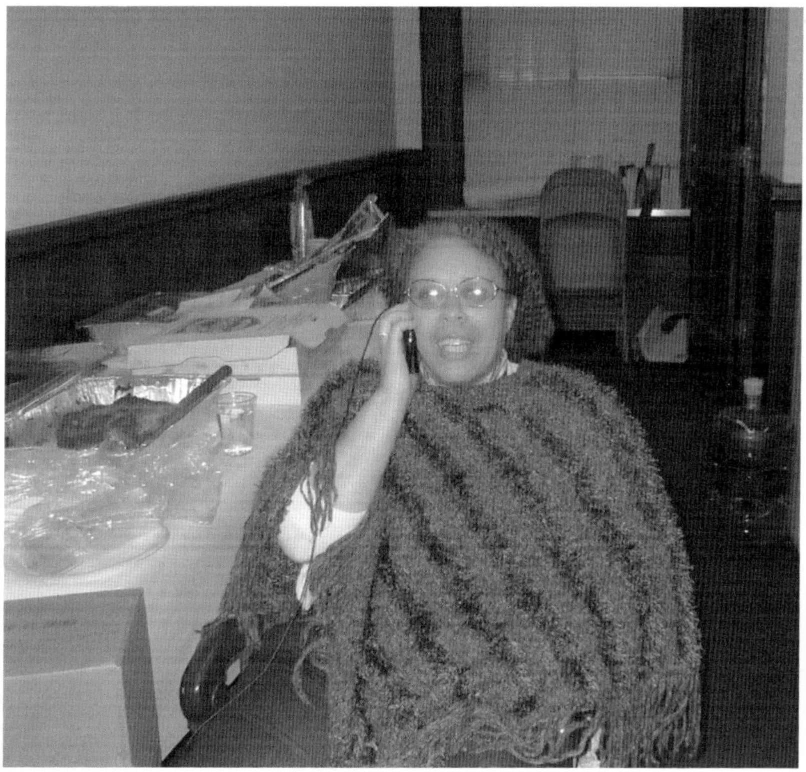

Sheila Hayes

Sheila Hayes is a civic volunteer who willingly accepts the clerical challenges of filing, answering phone calls, and fact-checking. Such duties help avoid delays that can stall community projects. When the work for one project is complete, Hayes goes on to the next project or task. This allows for simultaneous projects to move along more rapidly. Her dedication to the Bell Before City Hall project was completed in fewer than two years, from concept and fundraising, to completion and dedication.

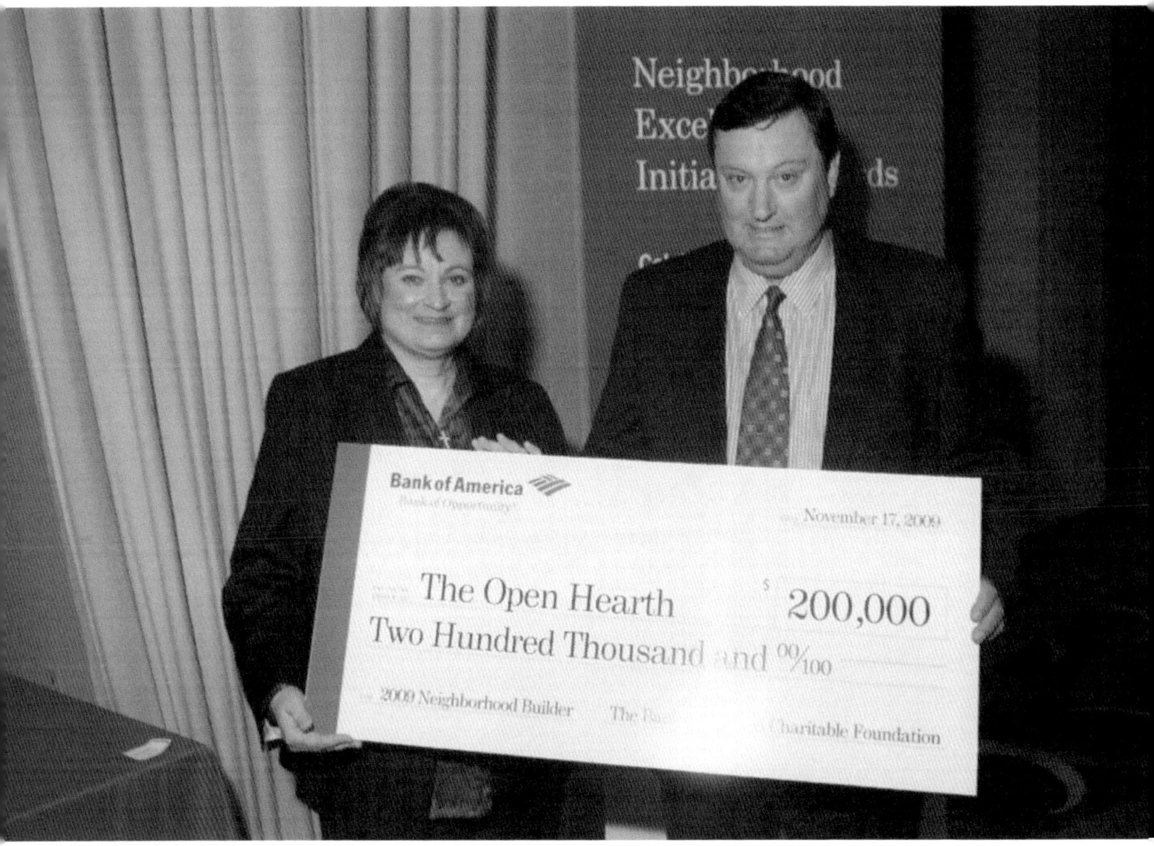

Nancy Irene Herbert

Nancy Irene Herbert has advocated for homeless shelters abroad and in Connecticut, honing her skills as a successful grant writer by presenting appealing applications that result in grants of over six figures. She is currently discovering new opportunity potentials for the Chamber of Commerce of Eastern Connecticut as their grant coordinator. Herbert is pictured here with Kevin Cunningham, Connecticut state president of Bank of America. (Courtesy Nancy I. Herbert.)

Peter Nystrom

Nystrom has lived a life of public service to the community of Norwich since first being elected to the city council in 1979. He has also served as a state representative (1984–2002) and as mayor (2009). Residents are comfortable discussing issues with Nystrom, whether in agreement or not. And they know that he could be counted on to help, even when it comes to the city's four-legged citizens. Elliott the cat had been shot with a target arrow. Seeing the cat, Mayor Nystrom took immediate charge, calling Norwich Animal Control and seeing that Elliott had immediate surgery at All Friends Animal Hospital, where he recovered and was returned to his owners. (Courtesy of Linda Nystrom.)

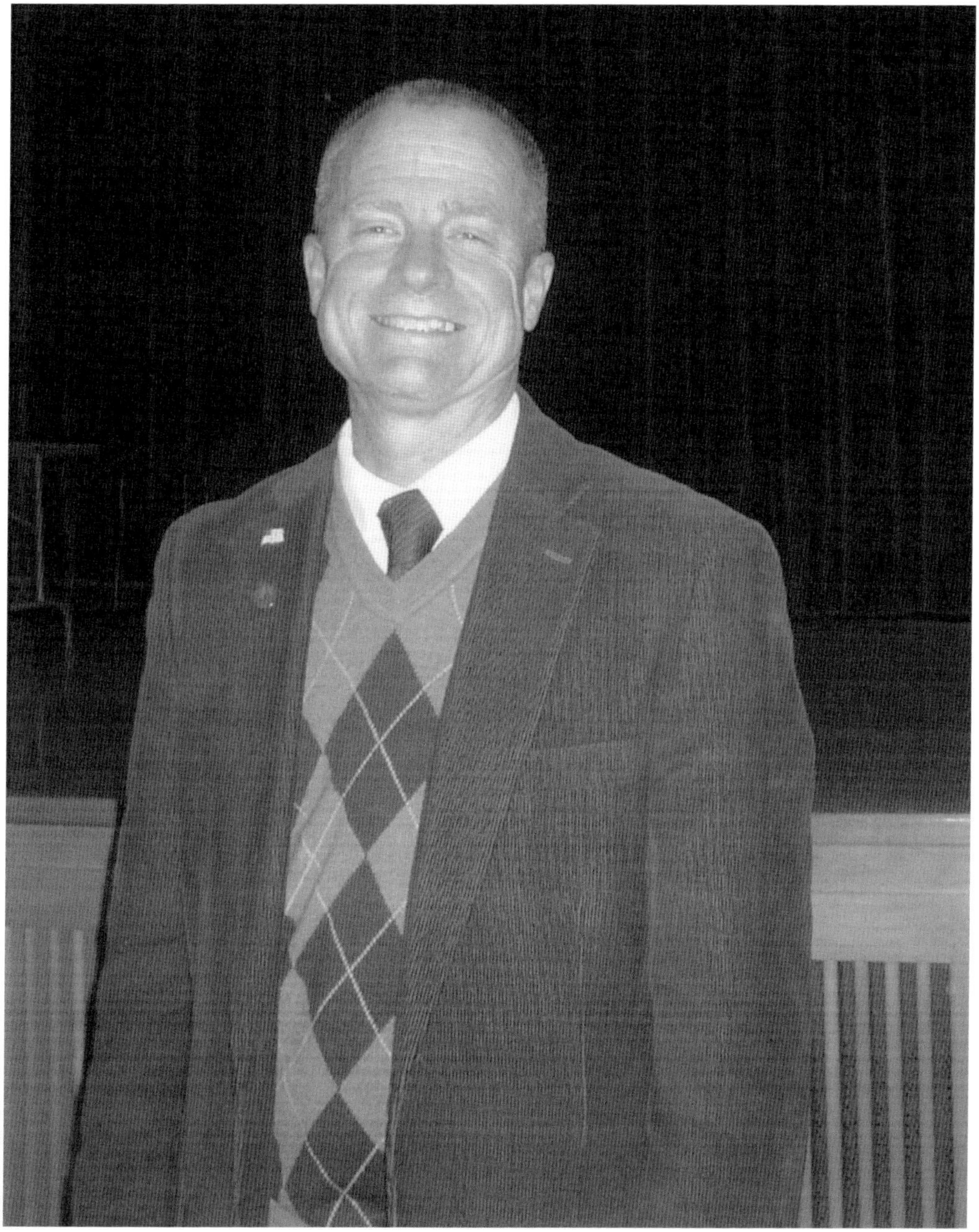

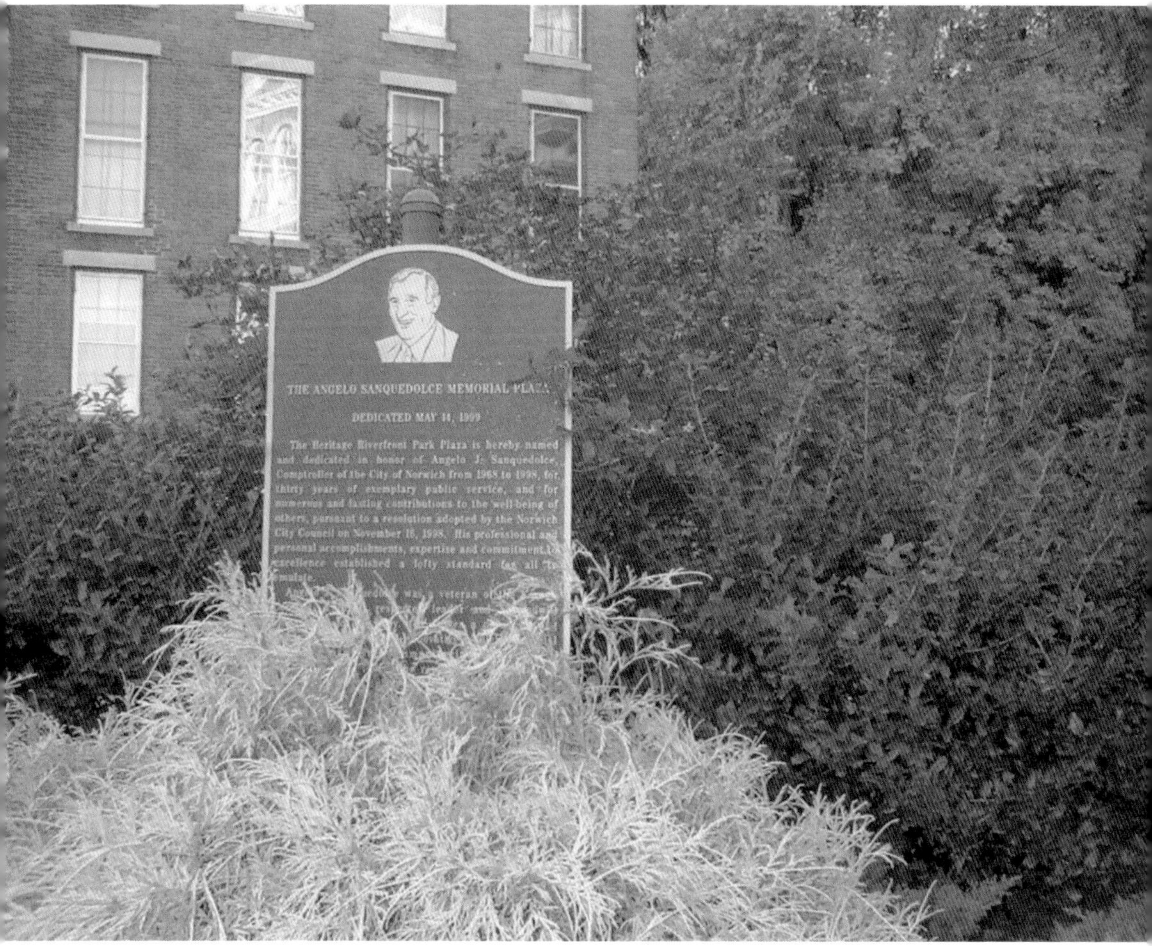

Angelo Sanquedolce

Sanquedolce was the comptroller for the City of Norwich from 1968 to 1998. But to many, he was chief mediator of disputes. His calm, good-natured demeanor and skills at mediation and finance allowed him to find the situations where everyone, or at least most of the parties involved, were winners. He worked with individuals, groups, banks, churches, fire departments, education departments, and taxpayers. Under his direction, Norwich received its first certificate of achievement for excellence in financial reporting, and an AA bond rating (the highest a city of Norwich's size can attain). The plaza in front of Norwich City Hall was named in his honor and has the only sign in the city with a smiling face.

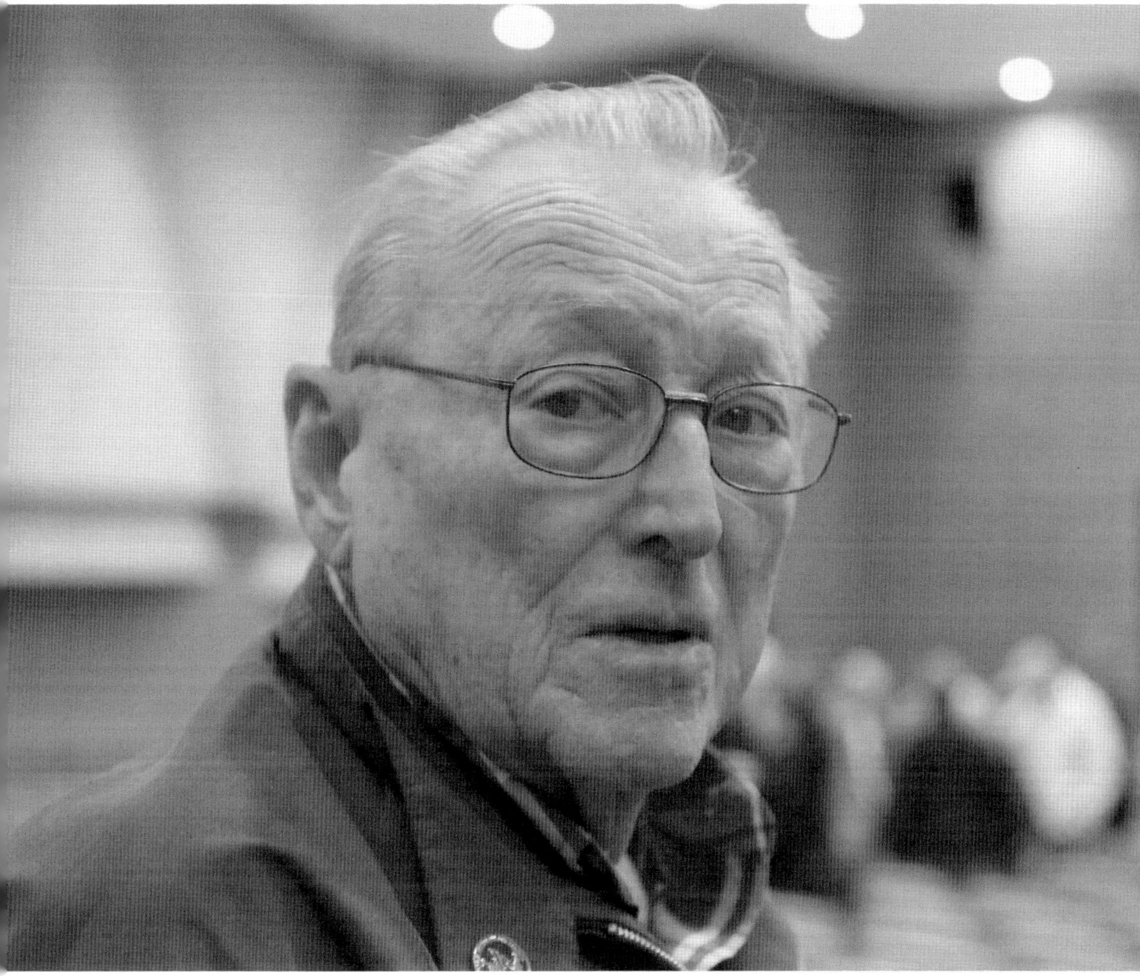

"Red" McKeon

McKeon has dedicated his life to his family, to the public, and to safety. He served as chief of the Occum Fire Department from 1960 through 1994 and founded an ambulance company in 1970. He was one of the first responders to the Van Tassel Warehouse explosion and fire on April 3, 1962, the second-worst fire in the history of Connecticut.

"Red" was an early and longstanding member of the Community Development Advisory Council for the city. When a fire destroyed the Roto Print Textile Factory in 1985, he used his experience to fight to create a safe, green park for the residents of Occum following an extensive pollutant cleanup. The space includes basketball courts, picnic tables, a playscape, a running/walking track, a boat launch, and fishing locations. The "Red" McKeon Park officially opened to the public in 1997. (Courtesy of Brian Kobylarz.)

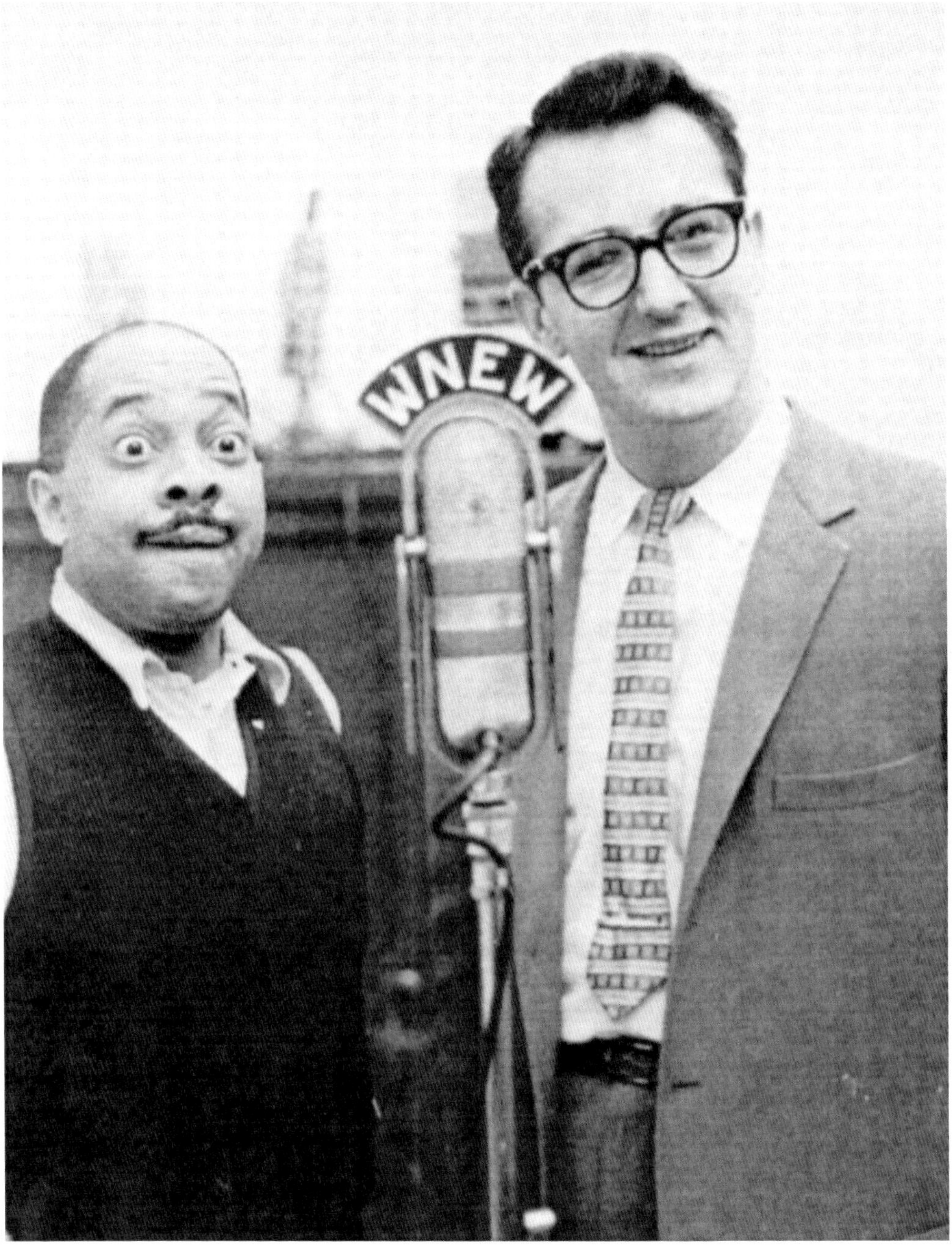

Jim Stanley

Jim Stanley (right) was full of unexpected fun and adventure. When Norwich celebrated the 300th anniversary of its settling, Stanley convinced the celebration committee to paint a street gold. The project was quickly approved and, when the time came, a crowd assembled just to watch the application of the gold leaf to the tar road near Chelsea Parade. Then, members of the crowd scraped the gold up as souvenirs as proof they were there. Stanley is pictured here with Bob Hodges. (Courtesy of Vivian Stanley-Olson.)

Harold Ross

Harold Ross retired as the owner of the H. Willey Tobacco & Candy Wholesale business and decided to pay the community back for some of his good fortune.

He joined a small group of investors to help establish The Community Foundation of Eastern Connecticut, a public charity that encourages community investment through philanthropic giving. Then, he quietly established the Harold Ross Institute for Preventive Care at the William W. Backus Hospital, which funds healthcare programs. He then helped to establish an adult daycare center at a local home for the elderly. When thanked, Ross's only comment was, "I've been well repaid in doing everything I did by meeting you." (Courtesy of United Community Services.)

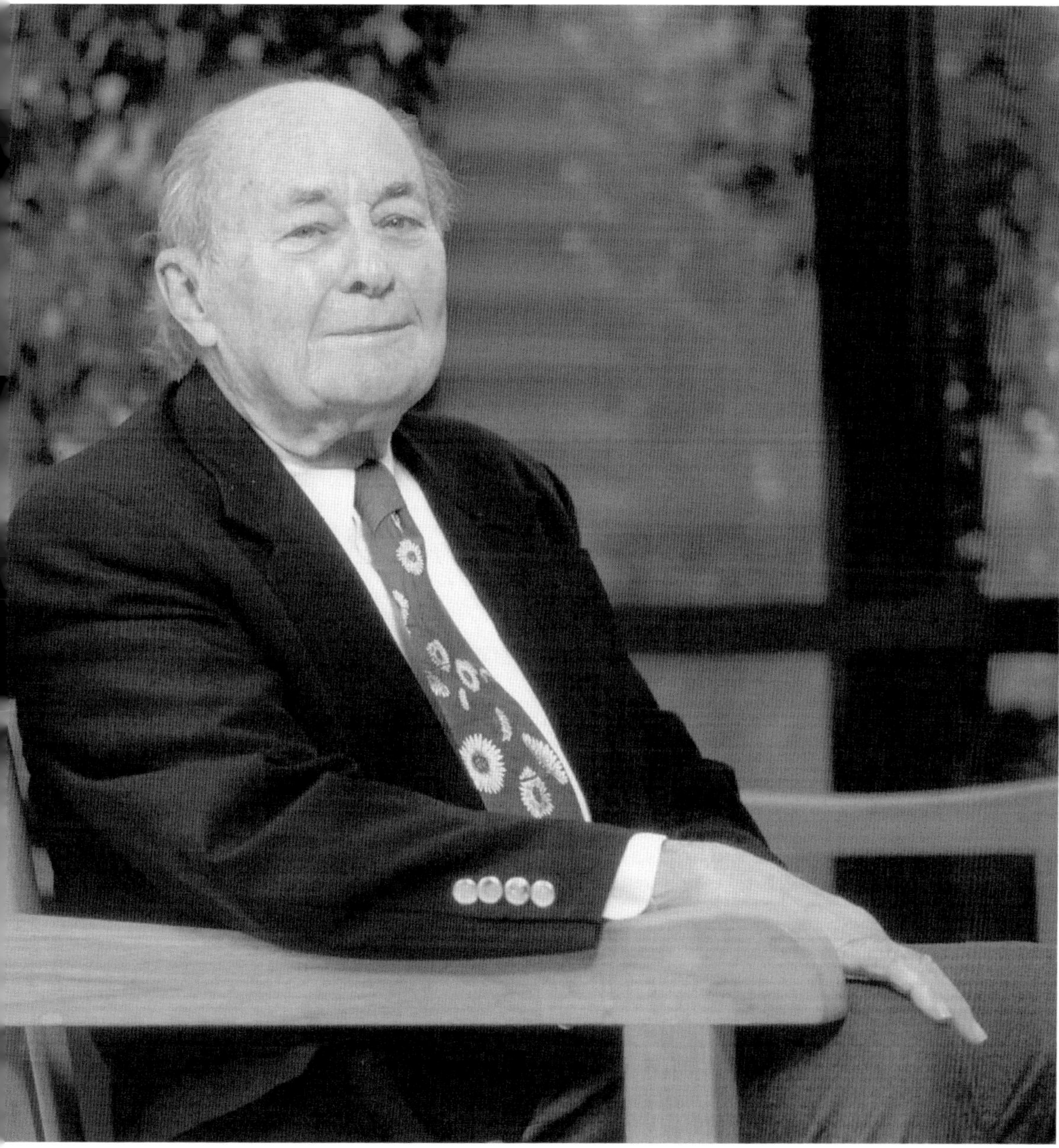

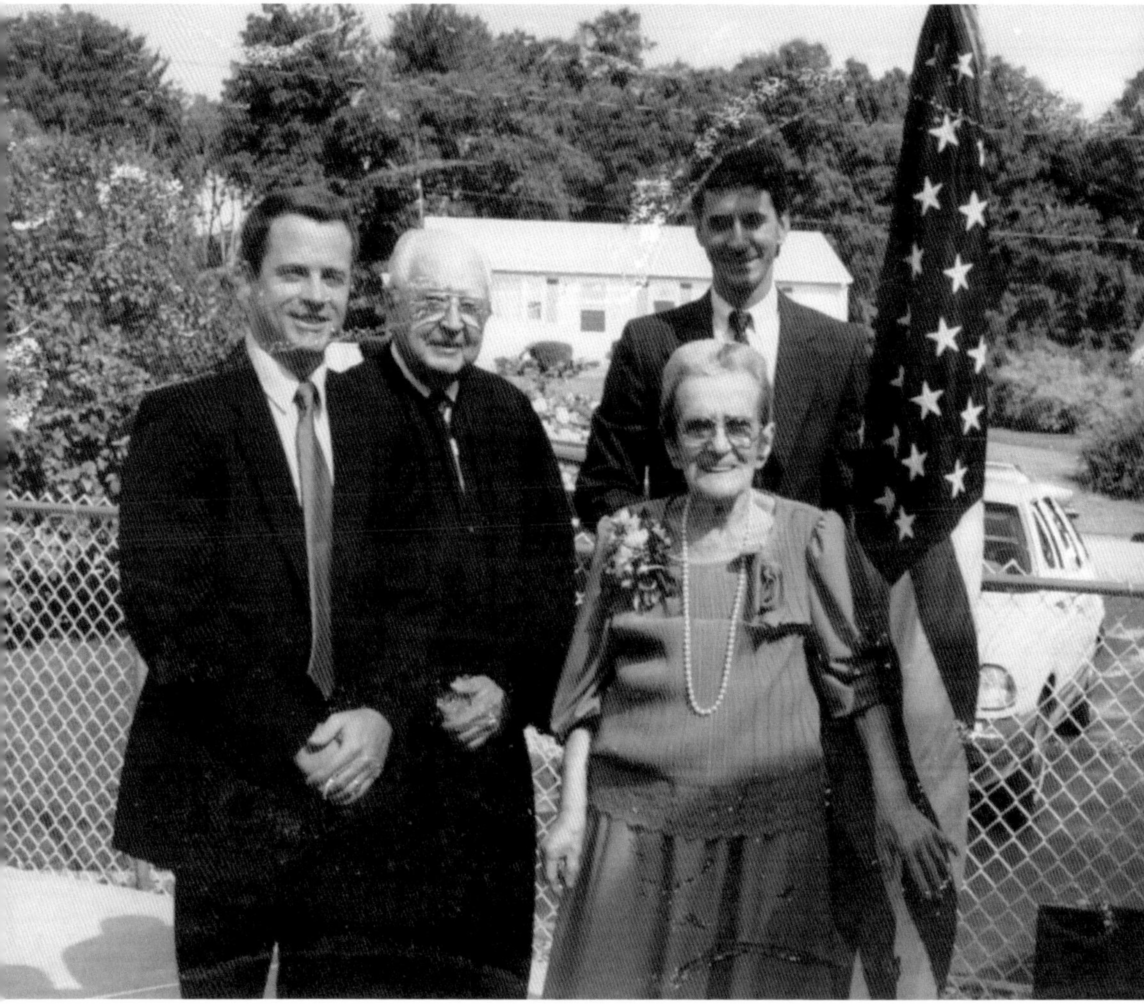

Clodia Emma Schofield

Clodia Schofield and her granddaughter, Edith Mobley, spent years requesting a marriage certificate from the church as proof of her Canadian-born grandmother's marriage in 1916 to her American husband. They were told that the church had burned down and that all the records had been lost. The women then spoke with newly elected Connecticut state representative Peter Nystrom. For two years, Nystrom and his aide Carolyn Caron made inquiries, hearing the same replies from officials. Then, one day, they asked about stored records and were directed to an old storage attic in another church, where they found the marriage license of Clodia Emma and Albert Schofield, who were wed on February 2, 1916.

On August 4, 1990, at the age of 92, Clodia Emma Schofield took the oath of allegiance as a US citizen from a federal judge from New Haven in her granddaughter's backyard, surrounded by friends and family. She is pictured here on the occasion with state representative Peter Nystrom (far left). (Courtesy of Peter Nystrom.)

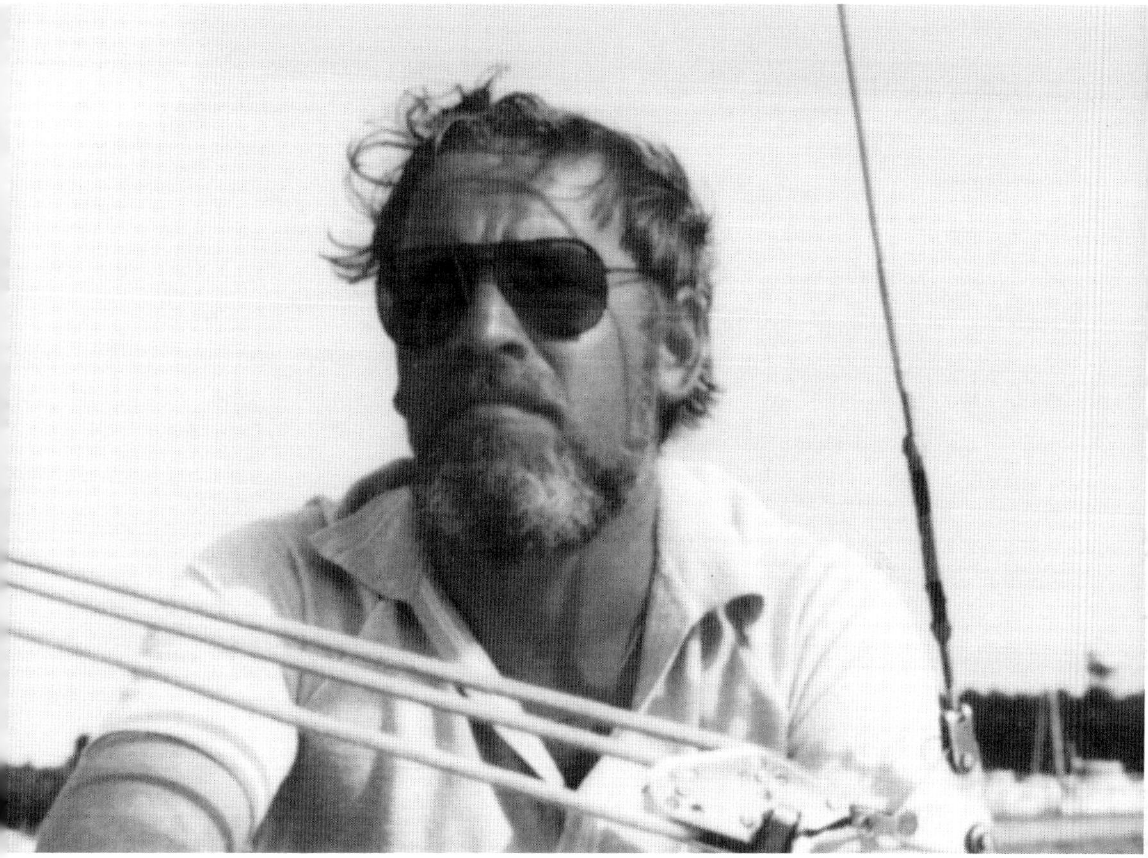

Leo Geer

"Joe" Geer began working with machines in school, during his time in Vietnam, and when he returned home and worked in many jobs before settling into the print industry. As the second of 12 children, he was a natural leader with an easy, quick wit. Geer liked to keep busy and always had the time and energy to help his family, friends, and neighbors with their homes, boats, and projects. He also worked on construction and remodeling of his own homes. Geer was the man with the tools who knew how to use them.

No stranger to mischief, he once built a "cannon" of PVC pipe, a soda cup, pizza pie plates, and a Whiffle ball for the Leffingwell House Colonial Museum Halloween display. It was so realistic that a neighbor called, requesting it not be pointed at her house in case it went off. (Courtesy of Terri Geer.)

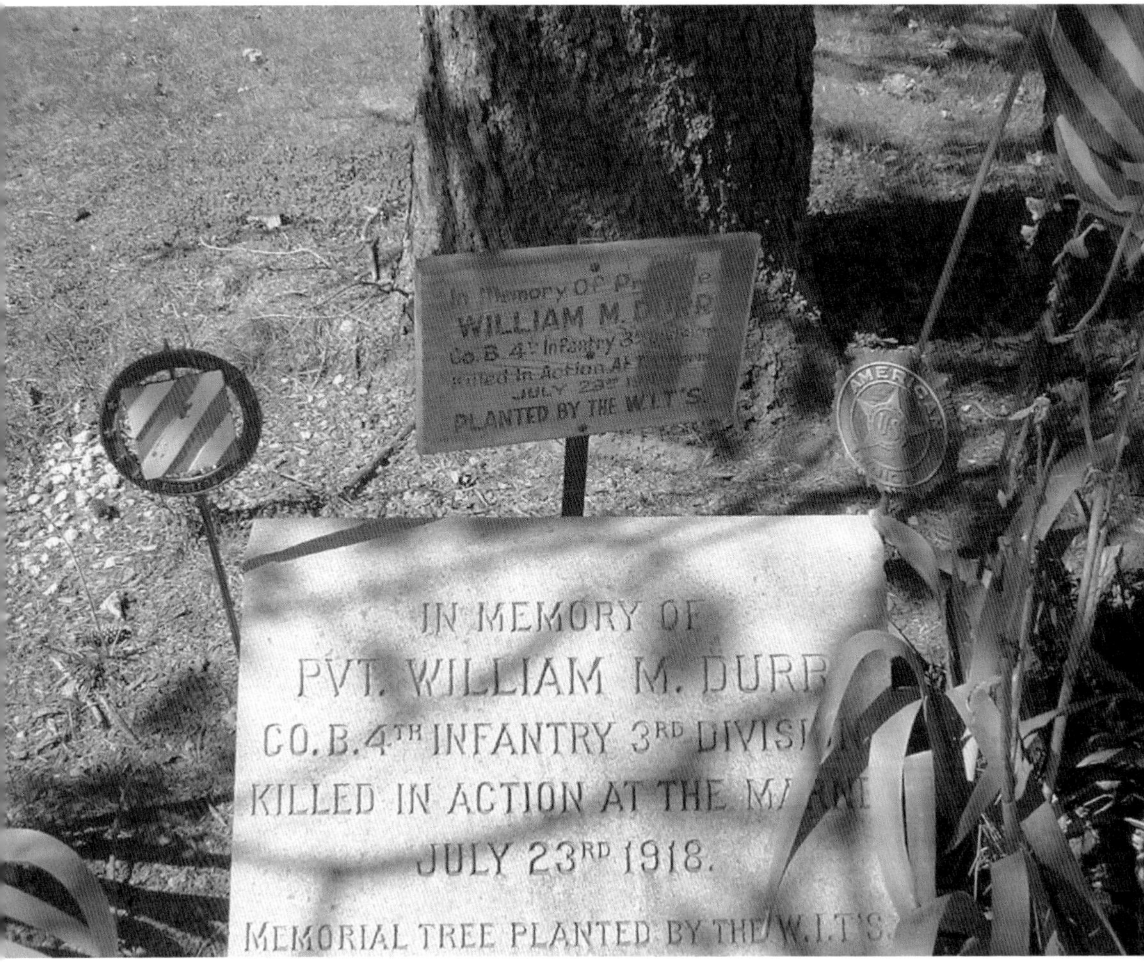

William Morton Durr

William Durr was the first in his family to complete his education, and he was even valedictorian of his Town Street School class. He was an active member of Jessie E. Hyde's Sunday school class at the First Congregational Church. In February 1918, at 19 years old, Durr enlisted in the Army. By April, he was shipped to France as part of the 28,000-man 3rd Division. On July 23, after several days of fierce fighting and facing heavy machine-gun and artillery fire, Pvt. William Durr was killed in action. His body was not recovered.

The members of the Workers in Training club honored their friend, first club president, Sunday school officer, and Christian Endeavor Society member on May 31, 1925, by planting a Colorado spruce tree that would grow tall and strong and would protect those who sought shelter beneath its limbs.

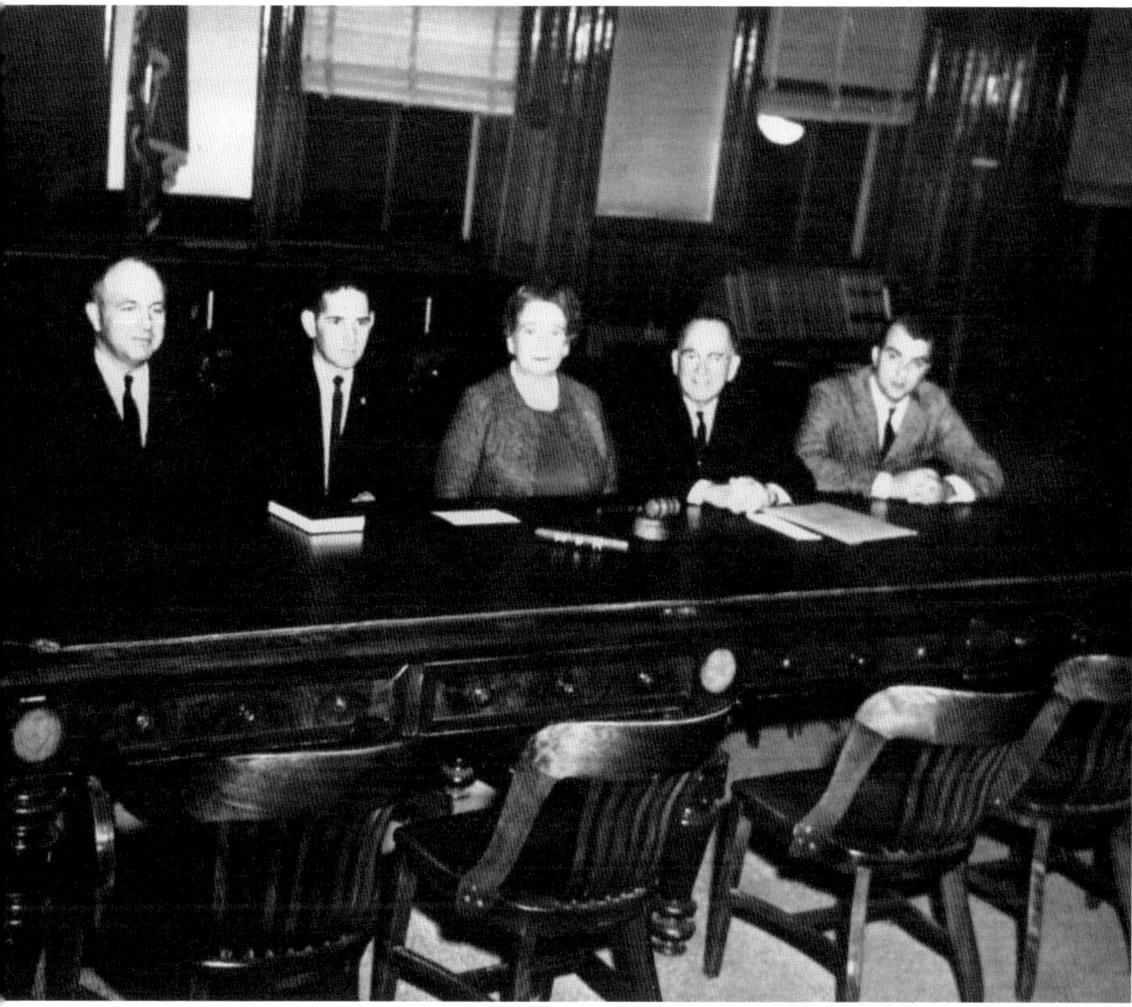

Ethel V. McWilliams

Between 1953 and 1963, Ethel McWilliams was elected to four consecutive terms on the city council. She was elected president of the city council in 1963.

She voiced her opinions with a firm, distinctive voice, never hesitating to make a quiet correction or to bring a discussion back to its topic. After leaving elective office, she was active in the community. Many recall her as being "the lady with the hat that helped the children cross the street near the Samuel Huntington School." She also phoned in regularly to an evening radio call-in program on WICH-AM to set a story straight. Her distinctive voice reminded listeners, "Facts are facts and need to be dealt with as they are and not how we wish them to be."

Pictured here are Paul Morosky, J. Longo III, Ethel V. McWilliams, Armand Beauregard, and Richard F. Jaskiewicz. (Courtesy of City of Norwich Mayor's Office.)

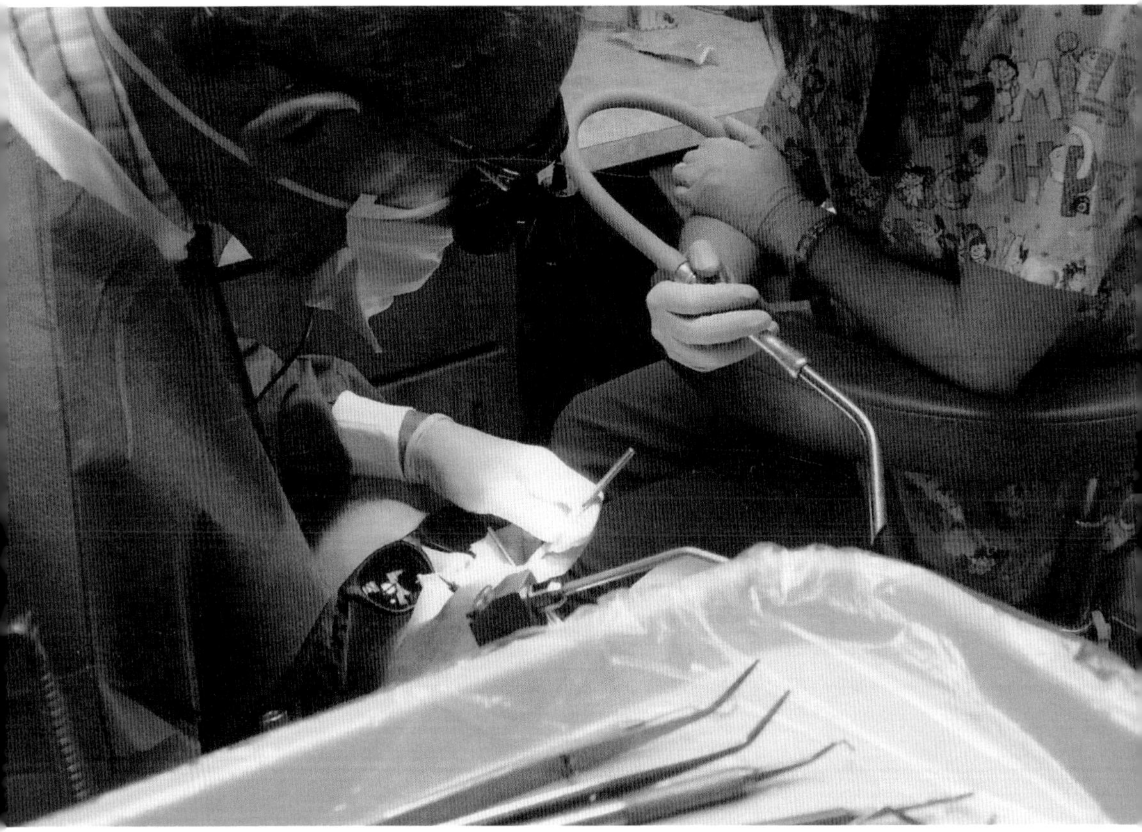

Dr. Robert Strick

Dr. Strick began Give Kids a Smile in Norwich as a single-day community event sponsored by the Connecticut State Dental Association. But with the dedication of Dr. Strick, his staff, and the Norwich United Community and Family Services organization, it is now a year-round program providing free oral healthcare to children in low-income families. The program also encourages parents, healthcare professionals, and policy makers to address the constant need for oral healthcare for underserved children. (Courtesy of Dr. Robert Strick.)

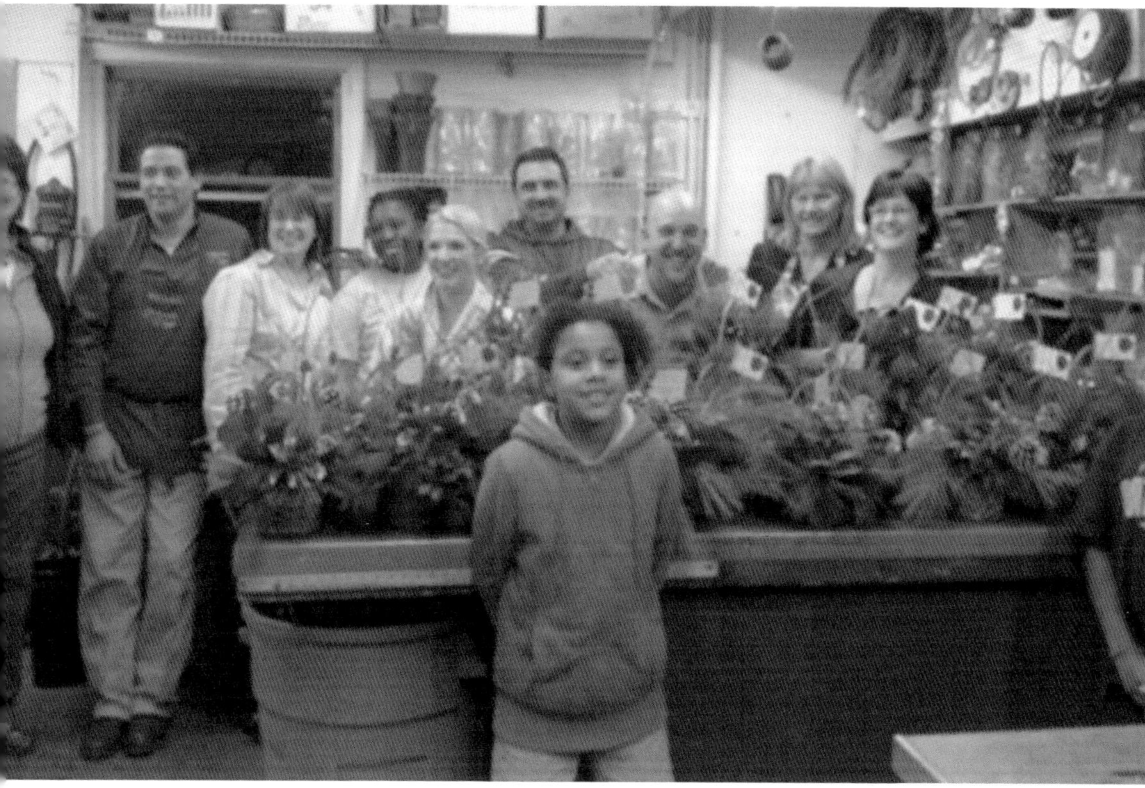

Rose City Chapter of BNI

Since 1985, the members of the Rose City Chapter of BNI (Business Networking International) have met weekly, sharing the philosophy that, by giving business to others, you will get business in return. The organization's status as the largest chapter in Connecticut is testament to its success. Amid much laughter and good-natured ribbing, each person is allowed 30 seconds to inform the group how their business is growing, what help they need, or what help they can provide.

The chapter's activities are not limited to scholarships for local students with a dream to own their own business. It also helps other community organizations achieve their goals. (Courtesy Rose City Business Networking International.)

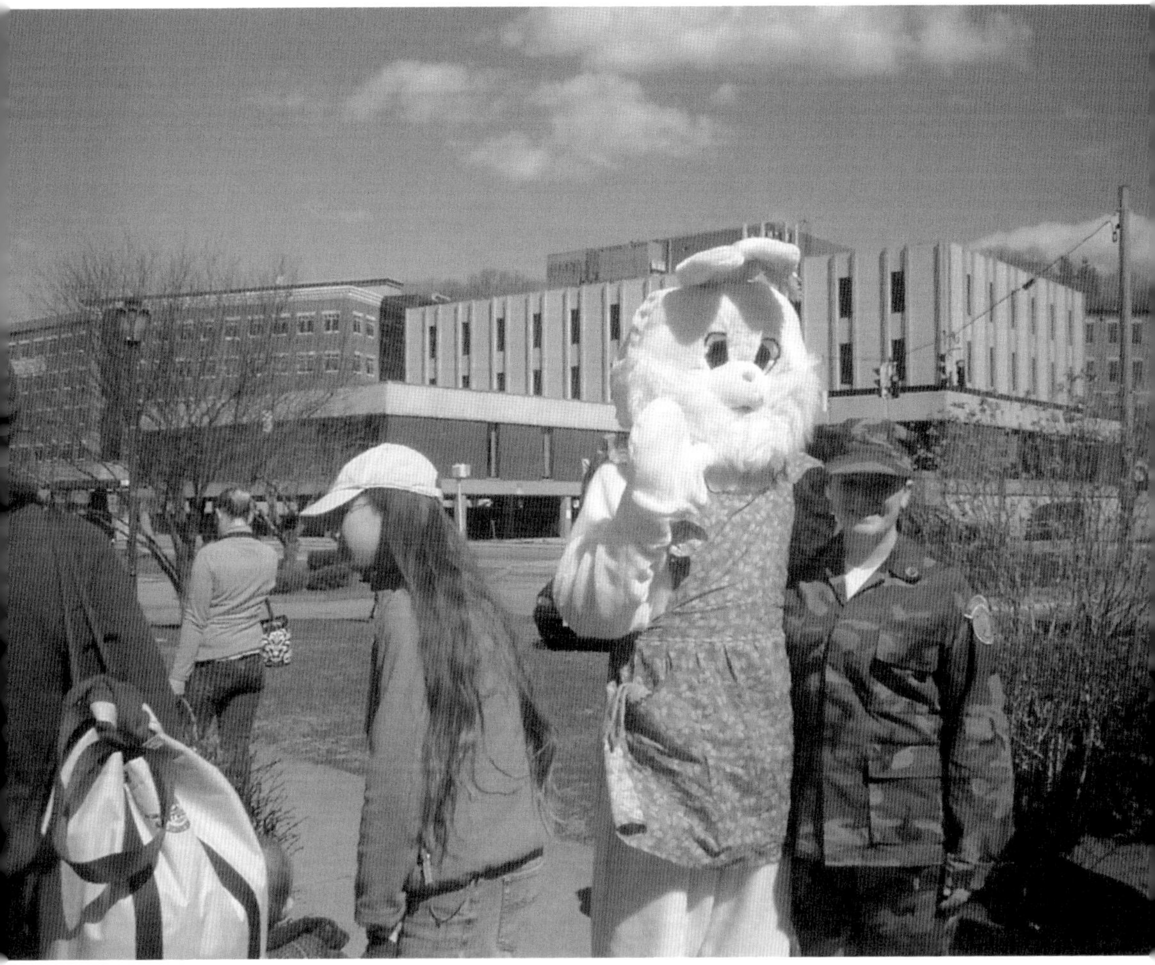

Three Rivers Young Marines

Three Rivers Young Marines is a group of teenaged men and women participating in physical challenges and exercises that stretch their minds. Paige LaFlamme (pictured above in uniform) also served as the official escort of the bunny at the Norwich Annual Egg Hunt. "The best part is the team building," she says. Everything that the Three Rivers Young Marines do, they do together. "You learn that there are jobs to do with everything and some jobs are more fun than others, but when you do them together as a team, it's easier and becomes fun. More interesting." (Courtesy of Three Rivers Young Marines.)

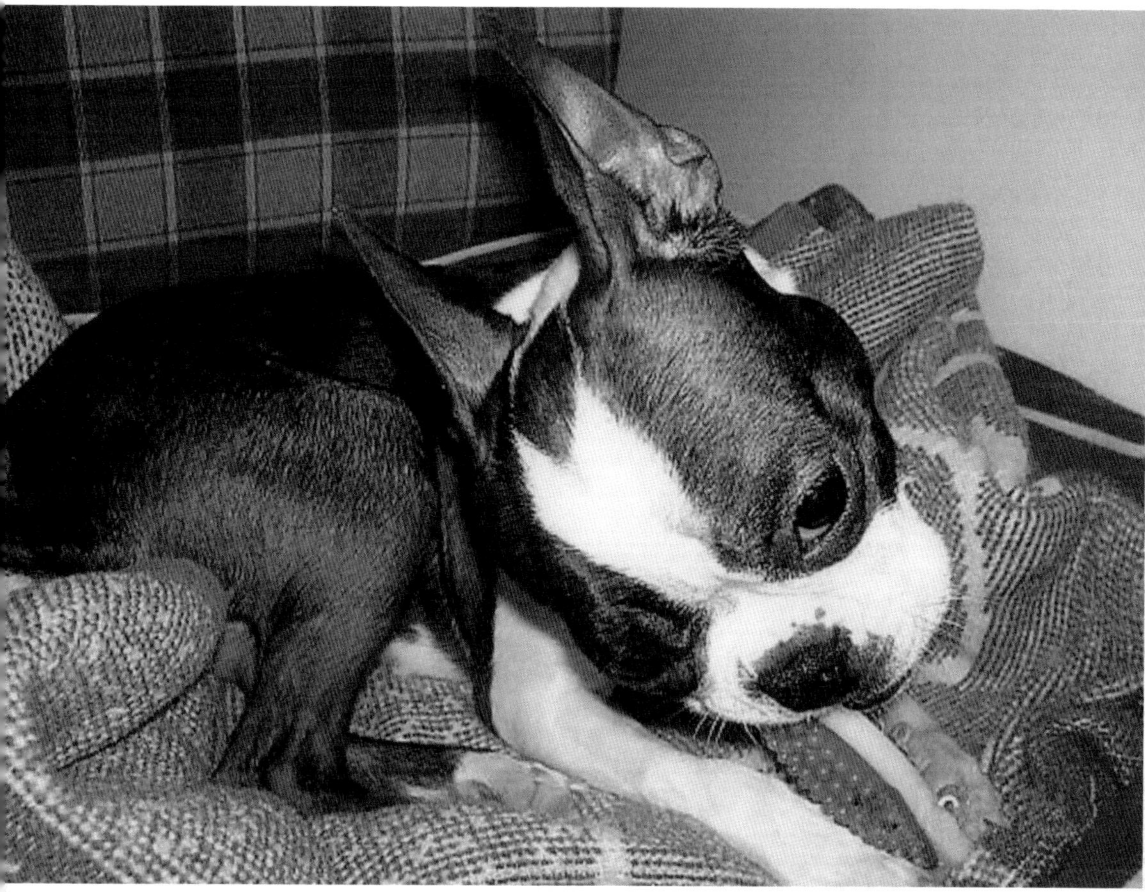

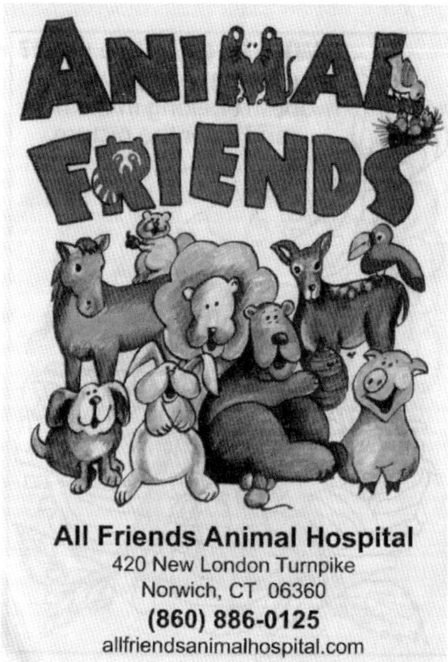

Zoey and the All Friends Animal Hospital
Zoey (above) was the dog that inspired the All Friends Animal Hospital to go beyond just helping to spay and neuter the dogs and other animals for the animal shelter in Norwich.

All Friends has created an extensive animal education program and organized pet fairs to provide care not paid for through town funding. The education program has grown to include schools, senior citizen programs, rabies clinics, neutering programs, and pet adoption days. At the frequent pet adoption fairs, adults and children can interact with a variety of pets, including snakes, rabbits, mice, kittens, and puppies. Schools are regularly supplied with animal care information handouts, coloring books, and pet emergency stickers for homes with pets. Such items help to ensure the safety of the pets and the responders who may encounter a frightened animal. (Both images courtesy of All Friends Animal Hospital.)

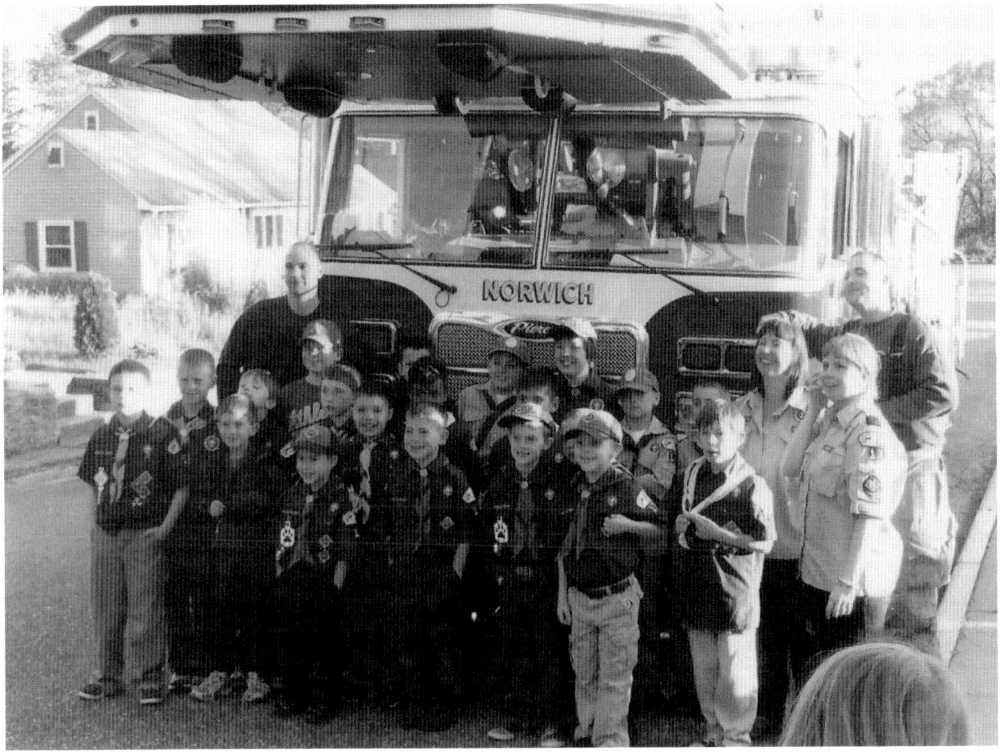

Boy Scouts of America Pack 17, Troop 4

Many of the dens in Boy Scout Pack 17 use the training room at the Norwich firehouse for meetings. The scouts knew only a few of the firefighters, but when a horrible accident took the life of Firefighter Ben Demond in March 2012, the scouts decided that their fundraising proceeds for camp should go instead to his children. Quickly earning additional funds from a pancake breakfast and a cake sale, they were able to present a check for $1,000 to the fund for Demond's children.

Shown in the above photograph are, from left to right, Lt. Mike Dziavit, Jared Michaud, Ethan Hester, Jonathan Simpson, Kyle Heard, Charisse Heard, Derrick Ouillette, Aidan O'Farrell, Andrew Rydell, Ryan Jakubielski, Brian So, Joseph Bell, Eduardo Ruud, Kole Thurston, Chance Fish, Ann Marie Jakubielski, Cooper Way, Aidan Jakubielski, Christopher Bacelar, Arthur Ruud, Cameron Busch, Skylar Bentley, and Christopher Grube. (Both images courtesy of Boy Scouts of America Pack 17, Troop 4.)

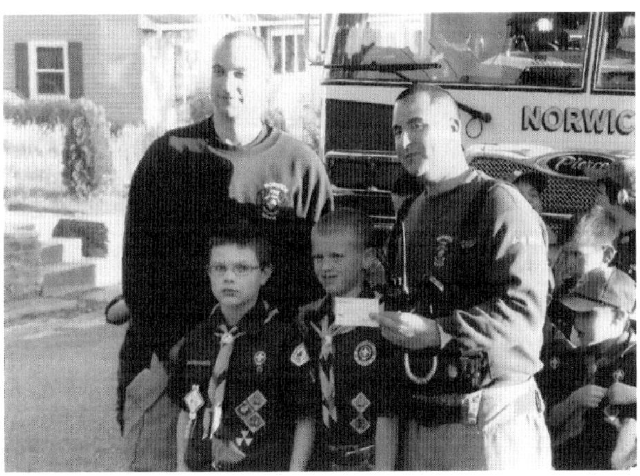

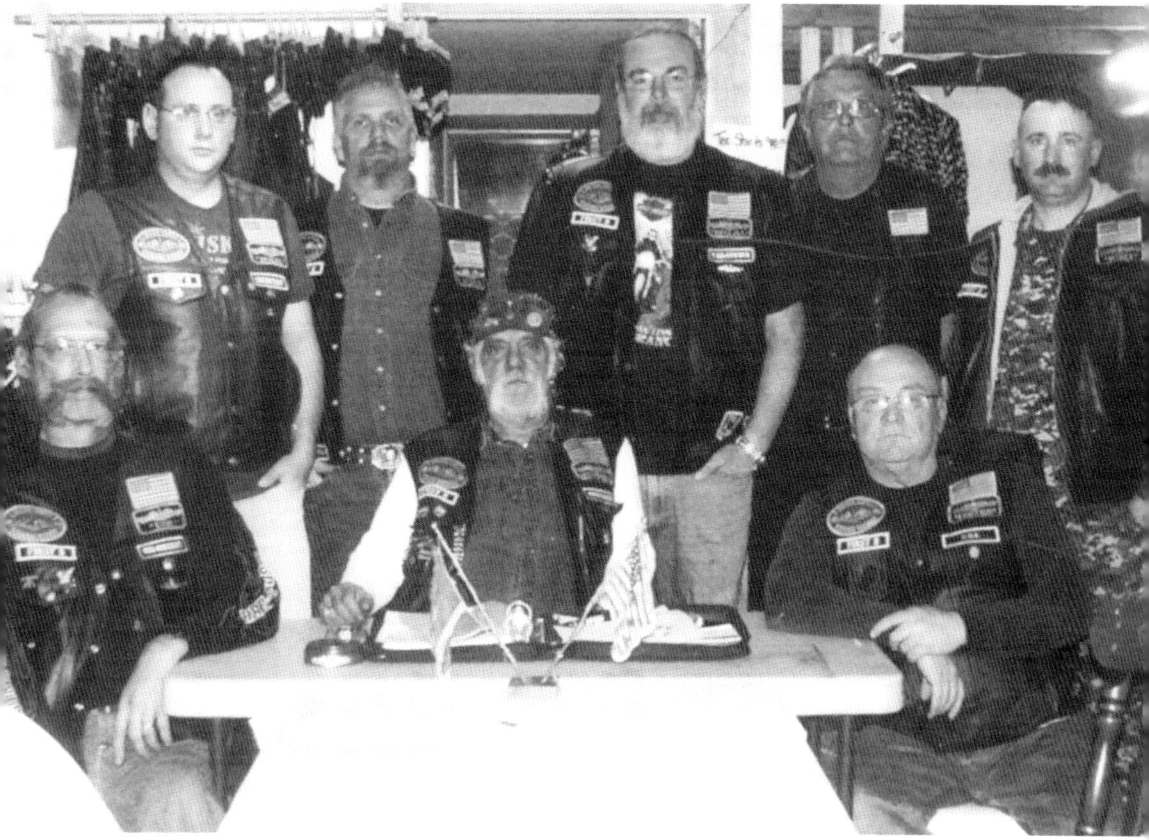

The Silent Service Motorcycle Club

Chartered on August 12, 2013, the Silent Service Motorcycle Club is made up mostly of US Navy submarine veterans. Their intention is to promote goodwill, preserve the proud heritage of the US Submarine Service, support veterans and children's groups, ride motorcycles, have fun, and drink beer.

They can be found on almost any weekend, keeping a watchful eye on other riders as they reinforce safe motorcycle-riding skills while traveling in a group, participating in a charity event.

After the ride, the men and their families can be found posing children on a Harley for a photograph or choosing a date and time to meet in support of a veteran who needs help. (Courtesy of Silent Service Motorcycle Club.)

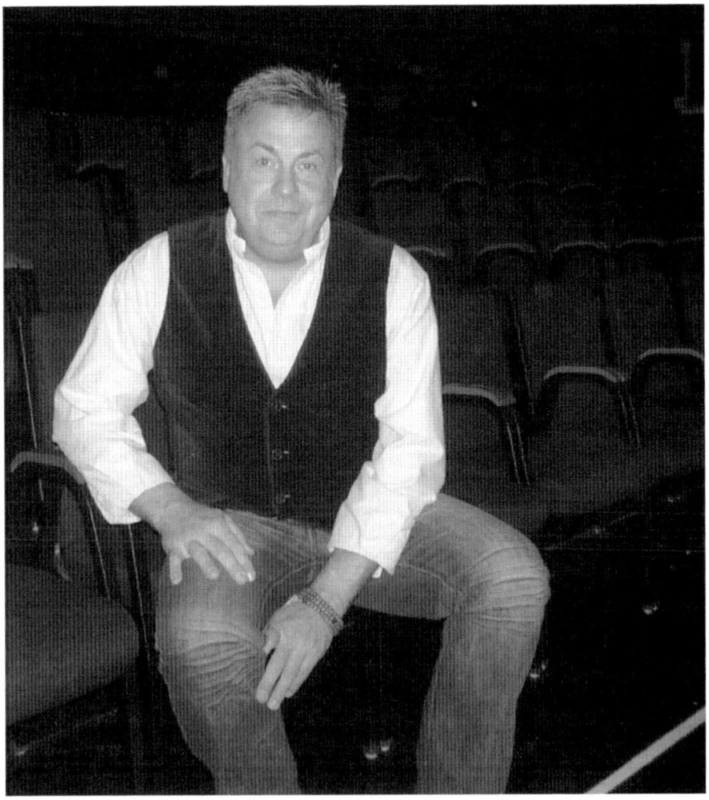

Brett Bernardini

Bernardini is the driving force behind the Spirit of Broadway theater and a constant and continuing source of strength, inspiration, and confidence to others in the field of art and in the nonprofit community. For years, he has been bringing his experience as well as a sense of warmth, style, and humor to long meetings of the Connecticut High School Musical Theater Awards, now five years old and involving 23 high schools from across Connecticut. He opens more than just the theater to writers, actors, and technicians; he opens his home, his heart, and his garden.

Every day, Bernardini posts a comment, quote, or phrase for his Facebook friends to read, react to, or ponder. It often has to do with facing the struggles of the day and balancing them with the dreams of tomorrow. Sometimes, he will write about the work he is doing on his house or the theater or how is garden is growing. His natural leadership as a communicator of thoughts and ideas encourages new thoughts and innovative ways of getting things done, as opposed to waiting for everything to be completely assembled or perfect. Bernardini is known for beginning rehearsals for a play before the complete cast has been selected. Namaste!

He is the Downtown Spirit of Broadway Theater creator, developer, and executive director. "As an artist, I do what I do because it is my voice; my way of communicating, exploring and discovering. I am an artist who uses my craft to provoke, to incite emotions and to challenge the status quo as my way of contributing to a larger conversation. Collaboratively, with other artists, I take your intangibles—your stories, your questions, your wonders—and form them into a momentary, visible reality. You don't understand me because I leap before there is a net: trusting that the plunge into the mystery is my next point of departure. You are fascinated by my world—superficially so abstract and random—and yet, from the chaos, I give birth to a living, breathing moment that otherwise would have never existed. I do what I do because it feeds my spirit—if not my stomach—and like any passion, it consumes me, demands more of me and I am the willing partner . . . never satiated, never content to rest. I am an artist . . . that's why I do what I do."

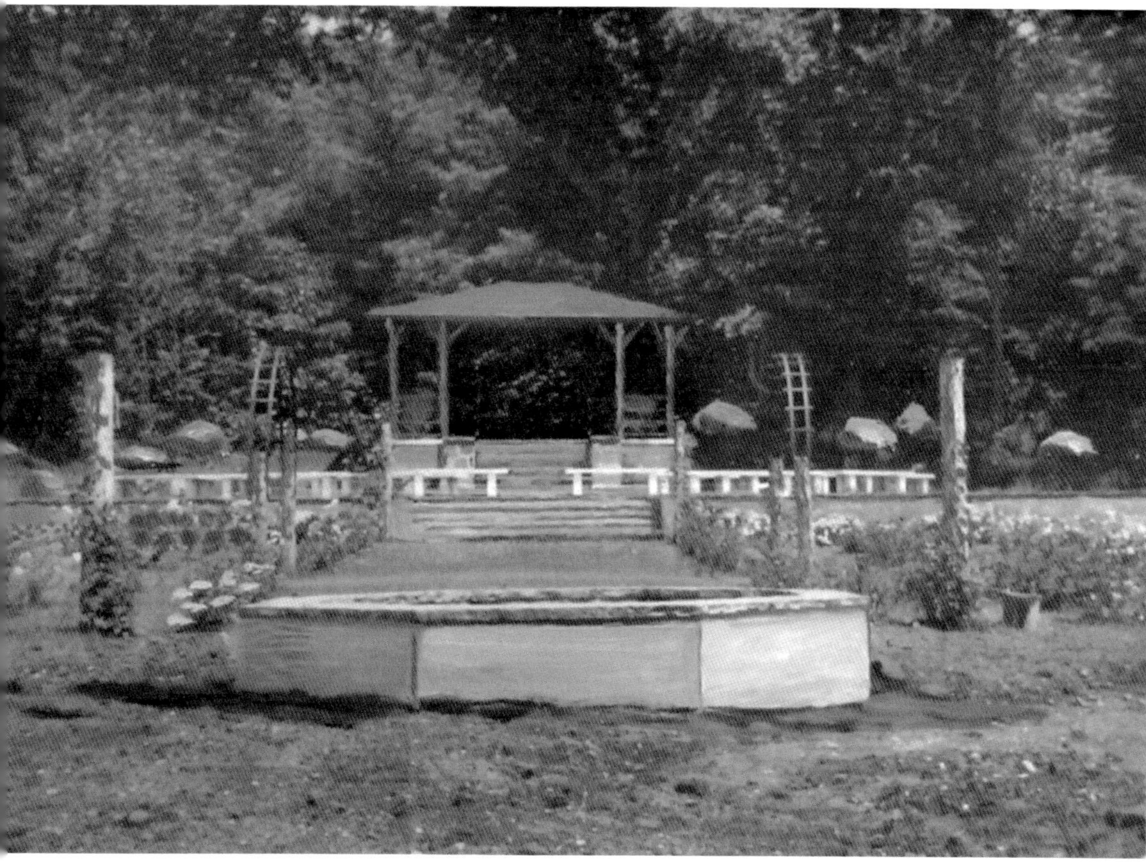

Roy Daniel Judd

Roy Judd saw his vision of a rose garden opened to the public on July 11, 1948. As a member of the Mohegan Park Board of Managers, he understood the potential of the 300-acre woodland in the center of the city, and he knew the value of an attractive and attention-getting entrance.

With help from his friends, fellow Norwich Rotarians, colleagues, and park board members, Judd collected donations and contributed much of the $20,000 for the project himself. Over 2,500 individual roses were planted in four large plots. Also installed were grass walks, a pergola, and a shelter house surrounded by a fence of trelliswork. It is now one of the most beautiful and popular gateways into the Mohegan Park. (Courtesy of Norwich, Connecticut, Mayor's Office.)

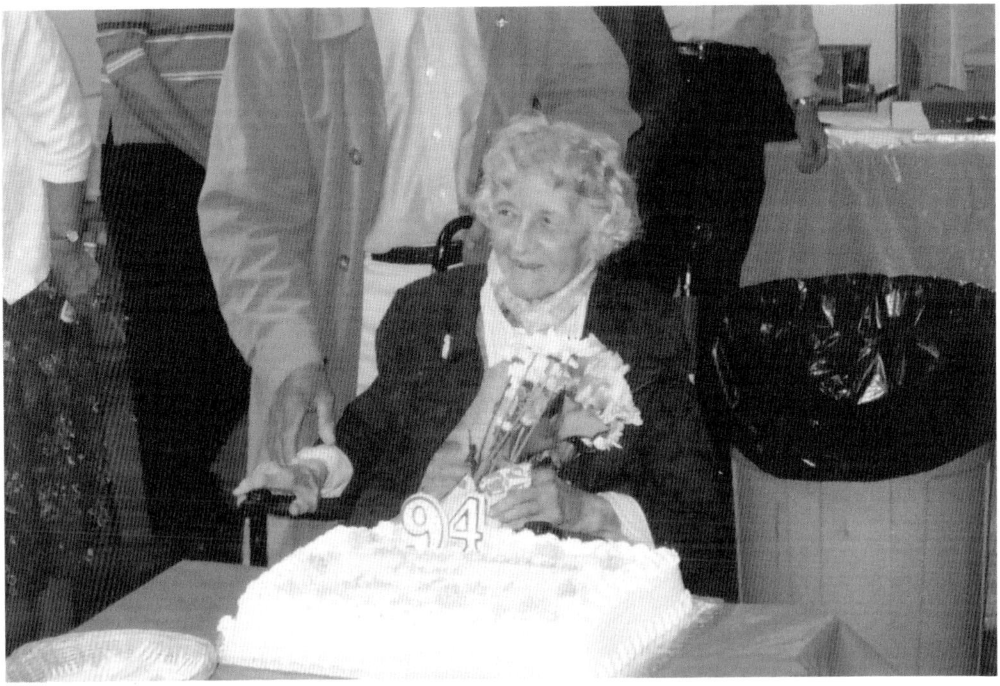

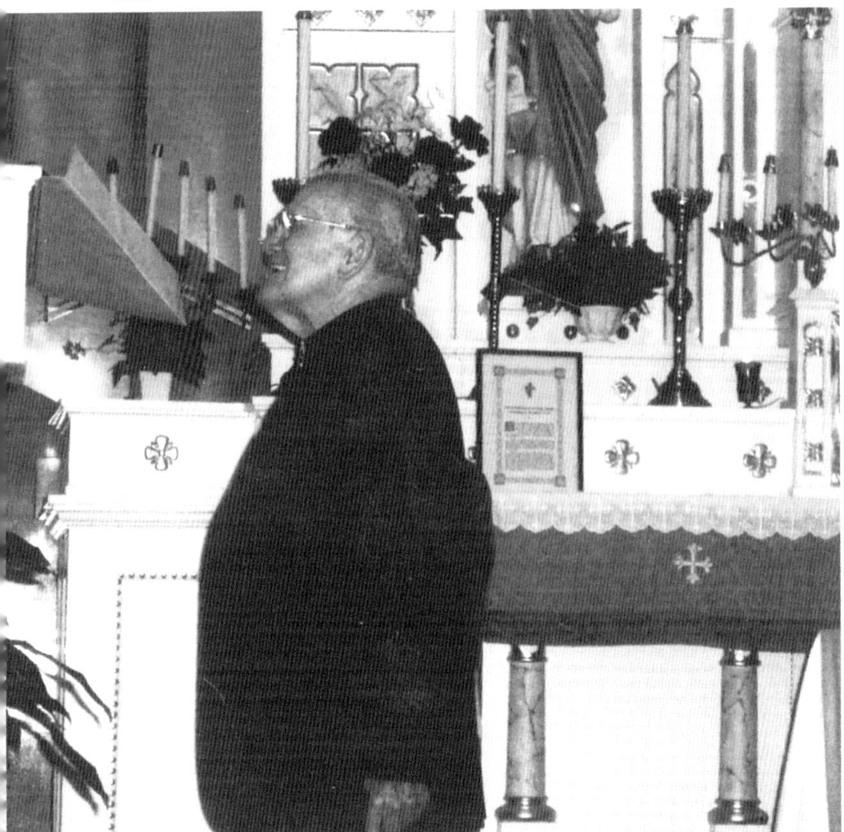

Rev. John Urban and Helen Urban
The Very Reverend John Urban and his wife, Helen, were more than just the pastor of the Divine Providence National Catholic Church in Greenville and his wife for over 60 years. They were a second set of parents to more than one generation, as well as leaders of their church and community. Life's lessons are not taught just in sermons, but are shown in the everyday actions while in school, on the playground, in old age, and even in the kitchen making pierogi. (Both images courtesy of Divine Providence National Catholic Church.)

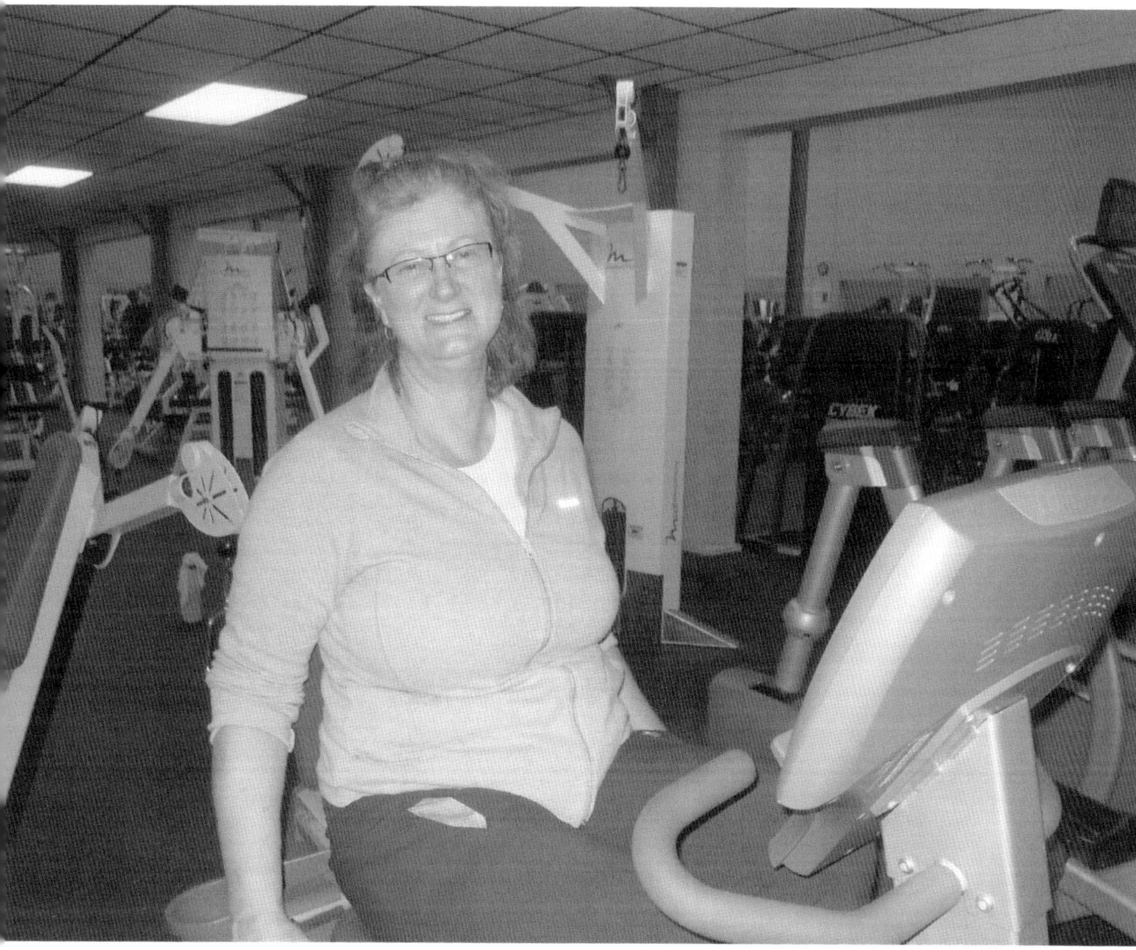

Jolene Bowers

Jolene Bowers keeps fit by always being in motion. She operates a 40,000-square-foot fitness and indoor soccer center, Summit Fitness, on the top of the business park hill. In addition, she attends meetings throughout Norwich to mentor new and small business entrepreneurs. She teaches them how to network, make friends, and maintain a healthy balance of family and exercise in order to achieve more in their business, all with a positive attitude.

Bowers demonstrates how taking the time to exercise and play with others is good for the mind, the body, and the family. "Starting and maintaining a business can be all-consuming. I remind people that they are not in business alone. Everyone is part of a team consisting of family, friends, clients and other business professionals. On a team, we all help each other to succeed."

INDEX

INDEX